ROLAND PARKER

Robotic Development with JavaScript

Building Intelligent Robots with Node.js, Johnny-Five, and Robotics-SDK

Contents

CHAPTER 1: INTRODUCTION TO ROBOTIC DEVEL-
OPMENT WITH...   1
CHAPTER 2: GETTING STARTED WITH NODE.JS FOR ROBOTICS 31
2.1 What is Node.js?   32
Key Features of Node.js: 33
Why Node.js is Ideal for Robotics   34
2.2 Installing and Configuring Node.js for Robotics Projects   35
Step 1: Installing Node.js   36
Installing Node.js on Windows: 37
Installing Node.js on macOS: 38
Installing Node.js on Linux (Ubuntu/Debian):   39
Step 2: Setting Up npm for Robotics Projects   41
Global Installation of npm Packages: 42
Installing Required npm Packages for Robotics: 44
Step 3: Setting Up an Integrated Development Environment...   46
Visual Studio Code (VS Code):   47
WebStorm: 48
Step 4: Testing the Installation   49
Summary   50
2.3 Working with npm and Package Management   51
2.3.1 What is npm?   52
Key Features of npm: 53
2.3.2 npm Initialization   54
2.3.3 Installing Packages with npm   56
Installing Local Packages   57
Installing Global Packages   58

Adding Dev Dependencies   59
Updating Packages   60
Removing Packages   61
2.3.5 Working with npm Scripts   62
Common npm Scripts for Robotics Projects: 63
2.3.6 Versioning and Lock Files   64
Summary   65
2.4 Asynchronous Programming in Node.js for Robotic Systems   66
2.4.1 Understanding Asynchronous Programming   67
2.4.2 Using Callbacks in Robotics   68
2.4.3 Promises in Robotics Programming   70
2.4.4 Async/Await for Cleaner Robotics Code   72
2.4.5 Event-Driven Architecture in Robotics   74
Summary   76
2.5 Event-Driven Architecture in Node.js   77
2.5.1 Understanding the Event-Driven Model   78
How It Works: 79
2.5.2 Basic Event-Driven Example in Node.js   80
2.5.3 Event-Driven Architecture in Robotics with Johnny-Five   82
Example: Reacting to Sensor Data Events   83
2.5.4 Reacting to Multiple Events in Robotics   85
Example: Coordinating Multiple Events   86
Benefits of Event-Driven Architecture in Robotics   88
2.5.5 Event-Driven Error Handling in Robotics   89
Example: Handling Errors in a Robotics System   90
Summary   91
2.6 Creating a Basic Node.js Robotics Application   92
Step 1: Setting Up the Project   93
Step 2: Writing the Application Code   94
Explanation of the Code: 96
Step 3: Running the Application   97
Summary   98
3.1 What is Johnny-Five?   99

3.1.1 Key Features of Johnny-Five: 100
3.1.2 How Johnny-Five Fits into JavaScript Robotics...   101
3.1.3 A Brief History of Johnny-Five: 102
3.1.4 Why Use Johnny-Five for Robotics Development?   103
3.1.5 Real-World Applications of Johnny-Five: 104
Summary   105
3.2 Hardware Requirements for Johnny-Five   106
3.2.1 Microcontrollers and Single-Board Computers (SBCs)   107
3.2.2 Firmata Protocol   109
3.2.3 Power Supply   110
3.2.4 Input and Output Components   111
3.2.5 Communication Interfaces   113
3.2.6 Additional Tools and Accessories   114
Summary   115
3.3 Installing Johnny-Five in Node.js   116
3.3.1 Prerequisites   117
3.3.2 Setting Up Your Project Directory   118
3.3.3 Installing Johnny-Five   120
3.3.4 Installing Firmata on Arduino (if applicable)   121
3.3.5 Testing Your Installation   122
3.3.6 Troubleshooting Common Installation Issues   124
Summary   125
3.4 Key Concepts and Components of Johnny-Five   126
3.4.1 Board   127
3.4.2 Pins   128
3.4.3 Components   129
3.4.4 Events   131
3.4.5 Using Libraries and Plugins   132
3.4.6 Working with Grids and Arrays   133
Summary   134
3.5 Building a Basic Robot with Johnny-Five   135
3.5.1 Project Overview   136
3.5.2 Wiring Setup   137

3.5.3 Code Implementation   139

3.5.4 Testing Your Robot   142

Summary   143

3.6 Understanding Johnny-Five Board Object and IO Plugins   144

3.6.1 The Board Object   145

3.6.2 Input/Output (IO) Plugins   147

Conclusion   149

4.1 Introduction to Sensors in Robotics   150

4.1.1 Types of Sensors   151

4.1.2 Integrating Sensors with Johnny-Five   153

4.1.3 Practical Applications of Sensors in Robotics   155

Summary   156

4.2 Working with Motors and Actuators   157

4.2.1 Types of Motors and Actuators   158

4.2.2 Integrating Motors and Actuators with Johnny-Five   159

4.2.3 Practical Applications of Motors and Actuators in...   163

Summary   164

4.3 Using LEDs and Displays for Feedback   165

4.3.1 Understanding LEDs in Robotics   166

4.3.2 Integrating LEDs with Johnny-Five   167

4.3.3 Using Displays for User Interaction   170

4.3.4 Practical Applications of LEDs and Displays in...   173

Summary   174

4.4 Integrating Cameras and Vision Systems   175

4.4.1 Importance of Vision Systems in Robotics   176

4.4.2 Types of Cameras Used in Robotics   177

4.4.3 Integrating a Camera with Johnny-Five   178

4.4.4 Processing Images with Computer Vision Libraries   180

4.4.5 Using Pre-trained Models for Object Detection   182

Summary   184

4.5 Understanding Servos and Stepper Motors   185

4.5.1 Introduction to Servos   186

4.5.2 Introduction to Stepper Motors   187

4.5.3 Applications of Servos and Stepper Motors in Robotics   188

4.5.4 Connecting and Controlling Servos with Johnny-Five   189

4.5.5 Controlling Stepper Motors with Johnny-Five   191

Summary   193

4.6 Connecting Bluetooth and Wi-Fi Modules   194

1. Introduction to Bluetooth and Wi-Fi Modules   195

2. Connecting Bluetooth Modules to a Robot   197

3. Connecting Wi-Fi Modules to a Robot   199

4. Bluetooth vs. Wi-Fi for Robotics   201

Conclusion   202

CHAPTER 5: DEVELOPING DECENTRALIZED APPLI-
CATIONS (DAPPS)   203

CHAPTER 6: EXPLORING HYPERLEDGER FABRIC   226

CHAPTER 7: BUILDING BLOCKCHAIN SOLUTIONS
WITH HYPERLEDGER   251

CHAPTER 8: INTRODUCTION TO CORDA BLOCKCHAIN   280

CHAPTER 9: DEVELOPING CORDAPPS WITH JAVASCRIPT   301

CHAPTER 10: INTEGRATING BLOCKCHAIN WITH
WEB TECHNOLOGIES   329

CHAPTER 11: SECURITY AND AUDITING IN
BLOCKCHAIN APPLICATIONS   356

CHAPTER 12: TESTING AND DEPLOYMENT IN
BLOCKCHAIN DEVELOPMENT   373

CHAPTER 13: BLOCKCHAIN INTEROPERABILITY
AND ORACLES   394

CHAPTER 14: ADVANCED TOPICS IN BLOCKCHAIN
DEVELOPMENT   420

CHAPTER 15: FUTURE OF BLOCKCHAIN AND JAVASCRIPT   446

APPENDIX A: GLOSSARY OF BLOCKCHAIN TERMS   466

APPENDIX B: JAVASCRIPT SYNTAX REFERENCE   467

APPENDIX C: ETHEREUM GAS PRICING AND OPTI-
MIZATION TECHNIQUES   469

APPENDIX D: HYPERLEDGER FABRIC CONFIGURA-
TION GUIDE   470
APPENDIX E: ADDITIONAL RESOURCES AND
LEARNING MATERIALS   471

CHAPTER 1: INTRODUCTION TO ROBOTIC DEVELOPMENT WITH JAVASCRIPT

1.1 The Evolution of Robotics

Robotics, as a field, has evolved dramatically over the past few decades, transforming from mechanical automation systems into sophisticated machines capable of intelligent behavior and real-world interactions. The journey of robotics is a story of continuous innovation, shaped by advancements in **mechanical engineering, electronics**, and, more recently, **software development**.

1.1.1 Early Beginnings: Mechanization and Automation

The roots of robotics can be traced back to early automata, mechanical devices designed to perform predefined tasks. These early machines were powered by simple mechanisms such as **gears, springs,** and **levers**. Examples of these automata can be found in ancient cultures, where they were used for entertainment or ritual purposes. By the 19th century, mechanization led to the first forms of **industrial automation**. Factories began using machines that could perform repetitive tasks more efficiently than human laborers, driving mass production.

The advent of electricity allowed further innovation. Machines could now be powered more effectively, and electrical controls could regulate their operations. However, it wasn't until the mid-20th century that true programmable robots were developed. Early programmable robots, such as **Unimate**—the first industrial robot used in a General Motors factory in

1961—were designed to perform repetitive tasks, such as welding or material handling.

1.1.2 The Rise of Computer Control and AI Integration

As computer technology progressed, robotics began to leverage **micro-controllers** and **computer processors**, enabling machines to execute more complex tasks through software. The 1980s saw significant breakthroughs in robotics with the rise of **CNC (Computer Numerical Control)** machines, which could be programmed to perform precise operations.

The introduction of **artificial intelligence (AI)** in the late 20th century pushed the boundaries of what robots could do. Robotics was no longer limited to fixed routines; with AI, robots could now process sensor data, make decisions, and adapt to changes in their environment. This allowed for the development of autonomous robots in industries like **automotive**, **aerospace**, and even **healthcare**.

The most significant leap in the field occurred with **machine learning (ML)** and **neural networks**, which allowed robots to learn from their experiences. This has enabled robots to perform tasks previously thought to be beyond their capability, such as natural language processing, visual recognition, and autonomous navigation.

1.1.3 Modern Robotics: Intelligent and Autonomous Systems

In the 21st century, robotics has moved from the factory floor into everyday life. **Personal robots**, such as **robotic vacuums (e.g., Roomba)** and **home assistants (e.g., Amazon Echo with Alexa)**, have become common household items. In parallel, **autonomous drones**, **robotic surgery systems**, and **self-driving cars** are revolutionizing industries.

With the integration of **Internet of Things (IoT)**, robots can now connect to other devices, creating more integrated and intelligent systems. IoT allows robots to access cloud-based services, communicate with other machines, and integrate into broader **smart environments**, making them part of an interconnected system.

1.1.4 The Emergence of Robotics Programming Frameworks

Programming has become the backbone of modern robotics. As the field has grown, so has the complexity of the software required to run these machines. **Robotic Operating Systems (ROS)** became popular as they offered a flexible framework for writing robot software. However, the field required languages that could handle both the web-based interfaces and the backend controls of robots.

With the rise of **JavaScript** and **Node.js**, robotics has entered a new phase. JavaScript, long associated with web development, has proven itself capable of interfacing with hardware through **Node.js**, a powerful runtime environment that allows JavaScript to run on the server and interact with devices. This opened the door for JavaScript developers to explore robotics and build intelligent robots using familiar web-based tools and programming methods.

1.2 Why Use JavaScript for Robotics?

JavaScript, traditionally a language for web development, is gaining traction in the world of robotics. Here's why:

- **Versatility**: JavaScript is a versatile, high-level language that can run on different environments, including browsers, servers, and now hardware.
- **Node.js Integration**: With the **Node.js** platform, JavaScript can communicate with hardware components, making it a great tool for building robotics applications.
- **Real-Time Applications**: JavaScript's event-driven, asynchronous architecture allows for **real-time processing**, which is essential for robotics, where sensors need to collect and process data continuously.
- **Rich Ecosystem**: JavaScript boasts a vast ecosystem of libraries and frameworks, many of which are designed to simplify hardware communication and robotic control.
- **Cross-Platform**: JavaScript is platform-agnostic. Whether you're developing for desktop, mobile, or embedded systems, JavaScript can work seamlessly across different environments.

1.2.1 JavaScript in Robotics: The Rise of Node.js and Johnny-Five

The emergence of **Node.js** and the **Johnny-Five** robotics framework revolutionized how developers build and program robots. These tools make it easier to control hardware components, such as **motors, servos, sensors,** and **LEDs** directly from JavaScript code. Node.js, known for its ability to handle concurrent processes, has made it an ideal choice for handling the asynchronous nature of robotics tasks like **sensor input**, **actuator control**, and **real-time decision-making**.

Johnny-Five, a JavaScript framework, enables developers to interact with microcontrollers like **Arduino** and **Raspberry Pi**, thus simplifying robotics development by offering easy-to-use APIs for controlling various components.

1.3 Overview of Key JavaScript Robotics Frameworks

There are several powerful JavaScript frameworks that are used to develop robotic systems, allowing developers to control hardware components with relative ease. The most popular ones include:

- **Johnny-Five**: A JavaScript framework for robotics that simplifies communication with microcontrollers such as **Arduino, Raspberry Pi**, and **Intel Galileo**. It provides a powerful abstraction layer that makes programming hardware more intuitive.
- **Cylon.js**: A framework that makes it possible to build robotics, IoT, and physical computing applications using JavaScript. Cylon.js supports a wide range of hardware platforms, from microcontrollers to complex robot systems.
- **NodeBots**: A group of JavaScript-based tools and libraries designed for building robots with Node.js. NodeBots emphasizes building **physical robots** controlled by JavaScript.

1.4 The Role of Node.js in Robotics

Node.js has emerged as a critical player in the world of robotics, thanks to its **non-blocking I/O**, event-driven architecture, and ability to handle multiple processes simultaneously. In robotics, where many components must communicate and act simultaneously, Node.js provides the speed and efficiency necessary for processing real-time data.

1.4.1 Benefits of Node.js for Robotics

- **Asynchronous Programming**: This enables robots to handle multiple tasks concurrently, such as monitoring sensor input while controlling actuators.
- **Modular Design**: Node.js offers a modular approach, which allows developers to write clean, maintainable code with reusable components.
- **Web Integration**: Node.js makes it easier to integrate robots with web interfaces, enabling users to control robots remotely through web applications or mobile devices.

1.4.2 Key Features of Johnny-Five and Node.js for Robotics

Johnny-Five, working with Node.js, allows you to build robotic systems with simple JavaScript syntax. Here are some core features:

- **Plug-and-Play Components**: Johnny-Five simplifies the process of connecting sensors, actuators, and other devices by abstracting low-level hardware protocols.
- **Extensive Hardware Support**: Johnny-Five works with numerous hardware platforms and microcontrollers, making it a versatile tool for building different types of robots.
- **Real-Time Data Processing**: With Node.js's event-driven model, robotic systems can process sensor data and make real-time decisions based on inputs from the environment.

1.5 Conclusion: Why Learn JavaScript for Robotics?

Learning JavaScript for robotics opens the door to a wide range of opportunities in **embedded systems, IoT**, and **AI-driven applications**. JavaScript, in combination with powerful frameworks like **Johnny-Five** and **Node.js**, allows developers to create robots that are both intelligent and efficient.

In this book, you will learn how to harness the power of JavaScript to control robots, work with sensors, actuators, and microcontrollers, and build intelligent systems. By mastering these tools, you will be able to bring your robotics ideas to life, pushing the boundaries of innovation.

This introduction lays the groundwork for the book and sets the stage for the more technical chapters that follow.

1.2 Why JavaScript for Robotics?

JavaScript, traditionally recognized as a language for web development, has become increasingly prominent in robotics development, primarily due to the rise of **Node.js** and other JavaScript-based frameworks that interact seamlessly with hardware. So why use JavaScript for robotics? In this section, we'll explore why JavaScript has gained popularity in this domain and the specific benefits it brings to robotic development.

1.2.1 JavaScript's Versatility and Accessibility

One of the key reasons JavaScript is so effective for robotics is its **versatility**. Originally designed for creating dynamic web pages, JavaScript has evolved into a full-fledged programming language that runs not only in the browser but also on servers, desktop applications, mobile platforms, and now **embedded systems**.

- **Cross-Platform Compatibility**: JavaScript's ability to run across different platforms makes it a powerful tool for robotic developers who may need to design robots that interact with various devices, such as smartphones, tablets, or web browsers.
- **Ease of Learning and Use**: JavaScript's syntax is simple, especially for those coming from web development backgrounds. Its wide adoption means there's a large developer community, abundant learning resources, and numerous libraries available to aid in the development of robotic systems.
- **Community Support and Ecosystem**: JavaScript has an enormous global community, providing support, code libraries, and frameworks for faster development. Whether it's libraries for managing hardware (like **Johnny-Five**), or frameworks for real-time communication (like **Socket.IO**), the JavaScript ecosystem offers a wealth of tools to simplify robotics development.

1.2.2 Real-Time Event-Driven Programming

In robotics, real-time control is crucial. Robots need to respond to external stimuli like sensor input, motor control, and user commands, often simultaneously. JavaScript, with its **event-driven architecture** and asynchronous programming model, is well-suited for handling these kinds of real-time tasks efficiently.

- **Non-Blocking I/O**: JavaScript's event-driven architecture (via **Node.js**) allows for non-blocking operations, meaning robots can handle multiple operations simultaneously. For instance, a robot can monitor temperature sensors, detect obstacles, and move motors all at once without lag or performance degradation.
- **Asynchronous Code**: With asynchronous operations (such as **callbacks**, **Promises**, and **async/await**), JavaScript can handle multiple tasks efficiently. In a robot, this could mean managing sensor data while controlling a motor without slowing down the robot's overall performance.

1.2.3 Node.js: The Powerhouse for JavaScript in Robotics

The biggest leap for JavaScript's role in robotics comes from **Node.js**, a runtime environment that allows JavaScript to run outside the browser. Node.js has several advantages for robotics:

- **Low Latency and High Performance**: Node.js is designed for building scalable, high-performance applications, and this translates well into robotics, where responsiveness and performance are critical.
- **Modular Development**: The Node.js ecosystem supports modular code development, allowing roboticists to build systems that are scalable and maintainable. You can develop different components of the robot, such as motor control, sensors, and data processing, separately and then integrate them smoothly.
- **Streamlined I/O Operations**: Node.js excels at handling input/output operations efficiently, which is crucial when dealing with real-time sensor data in a robot. By using **event-driven programming**, it allows multiple

I/O processes, such as reading sensor data or controlling motors, to run concurrently without slowing down the system.

1.2.4 Robotics Frameworks in JavaScript

Several JavaScript-based frameworks have emerged to simplify hardware interaction, making JavaScript a powerful language for controlling robotics. Among the most prominent frameworks are:

- **Johnny-Five**: Johnny-Five is one of the most popular robotics and IoT libraries for JavaScript. It provides easy-to-use APIs for controlling various hardware components, including microcontrollers like **Arduino** and **Raspberry Pi**. Its well-documented interface allows you to interact with sensors, motors, LEDs, and more, using simple JavaScript commands.
- **Cylon.js**: Cylon.js is another powerful JavaScript framework designed to simplify robotics and IoT development. It supports a wide range of hardware devices and platforms and allows for easy cross-device communication and coordination.
- **NodeBots**: The **NodeBots** community focuses on building robots powered by Node.js. It emphasizes hands-on development and encourages collaboration among developers, providing numerous resources for building everything from simple bots to complex robotic systems.

These frameworks abstract much of the complexity involved in interacting with hardware, allowing JavaScript developers to focus on building higher-level robotic behaviors and functionality.

1.2.5 Advantages of Using JavaScript for Robotics

There are several clear advantages to using JavaScript for robotic development, including:

- **Fast Prototyping**: JavaScript, combined with frameworks like Johnny-Five and Node.js, allows developers to quickly build and iterate on prototypes. Developers can set up the basics of a robot—such as motor control and sensor interaction—rapidly, and then refine the robot's behavior as needed.

- **Real-Time Web and Mobile Control**: JavaScript's dominance in web and mobile development provides robotic developers with a unique advantage. Using technologies like **WebSockets**, you can control and monitor your robot from a web browser or mobile application in real-time, making remote operation and data visualization simple.

- **Integration with Cloud Services**: JavaScript excels in connecting to APIs and cloud services, which is becoming increasingly important in modern robotics. Robots can use cloud-based AI systems to process large datasets, use IoT platforms to integrate into larger ecosystems, or send and receive real-time data for distributed control systems.

- **Event-Driven Interaction**: Robots often need to respond to environmental triggers, such as detecting obstacles, changes in light, or receiving input from users. JavaScript's event-driven model allows these triggers to be processed in real-time, giving your robot a more intelligent and responsive behavior.

1.2.6 Key Use Cases for JavaScript in Robotics

JavaScript has been successfully employed in various robotic applications, from **home automation** to **educational robots** and **industrial automation systems**. Some key areas where JavaScript plays an important role include:

- **Internet of Things (IoT)**: JavaScript, thanks to frameworks like **Cylon.js** and **Johnny-Five**, can control IoT devices and robots, making it a go-to language for developing smart homes, autonomous sensors, and automated factory equipment.

- **Educational Robotics**: Platforms like **TinkerBots** and **NodeBots** use JavaScript to teach programming and robotics concepts to students. Its ease of use, combined with the large number of available libraries, makes it ideal for beginners looking to learn both coding and robotics.

- **Remote-Controlled Robots**: JavaScript's ability to interact with web browsers allows developers to create interfaces that enable the remote control of robots from anywhere in the world. This is especially useful in applications like **drone navigation, telepresence robots**, and **robotic surgery**.

- **Research and Prototyping**: JavaScript is often used in research settings for rapid prototyping of new robotic designs. Its simplicity allows researchers to quickly test new ideas and technologies without needing to invest heavily in complex, low-level programming.

Summary

JavaScript has moved far beyond the browser and now plays a central role in robotics development, offering flexibility, real-time capabilities, and ease of use. With its strong support from Node.js and frameworks like Johnny-Five and Cylon.js, JavaScript allows developers to control complex hardware systems with just a few lines of code. Whether you're a web developer looking to transition into robotics or an experienced roboticist exploring new tools, JavaScript offers an accessible and powerful platform for building intelligent, responsive robots.

1.3 Overview of Node.js and Robotics Frameworks

JavaScript's growth in robotics development is largely driven by **Node.js**, an asynchronous, event-driven runtime environment that enables JavaScript to be used for backend development and hardware control. Combining Node.js with specialized robotics frameworks allows developers to harness the full potential of JavaScript for creating intelligent robots.

In this section, we'll explore the fundamentals of Node.js and discuss the most prominent robotics frameworks that enable JavaScript to interact seamlessly with hardware components like sensors, motors, and controllers.

1.3.1 Understanding Node.js for Robotics

Node.js is a powerful platform built on Chrome's **V8 JavaScript engine**. Initially designed for building fast and scalable network applications, its strengths also make it ideal for robotics development.

Here's why Node.js is a critical part of robotic development:

- **Non-Blocking I/O**: Node.js uses a non-blocking, event-driven architecture. This means multiple tasks—such as monitoring sensors or controlling motors—can be handled concurrently without slowing down the robot's performance.

- **Package Management with npm**: Node.js has access to **npm** (Node Package Manager), the largest software registry in the world, with a wide array of packages specifically designed for hardware interaction and robotics. Libraries like **Johnny-Five** and **Cylon.js** can be easily installed via npm, simplifying the development process.

- **Modularity and Scalability**: Node.js is designed for creating modular, scalable applications. In a robotics context, this allows developers to build different components, such as motor control, sensor data processing, and communication systems, as separate modules, making them easier to manage and scale.

- **Real-Time Communication**: For robots that need to communicate with users or external systems in real-time (e.g., web interfaces, mobile apps), Node.js is perfect. Its ability to handle **WebSockets** allows for real-time control and monitoring of robots via web browsers or mobile apps.

- **Cross-Platform**: Node.js runs on multiple operating systems (Linux, macOS, Windows), making it easy to deploy across various platforms commonly used in robotics, including **Raspberry Pi** and other embedded systems.

1.3.2 Johnny-Five: A JavaScript Robotics Framework

Johnny-Five is one of the most popular JavaScript libraries for robotics and IoT development. Built on top of Node.js, it provides a high-level API for controlling a wide range of hardware devices, from microcontrollers to sensors and actuators. It abstracts much of the low-level complexity of hardware programming, allowing developers to build sophisticated robotic systems using simple JavaScript commands.

Key Features of Johnny-Five:

- **Hardware Support**: Johnny-Five supports numerous platforms, including **Arduino**, **Raspberry Pi**, and **BeagleBone**, enabling developers to control a variety of devices from a single library.

- **Simplified Commands**: With Johnny-Five, interacting with hardware components is as simple as writing JavaScript functions. For example, turning on an LED or reading sensor data can be done with just a few lines of code.
- **Event-Driven Architecture**: Johnny-Five takes full advantage of Node.js's event-driven model, allowing developers to write non-blocking, responsive applications where robots can react to environmental stimuli, such as changes in sensor data.
- **Large Community and Documentation**: Johnny-Five has a thriving community that contributes to its development and provides extensive documentation. This makes it a great starting point for developers who are new to robotics.

Example: Controlling an LED with Johnny-Five

Here's a basic example of controlling an LED using Johnny-Five:

javascript

Copy code

```
const { Board, Led } = require("johnny-five");
const board = new Board();

board.on("ready", () => {
  const led = new Led(13); // Pin 13 on Arduino
  led.blink(500); // Blink every 500ms
});
```

In this code, we create a new **Johnny-Five Board** instance that represents the connected hardware. Once the board is ready, we initialize an **LED** on pin 13 of an Arduino and make it blink every 500 milliseconds.

1.3.3 Cylon.js: A Framework for Robotics and IoT

Cylon.js is another powerful robotics and IoT framework that allows developers to control hardware devices using JavaScript. It supports a wide range of hardware devices and platforms, making it a versatile tool for building robots and IoT systems.

Key Features of Cylon.js:

- **Multiple Hardware Platforms**: Cylon.js supports various hardware platforms, such as **Arduino, Raspberry Pi, Intel Edison**, and **Sphero**, providing flexibility in choosing the right hardware for your project.
- **Cross-Device Communication**: Cylon.js makes it easy to communicate between devices, allowing you to build distributed robotic systems where multiple robots or IoT devices work together.
- **Concurrency**: Like Johnny-Five, Cylon.js takes advantage of JavaScript's non-blocking I/O to handle concurrent tasks. This makes it ideal for real-time robotics applications that require constant monitoring and control of multiple sensors and actuators.
- **Web Integration**: Cylon.js integrates seamlessly with web technologies, making it easy to control robots or IoT devices through web interfaces. This is particularly useful for applications that require remote control via a browser or a mobile device.

Example: Controlling a Servo with Cylon.js

Here's an example of how to control a servo motor with Cylon.js:

javascript

Copy code

```
const Cylon = require("cylon");

Cylon.robot({
  connections: {
  arduino: { adaptor: "firmata", port: "/dev/ttyACM0" }
  },
  devices: {
  servo: { driver: "servo", pin: 9 }
  },
  work: function(my) {
  let angle = 0;
  every((1).second(), () => {
```

```
my.servo.angle(angle);
angle = (angle + 45) % 180; // Move between 0 and 180 degrees
});
}
}).start();
```

In this code, Cylon.js is used to control a servo motor connected to an Arduino. The servo moves between 0 and 180 degrees every second.

1.3.4 NodeBots: JavaScript Robotics Community

NodeBots is not just a framework but a movement within the JavaScript and robotics communities. The NodeBots project is built around the idea of using **JavaScript-powered robots** with Node.js and Johnny-Five. The community regularly hosts workshops, hackathons, and events to promote hands-on learning and collaboration in robotics.

Key Aspects of NodeBots:

- **Collaborative Learning**: The NodeBots community encourages collaborative learning, making it easier for newcomers to get involved in robotics and build robots using JavaScript.
- **Educational Focus**: NodeBots events often target students, hobbyists, and beginners, teaching them the fundamentals of robotics, hardware programming, and JavaScript.
- **Variety of Projects**: NodeBots participants build a wide range of projects, from simple line-following robots to more complex machines capable of real-world tasks. This variety demonstrates the flexibility of JavaScript in robotics development.

1.3.5 Other JavaScript Robotics Tools

While Johnny-Five and Cylon.js are the most popular JavaScript-based robotics frameworks, there are other tools worth mentioning:

- **Noduino**: A simple and lightweight JavaScript framework for controlling Arduino using Node.js and WebSockets.
- **Espruino**: A JavaScript interpreter that runs directly on low-power

microcontrollers. Espruino is perfect for resource-constrained environ-ments where you need to run JavaScript directly on embedded hardware without a full Node.js runtime.

- **Tessel**: Tessel is a hardware platform that runs JavaScript on embedded devices. It's designed to make hardware development as easy as web development, with a plug-and-play system for attaching modules like cameras, sensors, and more.

Summary

In summary, JavaScript's ability to interact with hardware through powerful frameworks like **Johnny-Five** and **Cylon.js**, combined with the performance and scalability of **Node.js**, makes it a great choice for building robots. Whether you're looking to build simple IoT devices or complex robotic systems, these frameworks provide the tools you need to get started quickly and scale your projects efficiently.

1.4 Introduction to Johnny-Five and Robotics-SDK

In this section, we will take a closer look at two key tools that make JavaScript an ideal language for robotic development: **Johnny-Five** and **Robotics-SDK**. These frameworks are fundamental to building robots and controlling hardware using JavaScript, offering abstraction layers that simplify the interaction between software and physical devices.

1.4.1 What is Johnny-Five?

Johnny-Five is an open-source JavaScript framework for robotics and the Internet of Things (IoT) built on top of Node.js. It provides a rich API to interact with a wide variety of hardware, including microcontrollers, sensors, motors, and LEDs. By leveraging JavaScript's event-driven and asynchronous nature, Johnny-Five allows developers to build responsive, non-blocking robotic applications easily.

Key Features of Johnny-Five:

- **Cross-Platform Hardware Support**: Johnny-Five supports multiple microcontroller platforms, including **Arduino**, **Raspberry Pi**, **Beagle-Bone**, and **Intel Galileo**. This flexibility makes it an excellent choice for developers who want to experiment with different hardware without switching tools.

- **Plug-and-Play**: Johnny-Five simplifies hardware integration. It abstracts away the complexities of hardware communication, allowing you to get started quickly with basic robotics projects. For example, turning on an LED or reading sensor data can be done in just a few lines of code.
- **Event-Driven Architecture**: The event-driven model of Johnny-Five means that robots can easily react to real-time changes in their environment. For example, when a sensor detects an obstacle, an event can trigger the robot to change its course or speed.
- **Modular and Scalable**: Johnny-Five is built on top of Node.js, making it modular and scalable. You can organize your code into modules, manage different components of your robot separately, and even scale your application to include multiple robots or devices.

How Johnny-Five Works:

Johnny-Five acts as a middle layer between the hardware and JavaScript code. It communicates with microcontrollers via **Firmata**, a protocol that allows Johnny-Five to control hardware components without needing to write low-level firmware.

Here's a basic flow of how Johnny-Five works:

1. **Connect the Hardware**: Attach sensors, motors, or actuators to a microcontroller (e.g., Arduino).
2. **Install Johnny-Five**: Set up Johnny-Five using Node.js.
3. **Write JavaScript Code**: Use Johnny-Five's API to control the hardware.
4. **Deploy**: Upload the code to the microcontroller and observe the robot's behavior in real-time.

Example: Blinking an LED with Johnny-Five

Here's a basic example of how Johnny-Five can be used to blink an LED:
javascript
Copy code

```
const { Board, Led } = require("johnny-five");
const board = new Board();

board.on("ready", () => {
    const led = new Led(13); // Connect LED to pin 13 on Arduino
    led.blink(500); // Blink every 500 milliseconds
});
```

In this example, an LED connected to pin 13 of an Arduino board will blink on and off every 500 milliseconds. This demonstrates how easy it is to control hardware with Johnny-Five using only a few lines of JavaScript.

1.4.2 Introduction to Robotics-SDK

While Johnny-Five is widely known for its ease of use in small-scale robotics projects, **Robotics-SDK** is designed to handle more complex and enterprise-level robotic applications. Robotics-SDK is a modular framework that allows developers to build and manage robotic systems that are both intelligent and scalable. It provides the tools necessary to integrate various robotic components, manage complex workflows, and facilitate communication between hardware and software layers.

Key Features of Robotics-SDK:

- **High-Level Abstraction**: Robotics-SDK provides a high-level abstraction layer, making it easy to manage robotic components such as sensors, actuators, and control systems. Developers can focus on building intelligent robotic behaviors rather than dealing with low-level hardware communication.
- **Modular Architecture**: Robotics-SDK is built with a modular design, enabling developers to mix and match different components and libraries. This modularity simplifies the integration of various hardware and software tools into one cohesive system.
- **Advanced Robotic Algorithms**: Robotics-SDK comes with built-in support for advanced robotic algorithms like **SLAM (Simultaneous Localization and Mapping)**, **path planning**, and **object recognition**. This makes it easier to build autonomous robots capable of navigating

complex environments.

- **Support for Multiple Platforms**: Robotics-SDK is cross-platform, supporting a wide range of operating systems and hardware platforms, from **embedded systems** to **cloud-based servers**. Whether you're developing robots for industrial automation or personal projects, Robotics-SDK provides the flexibility to deploy across various environments.
- **AI and Machine Learning Integration**: Robotics-SDK also supports the integration of AI and machine learning models, enabling robots to make decisions based on real-time data. This is especially important in applications such as autonomous navigation, human-robot interaction, and predictive maintenance.

Robotics-SDK Architecture:

At its core, Robotics-SDK provides an **API layer** that allows developers to control hardware, process sensor data, and manage robotic workflows. The framework is divided into several key components:

1. **Device Layer**: This is where low-level hardware interaction occurs. The device layer communicates with motors, sensors, cameras, and other hardware devices.
2. **Control Layer**: The control layer manages the logic behind how robots behave. This includes algorithms for controlling motors, making decisions based on sensor inputs, and executing robotic tasks.
3. **Communication Layer**: Robotics-SDK includes built-in support for communication protocols like **ROS (Robot Operating System)** and **MQTT,** allowing for distributed control and communication between robots or between robots and cloud systems.
4. **Application Layer**: This is where developers can define the high-level behavior of the robot, such as task automation, interaction with users, or real-time response to environmental changes.

Example Use Case of Robotics-SDK:

Imagine a warehouse with autonomous robots responsible for moving goods from one location to another. Using Robotics-SDK, developers can:

- Integrate sensors to detect obstacles in the robot's path.
- Use SLAM algorithms to help the robot navigate the warehouse without getting lost.
- Employ machine learning models to optimize the robot's route for efficiency.
- Monitor and control multiple robots from a centralized dashboard using the Robotics-SDK API.

This shows how Robotics-SDK can be used to build complex, intelligent robotic systems capable of operating autonomously in real-world environments.

1.4.3 Johnny-Five vs. Robotics-SDK: When to Use Each

While both Johnny-Five and Robotics-SDK are powerful tools for robotic development, they serve slightly different purposes:

- **Johnny-Five**: Ideal for beginners or small-scale projects, Johnny-Five simplifies hardware programming with an easy-to-use API. If you're building a hobbyist robot, a simple IoT device, or just getting started with robotics, Johnny-Five is the perfect choice.
- **Robotics-SDK**: Designed for more complex and large-scale robotic systems, Robotics-SDK is suitable for professional applications. If you're building industrial robots, autonomous systems, or require integration with advanced algorithms and AI, Robotics-SDK offers the flexibility and tools needed for those environments.

Both frameworks complement each other and can even be used together in certain projects. For instance, you might start by prototyping with Johnny-Five and then scale your project using Robotics-SDK when more complex functionality is required.

Summary

In this section, we explored **Johnny-Five** and **Robotics-SDK**, two essential tools for JavaScript-based robotic development. **Johnny-Five** offers simplicity and ease of use for beginners and hobbyists, while **Robotics-SDK** provides the modularity and advanced features required for professional and large-scale robotic systems. Together, these frameworks enable developers to build anything from small IoT devices to complex autonomous robots using the JavaScript ecosystem.

1.5 Setting Up Your Development Environment for Robotics

Before diving into building intelligent robots with JavaScript, it is essential to set up a proper development environment. In this section, we will guide you through setting up the necessary tools and libraries for robotic development using JavaScript, focusing on **Node.js**, **Johnny-Five**, and **Robotics-SDK**. A well-configured environment will ensure you can efficiently code, test, and deploy your robotic applications.

1.5.1 Installing Node.js

Node.js is the backbone of our JavaScript-based robotic development. It allows us to run JavaScript code outside of the browser and has a rich ecosystem of libraries and frameworks, such as Johnny-Five and Robotics-SDK.

Step 1: Download and Install Node.js

1. **Download**: Visit the official Node.js website and download the latest stable version (LTS) for your operating system (Windows, macOS, or Linux).
2. **Install**: Follow the installation prompts to install Node.js. This will also install **npm** (Node Package Manager), which is essential for managing libraries and dependencies in your projects.

Step 2: Verify Installation

After installation, verify that Node.js and npm are correctly installed by running the following commands in your terminal or command prompt:

```
bash
Copy code
node -v
```

npm -v

These commands should return the versions of Node.js and npm, confirming successful installation.

1.5.2 Setting Up Johnny-Five

Johnny-Five requires both hardware (like an Arduino board) and software setup. The software side involves installing the Johnny-Five library and ensuring that your development environment can communicate with the hardware.

Step 1: Install Johnny-Five

After installing Node.js, you can install Johnny-Five using npm. Open your terminal or command prompt and run the following command:

bash

Copy code

npm install johnny-five

This will download and install Johnny-Five, along with its dependencies.

Step 2: Set Up the Hardware

Johnny-Five works with a variety of hardware, but the most common is **Arduino**. If you are using an Arduino, follow these steps:

1. **Install Arduino IDE**: Download and install the Arduino IDE, which you will use to upload the **Firmata** firmware to your board.
2. **Upload Firmata**: Firmata is a protocol that allows Johnny-Five to control your Arduino board. Open the Arduino IDE, go to File > Examples > Firmata > StandardFirmata, and upload it to your board.
3. **Connect the Hardware**: Connect your Arduino to your computer using a USB cable.

Step 3: Verify Johnny-Five Setup

Once Johnny-Five is installed and your Arduino board is ready, create a simple JavaScript file to test the setup:

javascript

Copy code

const { Board, Led } = require("johnny-five");

```
const board = new Board();
```

```
board.on("ready", () => {
    const led = new Led(13); // Pin 13 is typically connected to the onboard
LED on Arduino
    led.blink(500); // Blink every 500 milliseconds
});
```

Save this file as blink.js, then run it using Node.js:

bash

Copy code

node blink.js

If everything is set up correctly, the onboard LED on your Arduino should start blinking. This confirms that Johnny-Five is successfully communicating with your hardware.

1.5.3 Setting Up Robotics-SDK

Robotics-SDK is a more advanced framework, designed for larger, more complex robotic systems. Installing Robotics-SDK involves setting up a few dependencies and libraries specific to your project.

Step 1: Install Robotics-SDK

Robotics-SDK is typically distributed as a package on npm. To install it, run the following command:

bash

Copy code

npm install robotics-sdk

Step 2: Configure Dependencies

Depending on your hardware and the features of Robotics-SDK you intend to use (such as sensor data processing, motor control, etc.), you may need to install additional dependencies. Robotics-SDK often integrates with hardware drivers and communication protocols like **ROS** (Robot Operating System) or **MQTT**.

For example, if you are building a robot that uses MQTT for communication, you can install the MQTT package as follows:

bash

Copy code

npm install mqtt

Step 3: Set Up Robotics-SDK Project

To start working with Robotics-SDK, create a new Node.js project and initialize a project directory:

bash

Copy code

mkdir robotics-project

cd robotics-project

npm init -y

This creates a new project folder with a package.json file. You can then install any additional dependencies and configure your project accordingly.

1.5.4 Setting Up Integrated Development Environment (IDE)

Having a well-configured IDE can significantly boost productivity. Here are some popular IDEs and editors you can use for JavaScript-based robotic development:

- **Visual Studio Code (VS Code):** This is one of the most popular code editors for JavaScript development. It provides excellent support for Node.js, Johnny-Five, and Robotics-SDK, along with extensions for debugging, code formatting, and linting. You can download VS Code here.

Recommended Extensions for Robotics Development:

- **Node.js**: Provides debugging, IntelliSense, and other development features for Node.js.
- **Johnny-Five Extension**: Provides code snippets and autocompletion for Johnny-Five.
- **Prettier**: A code formatter that ensures consistent coding styles across your project.
- **WebStorm**: A powerful IDE from JetBrains, WebStorm is designed specifically for JavaScript development. It has built-in support for

Node.js, excellent debugging tools, and a rich plugin ecosystem. You can find WebStorm here.

- **Arduino IDE**: Although Arduino IDE is mainly for writing and uploading Arduino code, it is essential when working with microcontrollers. You can use it to upload Firmata firmware and perform basic testing of hardware components.

1.5.5 Connecting Hardware Components

To build more complex robots, you'll need to connect various hardware components, such as motors, sensors, and actuators. Here's how you can ensure your hardware setup is compatible with Johnny-Five and Robotics-SDK:

- **Motors**: Johnny-Five provides support for a variety of motors, including DC motors, stepper motors, and servos. Motors typically connect to a motor driver, which interfaces with your microcontroller.

Example of initializing a motor in Johnny-Five:

```javascript
Copy code
const { Board, Motor } = require("johnny-five");
const board = new Board();

board.on("ready", () => {
  const motor = new Motor(9); // Motor connected to pin 9
  motor.start(200); // Motor speed set to 200
});
```

- **Sensors**: Johnny-Five supports numerous sensors such as ultrasonic distance sensors, temperature sensors, and infrared detectors. Make sure to check the pin compatibility of your microcontroller with the sensor you plan to use.

Example of using an ultrasonic sensor:

```javascript
Copy code
const { Board, Proximity } = require("johnny-five");
const board = new Board();

board.on("ready", () => {
  const proximity = new Proximity({
  controller: "HCSR04", // Ultrasonic sensor type
  pin: 7 // Sensor connected to pin 7
  });

proximity.on("data", () => {
  console.log("Distance: " + proximity.cm + " cm");
  });
  });
```

1.5.6 Testing and Debugging

After setting up your development environment, testing and debugging will be critical as you build robotic projects. Node.js and Johnny-Five provide built-in tools for debugging and testing code in real-time.

Testing Hardware Components

- Use **Johnny-Five's REPL** (Read-Eval-Print-Loop) to test components interactively. After initializing the Board object, you can run commands directly in the REPL.
- Example: To test an LED connected to pin 13 interactively:

```bash
Copy code
led = new five.Led(13)
led.on()
led.off()
```

Debugging

- **VS Code Debugger**: Use breakpoints in VS Code to pause your code and inspect variables, especially when dealing with asynchronous robotic events.
- **Console Logging**: In robotic projects, it's common to use console.log statements to monitor real-time sensor data or track the robot's state.

1.5.7 Version Control and Collaboration

Using **Git** for version control is highly recommended when working on robotics projects, especially if you're collaborating with others. Git enables you to track changes, work on different features in separate branches, and merge code efficiently.

1. Initialize Git in your project:

bash
```
Copy code
git init
```

1. Create a .gitignore file to exclude dependencies and node modules:

bash
```
Copy code
node_modules/
```

1. Push your project to a remote repository (e.g., GitHub, GitLab) to collaborate with others.

Summary

Setting up the development environment is a crucial first step in building robots using JavaScript. By installing Node.js, Johnny-Five, Robotics-SDK, and configuring the necessary hardware and software components, you create a foundation for success in robotic development. As you move forward, you will use this environment to build, test, and deploy increasingly sophisticated robotic systems.

1.6 Building Your First JavaScript Robot: A Simple Example

Now that your development environment is set up, it's time to build your first simple robot using JavaScript and Johnny-Five. In this example, we'll create a basic robot that responds to user input by moving forward or backward and blinking an LED. This project will give you hands-on experience in controlling hardware through code, providing a solid foundation for more complex robotic applications.

1.6.1 Hardware Requirements

To build this robot, you will need the following hardware components:

- **Arduino Uno (or any compatible microcontroller)**
- **Breadboard**
- **LED**
- **Resistor (220 ohms)**
- **DC motor**
- **Motor driver (such as L298N or H-bridge)**
- **Jumper wires**
- **USB cable** (for connecting the Arduino to your computer)

1.6.2 Circuit Setup

1. **LED Setup**: Connect the LED to pin 13 on the Arduino, with the resistor between the anode (positive leg) of the LED and the pin. The cathode (negative leg) should be connected to the ground (GND) on the Arduino.
2. **Motor Setup**:

- Connect the DC motor to the motor driver. The motor driver allows the Arduino to control the motor's power.
- The motor driver will have two pins for power input from the Arduino (typically connected to pins 9 and 10) and additional pins for motor power and ground.

1. **Power and Ground**: Ensure that all components share a common ground and that the Arduino receives sufficient power from the USB connection to the computer.

1.6.3 Writing the Code

We'll write a simple Node.js program that allows the robot to move forward and backward and blink an LED. This code will control the motor speed and direction and make the LED blink continuously.

Step 1: Initialize Johnny-Five and Define Components

Start by initializing Johnny-Five and defining the LED and motor components:

```javascript
Copy code
const { Board, Led, Motor } = require("johnny-five");
const board = new Board();

board.on("ready", () => {
  const led = new Led(13); // Pin 13 for the LED
  const motor = new Motor({
  pins: {
  pwm: 9, // PWM control for motor speed
  dir: 10 // Direction control for motor
  }
  });

// Blink the LED every second
  led.blink(1000);

// Move motor forward for 2 seconds, then backward for 2 seconds
  motor.forward(255); // Full speed forward
  board.wait(2000, () => {
  motor.reverse(255); // Full speed reverse
  board.wait(2000, () => {
```

```
motor.stop(); // Stop the motor
});
});
});
```

Step 2: Running the Program

Save the file as robot.js and run it in your terminal:

bash

Copy code

node robot.js

When you run the code:

- The LED should start blinking at 1-second intervals.
- The motor will move forward for 2 seconds, reverse for 2 seconds, and then stop.

1.6.4 Extending the Robot's Functionality

This basic example can be easily extended to add more functionality. Here are a few ideas to explore:

- **Add a Sensor**: Attach an ultrasonic distance sensor to make the robot move forward only when there's no obstacle ahead.
- **Control Speed Dynamically**: Modify the motor speed based on sensor input or user commands.
- **Remote Control**: Use web interfaces or voice commands to control the robot remotely.

By expanding the project in these ways, you'll begin to see the versatility of JavaScript in robotic development, leveraging the full capabilities of Johnny-Five and Robotics-SDK.

Conclusion of Chapter 1

In this introductory chapter, we've covered the evolution of robotics, the advantages of using JavaScript for robotic development, and provided an overview of key frameworks like **Node.js**, **Johnny-Five**, and **Robotics-SDK**.

By walking through the process of setting up your development environment and building your first simple robot, you've taken the first step toward creating more sophisticated, intelligent robots.

Key takeaways include:

- Understanding why JavaScript is an excellent choice for robotic development due to its asynchronous nature and vast ecosystem.
- Gaining familiarity with essential frameworks like Johnny-Five, which simplifies the process of interacting with hardware components using JavaScript.
- Learning how to set up your environment, including installing Node.js, Johnny-Five, and configuring hardware components such as motors, LEDs, and sensors.
- Building and running a basic robot project that serves as a foundation for future, more advanced projects.

CHAPTER 2: GETTING STARTED WITH NODE.JS FOR ROBOTICS

I n this chapter, we will explore **Node.js** in detail, understanding why it is a powerful tool for robotic development. We will also set up and configure Node.js for use with robotics projects, laying the groundwork for building intelligent and efficient robots using JavaScript.

2.1 What is Node.js?

N ode.js is an open-source, cross-platform JavaScript runtime environment built on **Chrome's V8 JavaScript engine**. It allows developers to write server-side and networking applications using JavaScript. Unlike traditional JavaScript environments, which run in the browser, Node.js enables JavaScript to run on the server or directly on a machine, making it ideal for applications that require I/O operations, such as robotics.

Key Features of Node.js:

- **Non-blocking, Asynchronous I/O**: Node.js uses non-blocking, event-driven architecture, meaning that it can handle multiple operations without waiting for one to complete before starting another. This is particularly useful in robotics, where you may need to manage inputs from multiple sensors and actuators simultaneously.
- **Single-threaded Event Loop**: Node.js operates on a single thread, utilizing an event loop to process I/O operations. This simplicity makes it easier to write efficient, performant code for controlling robots, where tasks like reading sensor data, controlling motors, and interacting with external devices can happen without delays.
- **Extensive Ecosystem**: The **Node.js package manager (npm)** is the largest ecosystem of open-source libraries, including many modules specifically for robotics, IoT, and hardware control. For example, **Johnny-Five** and **Robotics-SDK** are libraries that make it easy to interact with hardware components.
- **JavaScript Everywhere**: With Node.js, you can use JavaScript for both front-end and back-end development. In the context of robotics, this means you can create seamless integration between robot control systems and user interfaces, such as web apps or mobile apps, all using JavaScript.

Why Node.js is Ideal for Robotics

Node.js's event-driven architecture and non-blocking I/O make it perfect for robotics applications. Robots often need to perform multiple tasks simultaneously, such as reading sensor data while controlling motors, which is where Node.js excels.

For example:

- **Sensor Data Handling**: You can handle input from multiple sensors without blocking other operations, ensuring your robot can respond in real-time to environmental changes.
- **Actuator Control**: Node.js can efficiently manage the control of motors, servos, and other actuators by running non-blocking operations.
- **Event-Based Triggers**: Node.js's event-driven model is ideal for setting up triggers based on sensor readings or user inputs, making it easy to build responsive robots.

With this understanding of Node.js, we can now move on to setting up and configuring your development environment for robotic projects.

2.2 Installing and Configuring Node.js for Robotics Projects

To begin building robotics projects with **Node.js**, it's essential to correctly install and configure the environment on your machine. This section will guide you through the process of setting up Node.js, configuring the necessary tools, and ensuring you have everything you need for seamless development.

Step 1: Installing Node.js

N ode.js can be installed on a variety of platforms, including **Windows**, **macOS**, and **Linux**. The following steps will help you install Node.js on each of these platforms.

Installing Node.js on Windows:

1. **Download the Installer**: Visit the official Node.js website and download the Windows installer. You'll see options for both LTS (Long-Term Support) and Current versions. It's recommended to use the **LTS version** for stability, especially in production environments.

2. **Run the Installer**: After downloading, run the installer. Follow the prompts in the installation wizard and ensure that the box to install **npm** (Node.js package manager) is checked. npm is essential for managing libraries like **Johnny-Five** and **Robotics-SDK**.

3. **Verify the Installation**: Open **Command Prompt** and type the following commands to verify that Node.js and npm were installed correctly:

b ash
    Copy code
    node -v
npm -v

You should see the versions of Node.js and npm displayed.

Installing Node.js on macOS:

1. **Use Homebrew**: On macOS, the easiest way to install Node.js is through **Homebrew**. If you don't have Homebrew installed, open Terminal and install it with the following command:

b ash
    Copy code
    /bin/bash -c "$(curl -fsSL https://raw.githubusercontent.com/Homebrew/install/HEAD/install.sh)"

1. **Install Node.js**: Once Homebrew is installed, use the following command to install Node.js and npm:

bash
    Copy code
    brew install node

1. **Verify Installation**: Run the following commands in Terminal to verify the installation:

bash
    Copy code
    node -v
    npm -v

Installing Node.js on Linux (Ubuntu/Debian):

1. **Update Package Lists**: First, update your system's package lists to ensure you have the latest versions available:

b
ash
   Copy code
   sudo apt update

1. **Install Node.js**: You can install Node.js from the official Node.js repository. First, add the repository:

bash
   Copy code
   curl -fsSL https://deb.nodesource.com/setup_lts.x | sudo -E bash -
   Then, install Node.js:
   bash
   Copy code
   sudo apt install -y nodejs

1. **Verify Installation**: Check the installation using:

bash

```
Copy code
node -v
npm -v
```

Step 2: Setting Up npm for Robotics Projects

After installing Node.js, npm (Node.js package manager) is automatically installed as well. npm is vital for managing dependencies and libraries used in your robotic projects, such as **Johnny-Five**, **Robotics-SDK**, and other hardware control libraries.

Global Installation of npm Packages:

T o ensure npm is set up correctly and to avoid permission errors, it's recommended to configure npm to install global packages without the need for root access (especially on Linux and macOS).

- **Create a Global Directory for npm**:

bash
  Copy code
  mkdir ~/.npm-global

- **Configure npm to Use the New Directory**:

bash
  Copy code
  npm config set prefix '~/.npm-global'

- **Update Your System's Path**: Add the following to your shell configuration file (e.g., ~/.bashrc, ~/.zshrc):

bash
  Copy code
  export PATH=~/.npm-global/bin:$PATH

- **Reload the Configuration**:

bash

Copy code

```
source ~/.bashrc # or ~/.zshrc for ZSH users
```

Installing Required npm Packages for Robotics:

N ow, let's install the key packages required for developing robotics applications.

1. **Johnny-Five**: Johnny-Five is a popular JavaScript robotics library that works with various hardware platforms like Arduino. Install it globally using:

bash
Copy code
npm install johnny-five

1. **Robotics-SDK**: Robotics-SDK provides an advanced framework for building complex robotics systems. Install it as well:

bash
Copy code
npm install robotics-sdk

1. **Additional Libraries**: Depending on the hardware you use (e.g., sensors, actuators, communication protocols), additional libraries may be needed. For example, for serial communication with Arduino, you might need:

bash

Copy code

npm install serialport

Step 3: Setting Up an Integrated Development Environment (IDE)

F or robotic development with Node.js, it's important to choose a powerful IDE or text editor that offers strong support for JavaScript and Node.js. Here are a few popular options:

Visual Studio Code (VS Code):

- **Free and Open Source**: VS Code is widely used for JavaScript and Node.js development, offering many extensions specifically for Node.js, debugging, and hardware integration.
- **Extensions for Robotics**: Install extensions like **Node.js Extension Pack** and **Johnny-Five Snippets** for enhanced productivity.
- **Serial Monitor**: The **Arduino extension** for VS Code adds support for controlling hardware and monitoring serial output directly from the IDE.

WebStorm:

- **Commercial IDE**: WebStorm, developed by JetBrains, is a professional IDE for JavaScript development, including Node.js.
- **Built-in Support for npm**: WebStorm provides integrated npm support, terminal access, and excellent JavaScript debugging tools, making it a great choice for robotic development.

Step 4: Testing the Installation

O nce Node.js and npm are properly installed and configured, it's important to test the environment by running a simple Node.js script to ensure everything is working correctly.

Create a new folder for your project and initialize it as a Node.js project:

bash

Copy code

```
mkdir my-first-robot
cd my-first-robot
npm init -y
```

Create a file called index.js and add the following basic Node.js script:

javascript

Copy code

```
console.log("Hello, Node.js for Robotics!");
```

Run the script with:

bash

Copy code

```
node index.js
```

If you see the message "Hello, Node.js for Robotics!" in the console, then you've successfully set up Node.js for robotic development!

Summary

B y completing this section, you've successfully installed and configured Node.js for use in robotic projects. You're now ready to start working with JavaScript and hardware, utilizing Node.js's non-blocking I/O model, rich library ecosystem, and event-driven architecture to build intelligent robots. In the next section, we will dive deeper into the basics of JavaScript programming for robotics, focusing on key concepts you need to know to control hardware components.

2.3 Working with npm and Package Management

N ode.js relies heavily on its powerful package manager, **npm** (Node Package Manager), to handle dependencies and libraries. For robotic development, understanding how to work with npm is crucial since you'll be integrating various libraries like **Johnny-Five**, **Robotics-SDK**, and others that offer support for hardware control, sensors, and actuators.

In this section, we'll explore the basics of npm, how to manage dependencies, and some advanced techniques for using npm effectively in robotics projects.

2.3.1 What is npm?

n**pm** is the default package manager for Node.js, allowing developers to download, install, and manage third-party libraries (or "packages") from the **npm registry**. These packages can provide various functionalities, ranging from hardware control to communication protocols, without the need to reinvent the wheel.

For robotics projects, npm simplifies the process of adding libraries like Johnny-Five for Arduino control or serialport for serial communication.

Key Features of npm:

- **Dependency Management**: Automatically installs and manages project dependencies.
- **Version Control**: Ensures that your project always uses specific versions of packages.
- **Script Automation**: Allows you to run custom tasks using npm scripts (e.g., running tests or building the project).
- **Local and Global Packages**: Packages can be installed either locally (specific to a project) or globally (available system-wide).

2.3.2 npm Initialization

Every Node.js project starts with a file called package.json. This file acts as a configuration file, storing important information about your project, its dependencies, and scripts.

To initialize a new project and create package.json, navigate to your project folder in the terminal and run:

bash

Copy code

npm init

This command will prompt you to fill in details about your project (name, version, description, etc.). If you want to skip the prompts and use default values, use the -y flag:

bash

Copy code

npm init -y

After running this, you'll see a newly generated package.json file in your project directory. Here's an example of a basic package.json file:

json

Copy code

{

"name": "my-first-robot",

"version": "1.0.0",

"description": "A simple robot using Johnny-Five",

"main": "index.js",

"scripts": {

```
"start": "node index.js"
},
"dependencies": {},
"devDependencies": {}
}
```

2.3.3 Installing Packages with npm

The most common npm operation you'll perform is installing packages. There are two main types of package installations: **local** and **global**.

Installing Local Packages

L ocal packages are installed in the project's node_modules directory and are only available within the project. These are typically your dependencies (e.g., libraries like Johnny-Five, Robotics-SDK).
To install Johnny-Five locally:
bash
Copy code
npm install johnny-five
This command will:

1. Download the Johnny-Five package from the npm registry.
2. Install it in the node_modules folder.
3. Add Johnny-Five to the dependencies section of your package.json:

json
Copy code
```
{
"dependencies": {
"johnny-five": "^1.0.0"
}
}
```
This means that anyone who clones your project can run npm install to automatically install the same version of Johnny-Five used in your project.

Installing Global Packages

Global packages are installed system-wide and are available for any project. These are usually tools or utilities like **nodemon** (for automatic server restarts) or **robotics-cli**.

To install a package globally, use the -g flag:

bash

Copy code

npm install -g nodemon

Global packages are not listed in your project's package.json file since they are meant to be system-wide utilities.

Adding Dev Dependencies

In addition to regular dependencies (which are required for the project to run), you may also have **development dependencies**, which are only needed during development (e.g., testing frameworks or build tools).

To install a dev dependency, use the —save-dev flag:

bash

Copy code

npm install eslint —save-dev

This adds ESLint (a JavaScript linting tool) as a development dependency in your package.json:

json

Copy code

```
{
"devDependencies": {
"eslint": "^7.0.0"
}
}
```

Updating Packages

npm provides a built-in way to update packages to their latest versions. To update a specific package:

```bash
Copy code
npm update package-name
```

For example, to update Johnny-Five:

```bash
Copy code
npm update johnny-five
```

You can also check for outdated packages with:

```bash
Copy code
npm outdated
```

This will show you which of your installed packages have newer versions available.

Removing Packages

To uninstall a package:
bash
Copy code
npm uninstall package-name
For example, to uninstall Johnny-Five:
bash
Copy code
npm uninstall johnny-five
This will remove the package from the node_modules directory and also from package.json.

2.3.5 Working with npm Scripts

npm allows you to define and run custom scripts using the scripts section of your package.json. This is especially useful for running tasks like starting a server, testing, or even building your project. Here's an example package.json with npm scripts:

json

Copy code

```json
{
"scripts": {
"start": "node index.js",
"test": "echo 'No tests specified'",
"dev": "nodemon index.js"
}
}
```

To run a script, use the npm run command:

bash

Copy code

```bash
npm run dev
```

The above command will run nodemon index.js, automatically restarting the server when any files change.

Common npm Scripts for Robotics Projects:

- **Start Script**: Use this to start your robotics application:

j son
```
Copy code
"scripts": {
"start": "node robot.js"
}
```

- **Development Script**: Use nodemon to automatically restart the Node.js server when changes are made:

```
json
Copy code
"scripts": {
"dev": "nodemon robot.js"
}
```

2.3.6 Versioning and Lock Files

One of the key features of npm is its ability to lock down dependency versions, ensuring that all developers on a project use the same package versions. When npm installs a package, it creates a **package-lock.json** file that records the exact version of every installed package.

When someone else clones your project and runs npm install, npm uses this lock file to ensure that all dependencies are installed with the same versions, preventing any potential issues caused by newer, incompatible versions.

Best Practices for npm Versioning:

- Always commit your package.json and package-lock.json files to version control.
- Use **semantic versioning** (major.minor.patch) to track updates. For example, "^1.0.0" in package.json means npm will install any version 1.x.x, but not 2.0.0.

Summary

W orking with npm and understanding package management is a crucial aspect of building JavaScript-based robotics applications. npm simplifies the process of managing dependencies, versioning libraries, and automating development tasks through scripts. By mastering these tools, you will enhance your workflow and ensure that your robotics projects are scalable, maintainable, and easy to share with others.

2.4 Asynchronous Programming in Node.js for Robotic Systems

Asynchronous programming is one of the cornerstones of Node.js and plays a critical role in building responsive, efficient robotic systems. When developing robotics applications, you'll often encounter scenarios where you need to wait for input from sensors, perform time-sensitive actions, or handle multiple hardware components simultaneously. Node.js, with its non-blocking, event-driven architecture, is well-suited for such tasks.

In this section, we will explore the key concepts of asynchronous programming, including callbacks, promises, and async/await, and how they can be applied effectively in robotics.

2.4.1 Understanding Asynchronous Programming

I n contrast to synchronous programming, where tasks are executed one after another, **asynchronous programming** allows multiple tasks to run concurrently without blocking the main thread. This is essential in robotics, where actions such as reading sensor data, controlling motors, or communicating with other devices should not stop the entire system from functioning if a task takes time to complete.

Key Benefits of Asynchronous Programming for Robotics:

- **Non-Blocking I/O**: Asynchronous programming prevents I/O operations (such as reading from a sensor or network communication) from halting other tasks.
- **Concurrency**: Multiple tasks can run simultaneously, enabling robots to react quickly to real-world events, like object detection or environmental changes.
- **Efficiency**: Asynchronous code allows robots to manage their resources more efficiently, especially in real-time applications.

2.4.2 Using Callbacks in Robotics

Callbacks are one of the fundamental building blocks of asynchronous programming in Node.js. A callback is a function passed as an argument to another function and executed once a task is completed. In the context of robotics, callbacks are often used when interacting with hardware components like sensors, motors, or communication protocols.

Example: Controlling a Motor with a Callback Let's consider an example where you control a motor using Johnny-Five, a robotics framework for Node.js. The motor should start after reading a sensor, and a callback is used to execute an action once the sensor data is available.

```javascript
Copy code
const { Board, Sensor, Motor } = require("johnny-five");

const board = new Board();

board.on("ready", () => {
    const sensor = new Sensor("A0"); // Analog sensor
    const motor = new Motor(9); // Motor on pin 9

sensor.on("data", function() {
    if (this.value > 500) {
    motor.start(); // Start the motor if sensor value exceeds 500
    } else {
```

```
motor.stop(); // Stop the motor otherwise
   }
 });
 });
```

In this example, the sensor.on("data") event listener uses a callback function that checks the sensor value and controls the motor accordingly. This non-blocking behavior allows the system to continuously monitor sensor input and act on it in real-time.

2.4.3 Promises in Robotics Programming

Promises provide a more structured approach to handling asynchronous operations, especially when dealing with multiple dependent tasks. They represent a value that will be available in the future, either resolved (successful) or rejected (error).

Promises are particularly useful in robotics when you need to perform operations in sequence, such as connecting to multiple hardware components or executing a series of tasks with dependencies.

Example: Using Promises in Robotic Communication Imagine you need to establish a serial communication connection with a robot, and only after the connection is established, you can send a command to move the robot.

```javascript
Copy code
const SerialPort = require('serialport');

// Function to open a serial port and return a promise
function openSerialPort() {
return new Promise((resolve, reject) => {
const port = new SerialPort('/dev/tty-usbserial1', { baudRate: 9600 });

port.on('open', () => {
console.log('Serial port opened');
resolve(port); // Resolve the promise once the port is open
});
```

```
port.on('error', (err) => {
  reject(err); // Reject the promise in case of an error
  });
  });
  }
```

```
// Function to send a command once the serial port is open
  openSerialPort()
  .then((port) => {
  port.write('MOVE FORWARD\n', (err) => {
  if (err) {
  console.error('Error writing to port:', err);
  } else {
  console.log('Command sent');
  }
  });
  })
  .catch((err) => {
  console.error('Failed to open serial port:', err);
  });
```

In this example, the openSerialPort() function returns a promise that resolves once the serial port is successfully opened. The .then() method ensures that the robot's command is only sent once the communication channel is established, making the code more readable and manageable.

2.4.4 Async/Await for Cleaner Robotics Code

I ntroduced in ES6, **async/await** is a syntactic sugar on top of promises that allows you to write asynchronous code in a synchronous-like fashion. This makes the code easier to read and debug, which is particularly useful when dealing with complex robotic systems.

Example: Using Async/Await for Robotic Operations Let's rewrite the previous example using async/await for cleaner and more readable code.

```javascript
Copy code
const SerialPort = require('serialport');

// Function to open a serial port
async function openSerialPort() {
const port = new SerialPort('/dev/tty-usbserial1', { baudRate: 9600 });

return new Promise((resolve, reject) => {
  port.on('open', () => {
  console.log('Serial port opened');
  resolve(port);
  });

port.on('error', (err) => {
  reject(err);
```

```
});
});
}
```

```
// Async function to open port and send a command
async function controlRobot() {
try {
const port = await openSerialPort(); // Wait for the port to open
port.write('MOVE FORWARD\n'); // Send command to move the robot
console.log('Command sent');
} catch (error) {
console.error('Failed to open serial port:', error);
}
}
```

```
controlRobot(); // Execute the async function
```

Here, the openSerialPort() function returns a promise, but we handle it using await inside the controlRobot() function. This approach allows the code to flow more naturally without the nesting and chaining typical of callbacks and promises.

2.4.5 Event-Driven Architecture in Robotics

One of the most powerful features of Node.js is its event-driven architecture. Robotics often involves reacting to real-time events, such as a sensor detecting an object, a motor reaching a specific position, or a camera capturing an image. Node.js and its event system make it easy to handle such scenarios.

In Johnny-Five, for instance, every sensor or hardware component can trigger events, allowing you to write code that reacts to those events asynchronously. The on() method listens for specific events and executes a callback when the event is fired.

Example: Event-Driven Sensor Input

```javascript
Copy code
const { Board, Sensor } = require("johnny-five");

const board = new Board();

board.on("ready", () => {
    const proximity = new Sensor({
    pin: "A0",
    freq: 500 // Read the sensor every 500ms
    });
```

```
proximity.on("data", function() {
  console.log("Proximity: ", this.value);
  });

proximity.on("change", function() {
  console.log("Proximity sensor value changed");
  });
  });
```

In this example, the proximity sensor triggers two different events: data (which occurs at regular intervals) and change (which occurs whenever the sensor value changes). This event-driven approach is highly effective for real-time systems like robotics, where responsiveness is key.

Summary

A synchronous programming in Node.js provides the foundation for building responsive, real-time robotic systems. By leveraging callbacks, promises, and async/await, you can manage complex workflows, handle multiple components, and react to events efficiently. The non-blocking nature of Node.js makes it ideal for controlling hardware, reading sensor data, and communicating with various peripherals without sacrificing performance.

2.5 Event-Driven Architecture in Node.js

N ode.js is built around an **event-driven architecture** that enables it to handle asynchronous operations efficiently. This architecture is particularly beneficial for robotics, where real-time responsiveness is essential. In robotics applications, various components such as sensors, motors, and actuators constantly emit events, which need to be captured and responded to in a timely manner. Node.js, with its event-driven nature, allows developers to structure code in a way that reacts to these events without blocking other operations.

In this section, we'll explore the fundamentals of event-driven programming in Node.js and see how it applies to robotic systems using practical examples with Johnny-Five, a popular robotics framework for JavaScript.

2.5.1 Understanding the Event-Driven Model

The event-driven model in Node.js revolves around the concept of **event emitters** and **event listeners**. In this model, various components or objects can emit events, and you can register listeners to react when those events are fired.

In Node.js, the EventEmitter class (from the events module) is the core of this architecture. Many core modules in Node.js, such as HTTP servers, file systems, and even Johnny-Five components, extend EventEmitter to implement event-driven behavior.

How It Works:

1. **Event Emitters**: Objects that can trigger or "emit" events.
2. **Event Listeners**: Functions that are executed in response to a particular event being emitted.

A real-world analogy would be a doorbell (event emitter) and a person listening for the doorbell sound (event listener). When the doorbell rings (the event is emitted), the listener (person) responds by opening the door.

2.5.2 Basic Event-Driven Example in Node.js

To understand how events work, let's look at a basic example of an event emitter and listener in Node.js:
javascript

```
Copy code
const EventEmitter = require('events');

// Create an instance of the EventEmitter class
const emitter = new EventEmitter();

// Register an event listener for the 'robotStarted' event
emitter.on('robotStarted', () => {
console.log('The robot has started!');
});

// Emit the 'robotStarted' event
emitter.emit('robotStarted');
```

In this example:

- We create an instance of the EventEmitter class.
- We register an event listener using the on() method to listen for the event robotStarted.
- We emit the robotStarted event using the emit() method, which triggers

the event listener, causing the message "The robot has started!" to be logged.

This simple mechanism is the foundation of Node.js's event-driven architecture, and it becomes very powerful when applied to robotics.

2.5.3 Event-Driven Architecture in Robotics with Johnny-Five

J ohnny-Five is a robotics framework that fully embraces the event-driven nature of Node.js. It enables you to control various hardware components like motors, sensors, LEDs, and more, using event emitters and listeners. Every piece of hardware in Johnny-Five triggers events when it changes state or completes an action.

Example: Reacting to Sensor Data Events

L et's look at how a proximity sensor can trigger events, and how you can respond to them in real-time using Johnny-Five.
javascript
Copy code

```javascript
const { Board, Proximity } = require('johnny-five');

// Create a new board instance
const board = new Board();

board.on('ready', () => {
  // Create a new proximity sensor on pin A0
  const proximity = new Proximity({
  controller: 'HCSR04', // Using an ultrasonic sensor
  pin: 7
  });

// Listen for the 'data' event emitted by the sensor
  proximity.on('data', () => {
  console.log('Proximity detected: ${proximity.cm} cm away');
  });

// Listen for the 'change' event when the distance changes
  proximity.on('change', () => {
  console.log('Distance changed');
```

```
});
});
```

In this example:

- We initialize a proximity sensor using Johnny-Five.
- The sensor emits a data event every time it detects an object, providing the distance in centimeters. This data is printed out every time the event is emitted.
- The sensor also emits a change event when there is a significant change in the distance detected.

This kind of event-driven approach is ideal for robotics, where you often need to respond to constantly changing inputs from the environment.

2.5.4 Reacting to Multiple Events in Robotics

I n robotics, multiple components may need to work together, reacting to different events concurrently. For example, a robot might need to monitor several sensors and perform different actions based on input from each sensor, while simultaneously controlling motors.

Example: Coordinating Multiple Events

L et's consider a scenario where we monitor both a button press and a proximity sensor. When the button is pressed, the robot should move forward, but if an obstacle is detected by the proximity sensor, the robot should stop.

javascript

Copy code

```javascript
const { Board, Button, Motor, Proximity } = require('johnny-five');

const board = new Board();

board.on('ready', () => {
  // Set up the motor
  const motor = new Motor(9);

// Set up the button
  const button = new Button(7);

// Set up the proximity sensor
  const proximity = new Proximity({
  controller: 'HCSR04',
  pin: 8
  });

// Event listener for button press to start the motor
```

```
button.on('press', () => {
console.log('Button pressed, starting motor');
motor.start();
});
```

```
// Event listener for proximity sensor to stop the motor if an object is detected
proximity.on('data', () => {
if (proximity.cm < 20) { // If an object is detected within 20 cm
console.log('Object detected, stopping motor');
motor.stop();
}
});
});
```

In this code:

- The button emits a press event when it is pressed, causing the motor to start.
- The proximity sensor emits a data event continuously, and if an object is detected within 20 cm, the motor is stopped.

This event-driven approach allows us to handle real-time responses in robotics, reacting to input from different sensors and components simultaneously.

Benefits of Event-Driven Architecture in Robotics

The event-driven model offers several advantages when applied to robotics systems:

1. **Real-Time Responsiveness**: Event listeners allow robots to respond immediately to environmental changes, such as sensor input, user interactions, or motor feedback.

2. **Scalability**: As you add more components to your robotic system (e.g., additional sensors, actuators, or controllers), the event-driven architecture allows you to manage and coordinate them efficiently without complex polling mechanisms.

3. **Modularity**: Each component (sensor, motor, button, etc.) emits its own events and can be controlled independently, making it easier to modularize and debug the system.

4. **Efficiency**: Since events are emitted asynchronously, Node.js's event loop ensures that the system doesn't block while waiting for an event to occur, making efficient use of CPU and memory resources.

2.5.5 Event-Driven Error Handling in Robotics

H andling errors in an event-driven system is also crucial, especially in robotics, where hardware components might fail or behave unpredictably. Johnny-Five allows you to attach listeners to error events to ensure that your robot can handle such situations gracefully.

Example: Handling Errors in a Robotics System

javascript

Copy code

```javascript
const { Board, Motor } = require('johnny-five');

const board = new Board();

board.on('ready', () => {
  const motor = new Motor(9);

// Catch motor errors
  motor.on('error', (err) => {
  console.error('Motor error:', err);
  motor.stop();
  });

// Start the motor
  motor.start();
  });
```

In this example, the motor emits an error event if something goes wrong (e.g., a wiring issue or overload). We handle this error by stopping the motor and logging the error to avoid further damage to the system.

Summary

N ode.js's event-driven architecture provides a powerful and flexible framework for building responsive, real-time robotic systems. By leveraging event emitters and listeners, developers can write modular and scalable code that reacts to the ever-changing conditions of the physical world. Whether it's responding to sensor data, coordinating multiple components, or handling errors gracefully, the event-driven model ensures that robotic applications can perform efficiently and effectively in real-time environments.

2.6 Creating a Basic Node.js Robotics Application

I n this section, we'll bring together everything we've covered in the chapter and create a simple yet functional Node.js application to control a robot. We'll use Johnny-Five as the framework for interacting with hardware components and follow the event-driven principles we explored earlier. This basic robotics project will control an LED and a motor, responding to button presses in real time.

Step 1: Setting Up the Project

B efore writing any code, we need to initialize a new Node.js project and install the necessary dependencies. Here's how to set up the environment:

1. **Initialize a New Node.js Project:** Open your terminal and create a new project directory for your robotics application. Inside that directory, run the following command to initialize a new Node.js project:

bash

```
Copy code
mkdir basic-robotics-app
cd basic-robotics-app
npm init -y
```

This creates a package.json file, which manages the project's dependencies.

1. **Install Johnny-Five:** Johnny-Five is the robotics framework we'll use to interact with hardware. Install it using npm:

bash

```
Copy code
npm install johnny-five
```

Step 2: Writing the Application Code

Now that the environment is set up, let's create the basic Node.js application. The goal is to control an LED and a motor based on user input via a button press.

1. **Create a New JavaScript File:** In your project directory, create a new file called robot.js. This will contain the code for the robot.
2. **Write the Code:** Open robot.js and write the following code:

```javascript
Copy code
const { Board, Led, Button, Motor } = require('johnny-five');

// Create a new board instance
const board = new Board();

board.on('ready', () => {
  console.log('Board is ready!');

// Initialize the components
  const led = new Led(13); // LED connected to pin 13
  const button = new Button(7); // Button connected to pin 7
  const motor = new Motor(9); // Motor connected to pin 9

// Turn on the LED when the button is pressed
```

```
button.on('press', () => {
console.log('Button pressed!');
led.on(); // Turn on the LED
motor.start(255); // Start the motor at full speed
});
```

```
// Turn off the LED when the button is released
button.on('release', () => {
console.log('Button released!');
led.off(); // Turn off the LED
motor.stop(); // Stop the motor
});
});
```

Explanation of the Code:

- **Board Initialization:** The Board instance represents the Arduino or microcontroller board, and the code within the board.on('ready') block will execute once the board is ready for communication.
- **LED and Button Setup:** We define an LED on pin 13, a button on pin 7, and a motor on pin 9. These pins correspond to where each component is physically connected to the board.
- **Event-Driven Interaction:** The button has two event listeners:
- press: This event fires when the button is pressed. The LED turns on, and the motor starts.
- release: This event fires when the button is released. The LED turns off, and the motor stops.

This code demonstrates a simple event-driven robotics application using Johnny-Five.

Step 3: Running the Application

To run the application, ensure that your Arduino or compatible board is connected to your computer, and then execute the following command in your terminal:

bash

Copy code

node robot.js

If everything is set up correctly, you should be able to control the LED and motor by pressing and releasing the button. The LED will light up, and the motor will run while the button is pressed, and both will stop when the button is released.

Summary

In this chapter, we explored the fundamentals of using Node.js for robotics development. We covered:

- The basics of **Node.js**, including its event-driven architecture, which makes it ideal for real-time systems like robotics.
- How to **install and configure** Node.js for robotics projects and use **npm** to manage project dependencies.
- The importance of **asynchronous programming** and how Node.js handles non-blocking I/O operations, which are essential for smooth robotic control.
- The significance of **event-driven programming** in robotics, and how Johnny-Five embraces this paradigm to interact with hardware components.

We concluded with a practical example where you created a basic Node.js robotics application that controls an LED and a motor using a button.

This chapter laid the foundation for building more complex robotic systems. In the next chapter, we'll dive deeper into working with specific hardware components like sensors, motors, and servos, and how to programmatically control them to create more intelligent and interactive robots.

3.1 What is Johnny-Five?

Johnny-Five is an open-source JavaScript robotics framework that simplifies the process of controlling hardware components such as sensors, motors, and microcontrollers through JavaScript. Created by Rick Waldron in 2012, it enables developers to build and control robots using familiar JavaScript syntax and concepts, making robotics more accessible to the vast community of JavaScript developers.

Johnny-Five operates on top of Node.js and communicates with various microcontroller boards, most notably Arduino, but it also supports a wide range of other hardware platforms such as the Raspberry Pi, Tessel, Intel Galileo, and more. By abstracting low-level hardware protocols, Johnny-Five allows developers to focus on building intelligent applications rather than worrying about the underlying complexities of communication between software and hardware.

3.1.1 Key Features of Johnny-Five:

- **Cross-Platform Support:** Johnny-Five can control a variety of hardware platforms, including Arduino, BeagleBone, and Raspberry Pi. This cross-platform flexibility makes it a versatile tool for robotics development.
- **Real-Time Interaction:** Johnny-Five leverages Node.js's non-blocking, event-driven architecture, making it ideal for robotics, where real-time control and interaction are critical.
- **Modular Components:** Johnny-Five provides abstractions for many common hardware components, such as LEDs, motors, sensors, and servos. Developers can control these components with simple JavaScript code, without needing to write low-level microcontroller code.
- **Growing Ecosystem:** The Johnny-Five ecosystem is continuously growing, with an active developer community contributing new libraries, plugins, and hardware support. This makes it easier to experiment with and expand the functionality of robotic projects.
- **Extensibility:** Johnny-Five allows you to extend the functionality of its components by writing custom logic and combining different hardware modules, making it highly customizable for advanced projects.

Johnny-Five stands out as a powerful framework for those who are familiar with JavaScript and want to explore the exciting world of robotics without the steep learning curve typically associated with hardware programming.

3.1.2 How Johnny-Five Fits into JavaScript Robotics Development:

J avaScript has become a dominant language in web development, and with Johnny-Five, it has extended its reach into the world of robotics. For JavaScript developers, using Johnny-Five means leveraging existing JavaScript skills to build and control hardware, making it easier to develop powerful robotic systems.

Johnny-Five interacts with microcontrollers using the **Firmata protocol**, which allows the board to communicate with Johnny-Five over a serial connection. In a typical Johnny-Five setup, the JavaScript code runs on your computer (or server), and commands are sent to the microcontroller to execute actions, like turning on an LED or moving a motor.

3.1.3 A Brief History of Johnny-Five:

Named after the famous robot from the 1986 film *Short Circuit*, Johnny-Five was first introduced as a library for controlling Arduino boards using JavaScript. Since then, it has evolved into a full-fledged framework for robotics development. Over time, it has grown to support multiple platforms and hardware components, becoming the go-to solution for JavaScript-based robotics development.

Johnny-Five's rise in popularity is due to its simplicity and versatility. By lowering the barrier of entry into robotics, Johnny-Five has empowered a new wave of developers and hobbyists to experiment with building intelligent machines using JavaScript.

3.1.4 Why Use Johnny-Five for Robotics Development?

- **Ease of Use:** Johnny-Five makes controlling hardware components as easy as writing JavaScript code. There's no need for deep knowledge of electronics or microcontroller programming. If you're comfortable with JavaScript, you can get started with Johnny-Five quickly.
- **JavaScript Integration:** Many developers are already familiar with JavaScript and Node.js, making Johnny-Five a natural extension for building physical systems. It's a seamless way to apply web development skills to the world of robotics.
- **Wide Hardware Support:** Johnny-Five supports a range of microcontrollers and single-board computers, making it a flexible choice whether you're building small DIY projects or larger robotics systems.
- **Community and Resources:** The Johnny-Five community is active and supportive, with plenty of resources available to help you get started. Tutorials, documentation, and examples are widely available, reducing the learning curve.

3.1.5 Real-World Applications of Johnny-Five:

J ohnny-Five is used in a variety of fields, from educational robotics kits to advanced research and development projects. Some of the common applications include:

- **DIY Projects:** Johnny-Five is popular among hobbyists building robots, drones, and automated systems at home.
- **Education:** The framework is widely used in classrooms to teach students about electronics, robotics, and programming in a hands-on way.
- **Prototyping:** Johnny-Five is often used for rapid prototyping of robotics applications, where quick iterations are needed to test new ideas or designs.
- **Industrial Automation:** While Johnny-Five is more commonly seen in hobbyist and educational projects, its use in industrial automation and IoT (Internet of Things) applications is growing as the framework matures.

Summary

J ohnny-Five represents a shift in how robotics can be developed, democratizing access to the field by making it more approachable for software developers, particularly those in the JavaScript ecosystem. With its ability to communicate with a wide range of hardware platforms and its event-driven, real-time capabilities, Johnny-Five has opened up exciting possibilities for building intelligent robots.

3.2 Hardware Requirements for Johnny-Five

J ohnny-Five is a JavaScript framework that bridges the gap between software development and physical hardware control. Before diving into building robotics projects, it's essential to understand the hardware components that Johnny-Five works with and the requirements needed to set up your robotics projects.

3.2.1 Microcontrollers and Single-Board Computers (SBCs)

J ohnny-Five communicates with a variety of microcontrollers and single-board computers (SBCs). These devices act as the "brain" of your robot, processing commands and controlling connected hardware like sensors, motors, and LEDs.

Here are some of the most commonly used microcontrollers and SBCs with Johnny-Five:

- **Arduino**: The Arduino family (Uno, Mega, Nano, etc.) is one of the most popular platforms for Johnny-Five projects. It uses the Firmata protocol to allow Johnny-Five to send commands over a serial connection. The Arduino is excellent for small robotics projects where you need to control simple components like LEDs, motors, and basic sensors.
- **Raspberry Pi**: A powerful single-board computer that runs a full Linux operating system, the Raspberry Pi is commonly used in more advanced Johnny-Five projects. It can run Johnny-Five code directly without needing to communicate with a separate host computer, giving you more flexibility for larger projects or those requiring more processing power.
- **BeagleBone**: Another single-board computer similar to the Raspberry Pi, the BeagleBone provides more GPIO pins, making it suitable for larger robotics projects with many connected sensors and actuators.
- **Tessel**: Tessel is a microcontroller that's fully programmable in JavaScript and designed to integrate seamlessly with Node.js and Johnny-Five.

It's particularly useful for developers who want to stay entirely in the JavaScript ecosystem without needing a separate host computer.

- **Intel Galileo**: This is an Intel microcontroller board that is Arduino-compatible but offers more processing power and connectivity options, making it useful for more complex Johnny-Five robotics applications.

Each of these platforms has its strengths. For beginners, the Arduino is a great choice due to its simplicity, while more experienced developers working on advanced projects may prefer Raspberry Pi or BeagleBone for their flexibility and power.

3.2.2 Firmata Protocol

To communicate with microcontrollers like Arduino, Johnny-Five uses the **Firmata** protocol. Firmata is a standard protocol for communicating with microcontrollers from software running on a computer, such as Node.js with Johnny-Five.

The most common use of Firmata with Johnny-Five is to send commands to an Arduino board over USB. Before using Johnny-Five, you need to upload the StandardFirmata firmware to your Arduino board using the Arduino IDE. Once Firmata is installed on the board, Johnny-Five can send commands directly to the hardware, allowing you to control components like motors, servos, and sensors.

3.2.3 Power Supply

Your robot will need a power supply to run both the microcontroller and any attached components, such as motors or sensors. Depending on your project, the power requirements can vary greatly. Here's a breakdown of typical power needs:

- **Microcontrollers** like Arduino typically require between 5V and 9V DC power. You can power these devices through USB or a dedicated power source like a battery pack or an external power adapter.
- **Single-Board Computers** like the Raspberry Pi often require a stable 5V power supply delivered through a micro-USB or USB-C connection. For larger projects, you may need a power supply with more amperage, especially if you're connecting additional components that require significant power (such as cameras or high-power sensors).
- **Motors and Actuators**: If your robot includes motors, you'll likely need an external power supply to handle their current requirements, as most microcontrollers can't directly power motors. Motor drivers or H-bridge circuits are typically used to control motors from a microcontroller.

Make sure to provide a separate power source for high-power components like motors or servos to avoid overloading your microcontroller.

3.2.4 Input and Output Components

To build robots, you'll need to interact with the physical world using input and output (I/O) components. Here are some common hardware components you'll use with Johnny-Five:

- **Sensors**: Sensors allow your robot to perceive its environment by detecting various inputs, such as light, temperature, distance, or motion. Johnny-Five provides support for many common sensors, including:
- Ultrasonic distance sensors
- Infrared (IR) sensors
- Temperature and humidity sensors
- Light sensors (photocells)
- Accelerometers and gyroscopes (for motion detection)
- **Actuators**: These are the components that cause movement or action in your robot, such as motors and servos. Johnny-Five makes it easy to control these components programmatically.
- **Servos**: Rotational motors used to move robot arms, joints, or wheels.
- **DC Motors**: Used for continuous movement, such as driving wheels on a robot.
- **Stepper Motors**: Provide precise control over angular movement, used in robotic arms or 3D printers.
- **LEDs and Displays**: LEDs are often used for visual indicators, while displays like LCD screens allow your robot to present information to users.
- **LEDs**: Single-color or RGB (multicolor) LEDs are easy to control using

Johnny-Five for signaling or feedback purposes.

- **7-Segment Displays**: Simple numeric displays to show data like sensor readings or system status.
- **LCDs**: More advanced displays capable of showing custom text or graphics.

3.2.5 Communication Interfaces

R obots often need to communicate with other devices or systems. Johnny-Five supports a variety of communication interfaces to enable this:

- **Serial Communication (UART)**: This is the most common interface for communicating with microcontrollers. Johnny-Five can send and receive data over serial using the Firmata protocol.
- **I2C and SPI**: These protocols are used for communication between a microcontroller and sensors or other hardware modules. Many advanced sensors, like IMUs (Inertial Measurement Units) or environmental sensors, use I2C or SPI.
- **Wi-Fi and Bluetooth**: For projects that require wireless communication, Johnny-Five can integrate with modules like the ESP8266 or ESP32 to add Wi-Fi or Bluetooth capabilities. This is especially useful for building IoT-enabled robots.
- **GPIO Pins**: For SBCs like Raspberry Pi, Johnny-Five supports the use of GPIO (General Purpose Input/Output) pins, allowing you to directly control connected components like LEDs, motors, or relays.

3.2.6 Additional Tools and Accessories

While the core hardware components mentioned above are essential, there are some additional tools and accessories you'll likely need when working with Johnny-Five and robotics:

- **Breadboards and Jumper Wires**: Used for prototyping circuits and connecting components without soldering.
- **Resistors and Capacitors**: Basic electronic components that help manage current and voltage in your circuits.
- **H-Bridge or Motor Driver Circuits**: Necessary for controlling high-power DC motors from a microcontroller.
- **Multimeter**: An essential tool for debugging circuits and ensuring that your hardware is functioning properly.
- **Soldering Kit**: For more permanent connections in your robotics projects, especially when working with more advanced or custom-designed robots.

Summary

T he hardware components you choose are the foundation of your robotic systems, and understanding how to select, connect, and power these components is crucial for successful development with Johnny-Five. By using the right microcontroller, sensors, actuators, and communication protocols, you can bring your robotic ideas to life.

3.3 Installing Johnny-Five in Node.js

To begin developing robotics applications with Johnny-Five, you need to install the framework in your Node.js environment. This section will guide you through the installation process step by step, ensuring you have everything set up to start building intelligent robots.

3.3.1 Prerequisites

B efore you install Johnny-Five, ensure you have the following prerequisites in place:

- **Node.js**: Ensure you have Node.js installed on your system. You can download it from the official Node.js website. Johnny-Five requires Node.js version 10 or higher.
    - **npm (Node Package Manager)**: npm comes bundled with Node.js and is used to manage packages in your Node.js applications. It allows you to install Johnny-Five and its dependencies easily.
    - **A Supported Microcontroller or SBC**: Make sure you have a compatible microcontroller or single-board computer (like an Arduino, Raspberry Pi, or BeagleBone) that you can connect to your computer. Ensure that you have the necessary drivers installed if required.

3.3.2 Setting Up Your Project Directory

1. **Create a New Directory**: Start by creating a new directory for your robotics project. Open your terminal or command prompt and run the following command:

b ash
     Copy code
     mkdir my-johnny-five-robot
Replace my-johnny-five-robot with your preferred project name.

1. **Navigate to Your Project Directory**: Change into the new directory:

bash
     Copy code
     cd my-johnny-five-robot

1. **Initialize a New Node.js Project**: Initialize your project with npm to create a package.json file. Run the following command and follow the prompts:

bash
     Copy code
     npm init -y
The -y flag automatically answers "yes" to all prompts, creating a default

package.json file.

3.3.3 Installing Johnny-Five

Now that your project directory is set up, you can install the Johnny-Five framework:

1. **Install Johnny-Five**: Use npm to install Johnny-Five and its dependencies. Run the following command:

bash
Copy code
npm install johnny-five

This command will download and install the Johnny-Five library and its dependencies into your project directory, creating a node_modules folder where all packages will be stored.

1. **Verify the Installation**: Once the installation is complete, you can verify that Johnny-Five is installed correctly by checking your package.json file. Open package.json and look for "johnny-five" listed under dependencies. It should look something like this:

json
Copy code
"dependencies": {
"johnny-five": "^2.x.x" // Version may vary based on the latest release
}

3.3.4 Installing Firmata on Arduino (if applicable)

I f you are using an Arduino microcontroller, you need to upload the Firmata firmware to it. Follow these steps:

1. **Open the Arduino IDE**: Launch the Arduino Integrated Development Environment (IDE).

2. **Install Firmata Library**: If you haven't already installed it, go to Sketch > Include Library > Manage Libraries... and search for "Firmata." Install the "Firmata" library.

3. **Upload StandardFirmata**: Once Firmata is installed, open the example sketch by going to File > Examples > Firmata > StandardFirmata. Upload this sketch to your Arduino by selecting the appropriate board and port from the Tools menu and clicking the upload button (right arrow icon).

4. **Connect Your Arduino**: Make sure your Arduino is connected to your computer via USB. Once the upload is complete, your Arduino is ready to communicate with Johnny-Five.

3.3.5 Testing Your Installation

N ow that you have Johnny-Five installed and your microcontroller set up, you can write a simple script to test your installation:

1. **Create a New JavaScript File**: In your project directory, create a new file named test.js:

bash
Copy code
touch test.js

1. **Write a Simple Test Script**: Open test.js in your preferred code editor and add the following code:

javascript
Copy code
```
const { Board, Led } = require("johnny-five");
const board = new Board();

board.on("ready", function() {
    const led = new Led(13); // Use the onboard LED for testing
    led.blink(500); // Blink the LED every 500 milliseconds
});
```
This script initializes a board and blinks the onboard LED on pin 13.

1. **Run the Script**: Save your changes and return to your terminal. Run the script using Node.js:

bash

Copy code

node test.js

If everything is set up correctly, the onboard LED should start blinking, indicating that Johnny-Five is working as expected.

3.3.6 Troubleshooting Common Installation Issues

I f you encounter issues during installation or when running your test script, consider the following troubleshooting tips:

• **Check Node.js and npm Versions**: Ensure you have the correct versions of Node.js and npm installed. You can check your versions by running:

bash
Copy code
node -v
npm -v

- **Firmware Upload**: Make sure you have uploaded the Firmata firmware to your Arduino correctly. If the LED does not blink, double-check the connection and the code.
- **Check USB Connection**: Ensure your microcontroller is connected to your computer properly. If you are using an Arduino, the correct port must be selected in the Arduino IDE.
- **Consult the Documentation**: If issues persist, consult the Johnny-Five documentation and community forums for more help.

Summary

W ith Johnny-Five successfully installed and your development environment set up, you are now ready to start building intelligent robots using JavaScript. In the following sections, we will explore how to work with various sensors, motors, and other components in Johnny-Five, allowing you to create dynamic and interactive robotic systems.

3.4 Key Concepts and Components of Johnny-Five

J ohnny-Five is a powerful robotics framework that provides a high-level API for building interactive robots and hardware projects using JavaScript. Understanding the key concepts and components of Johnny-Five is essential for effectively leveraging its capabilities in your robotics applications. In this section, we will explore the fundamental concepts, essential components, and how they work together to enable robotic development.

3.4.1 Board

The Board class is the central component in Johnny-Five. It represents the physical hardware board (e.g., Arduino, Raspberry Pi) and serves as the communication interface between the JavaScript code and the hardware. The Board class initializes the board and manages the connection to it.

Key Features:

- Initializes the board and manages its state.
- Listens for hardware events (e.g., ready, error).
- Provides access to various hardware components (e.g., sensors, actuators).

Example:

```javascript
Copy code
const { Board } = require("johnny-five");
const board = new Board();

board.on("ready", function() {
  console.log("Board is ready!");
});
```

3.4.2 Pins

In Johnny-Five, pins are the physical connection points on a microcontroller. Each pin can serve different purposes, such as digital input/output, analog input, or PWM output. You can control these pins through Johnny-Five, allowing you to read sensor data or control motors and LEDs.

Types of Pins:

- **Digital Pins:** Used for digital input (high/low) and output (on/off).
- **Analog Pins:** Used for reading analog values (e.g., from sensors).
- **PWM Pins:** Used for pulse-width modulation to control motors and brightness.

Example:

```javascript
Copy code
const { Board, Led } = require("johnny-five");
const board = new Board();

board.on("ready", function() {
    const led = new Led(13); // Use digital pin 13 for the LED
    led.on(); // Turn the LED on
});
```

3.4.3 Components

J ohnny-Five provides various built-in components that simplify the interaction with hardware. Each component encapsulates the behavior of specific hardware elements, such as motors, sensors, and displays.

Common Components:

- **LED:** Represents an LED connected to a pin, enabling control over its state (on/off) and brightness.
- **Servo:** Controls the position of a servo motor, allowing for precise movement.
- **Motor:** Represents a DC motor, enabling forward and backward control.
- **Button:** Monitors the state of a push button, triggering events based on user input.
- **Sensor:** Represents various sensors (e.g., temperature, distance, light) for gathering data.

Example:

```javascript
Copy code
const { Board, Led, Button } = require("johnny-five");
const board = new Board();

board.on("ready", function() {
  const led = new Led(13);
  const button = new Button(2);
```

```javascript
button.on("press", function() {
  led.on(); // Turn LED on when button is pressed
  });

button.on("release", function() {
  led.off(); // Turn LED off when button is released
  });
  });
```

3.4.4 Events

J ohnny-Five employs an event-driven architecture, allowing you to respond to various events generated by hardware components. Events can trigger specific actions in your code, making your robotics applications more interactive.

Common Events:

- **"ready"**: Emitted when the board is ready for interaction.
- **"press"**: Emitted when a button is pressed.
- **"release"**: Emitted when a button is released.
- **"change"**: Emitted when the state of a sensor changes.

Example:

```javascript
Copy code
const { Board, Button } = require("johnny-five");
const board = new Board();

board.on("ready", function() {
  const button = new Button(2);

button.on("press", function() {
  console.log("Button pressed!");
  });
  });
```

3.4.5 Using Libraries and Plugins

Johnny-Five supports various libraries and plugins that enhance its functionality. You can integrate additional sensors, motors, and other hardware components through community-driven libraries, expanding your project's capabilities.

Example Libraries:

- **Firmata:** Enables communication between Johnny-Five and various microcontrollers.
- **ServoBlaster:** Allows control of servos on Raspberry Pi.

3.4.6 Working with Grids and Arrays

In robotics, it's often necessary to represent multiple components or sensors in a structured manner. Johnny-Five allows you to work with grids and arrays, enabling organized handling of multiple devices.

Example:

```javascript
Copy code
const { Board, Led } = require("johnny-five");
const board = new Board();

board.on("ready", function() {
  const leds = [];
  for (let i = 0; i < 5; i++) {
    leds[i] = new Led(i + 2); // Connect 5 LEDs to pins 2 to 6
    leds[i].on(); // Turn on all LEDs
  }
});
```

Summary

U nderstanding the key concepts and components of Johnny-Five is crucial for successful robotic development with JavaScript. The Board serves as the foundation, while pins and components enable interaction with hardware. Leveraging events and integrating additional libraries enhances the functionality and interactivity of your robotic applications. With this foundational knowledge, you are now prepared to dive deeper into using Johnny-Five for your robotics projects and explore the exciting possibilities it offers.

3.5 Building a Basic Robot with Johnny-Five

I n this section, we will guide you through the process of building a simple robot using the Johnny-Five framework. This example will demonstrate how to combine various components, such as motors and sensors, to create a functional robot. We will also cover the wiring setup, code implementation, and how to get your robot up and running.

3.5.1 Project Overview

For this example, we will create a basic robot that can move forward, backward, and turn. The robot will be equipped with two DC motors for movement and an ultrasonic distance sensor to detect obstacles. When an obstacle is detected within a certain distance, the robot will stop and reverse briefly before changing direction.

Components Needed:

- **Microcontroller:** Arduino Uno or compatible board
- **DC Motors:** 2
- **Motor Driver:** L298N or similar
- **Ultrasonic Distance Sensor:** HC-SR04
- **Chassis:** Any small robot chassis to hold components
- **Wires and Connectors:** To make connections
- **Power Supply:** Battery pack or power supply for the motors and microcontroller

3.5.2 Wiring Setup

T o build the robot, you will need to wire the components correctly. Here's a basic wiring setup for the robot:

1. **DC Motors:** Connect the motors to the motor driver.

- Motor 1 (Left) - Connect to Output A on the motor driver.
- Motor 2 (Right) - Connect to Output B on the motor driver.

1. **Motor Driver Connections:**

- Connect the motor driver's input pins to the Arduino. For example:
- IN1 (Motor 1) → Digital Pin 3
- IN2 (Motor 1) → Digital Pin 4
- IN3 (Motor 2) → Digital Pin 5
- IN4 (Motor 2) → Digital Pin 6
- Connect the motor driver's enable pins to the Arduino (if required) or to a power source for constant power.

1. **Ultrasonic Sensor:**

- VCC → 5V on the Arduino
- GND → GND on the Arduino
- Trig → Digital Pin 8
- Echo → Digital Pin 9

The wiring setup is summarized below:

```scss
Copy code
Arduino Pin | Motor Driver | Ultrasonic Sensor
———————|——————————|——————————-
3 | IN1 (Motor 1) |
4 | IN2 (Motor 1) |
5 | IN3 (Motor 2) |
6 | IN4 (Motor 2) |
8 | | Trig
9 | | Echo
5V | | VCC
GND | | GND
```

3.5.3 Code Implementation

Now that the hardware is set up, let's write the code to control the robot using Johnny-Five.

Installation: Ensure you have Johnny-Five installed in your Node.js environment. If not, you can install it via npm:

bash

Copy code

npm install johnny-five

Robot Code:

Here's a simple implementation of the robot's functionality:

javascript

Copy code

```javascript
const { Board, Motor, Proximity } = require("johnny-five");
const board = new Board();

board.on("ready", function() {
  // Create motors
  const motor1 = new Motor([3, 4]); // Pins for Motor 1
  const motor2 = new Motor([5, 6]); // Pins for Motor 2

  // Create proximity sensor
  const proximity = new Proximity({
  controller: "HCSR04",
  pin: 8
  });
```

```javascript
// Function to move forward
  function moveForward() {
  motor1.forward(255); // Set speed to max
  motor2.forward(255);
  }

// Function to stop
  function stop() {
  motor1.stop();
  motor2.stop();
  }

// Function to reverse
  function reverse() {
  motor1.reverse(255);
  motor2.reverse(255);
  board.wait(1000, stop); // Reverse for 1 second
  }

// Function to change direction
  function changeDirection() {
  motor1.reverse(255); // Move left motor backward
  motor2.forward(255); // Move right motor forward
  board.wait(500, stop); // Change direction for half a second
  }

// Move forward initially
  moveForward();

// Listen for proximity events
  proximity.on("data", function() {
  console.log("Distance: " + this.cm + " cm");
  if (this.cm < 15) { // If an obstacle is detected within 15 cm
```

```
stop();
reverse();
changeDirection();
moveForward(); // Resume moving forward
}
});
});
```

Explanation of the Code:

- **Board Initialization:** Initializes the board and sets up motors and sensors.
- **Motor Functions:** Defines functions to move the robot forward, stop, reverse, and change direction.
- **Proximity Sensor:** Listens for distance readings. If an obstacle is detected within 15 cm, the robot stops, reverses, changes direction, and resumes moving forward.

3.5.4 Testing Your Robot

1. **Upload the Code:** Use the Arduino IDE to upload any required setup code (such as the Firmata protocol if using Firmata with Johnny-Five) to the Arduino board.
2. **Run the Node.js Application:** Open a terminal and run your Node.js application using:

b ash
Copy code
node your-robot-code.js

1. **Observe Behavior:** Place the robot on a flat surface and observe its behavior. It should move forward and respond to obstacles by reversing and changing direction.

Summary

By following this guide, you have successfully built a basic robot using Johnny-Five. This project has introduced you to essential components like motors and sensors, as well as the core programming concepts of event handling and motor control. As you gain more experience with Johnny-Five and robotics, you can enhance this robot by adding more sensors, refining its movement, or integrating additional features like remote control or advanced AI behaviors.

3.6 Understanding Johnny-Five Board Object and IO Plugins

I n this section, we will explore the foundational aspects of the Johnny-Five framework, focusing on the Board object and Input/Output (IO) plugins that allow developers to connect various hardware components seamlessly. Understanding these components is crucial for effectively using Johnny-Five in your robotics projects.

3.6.1 The Board Object

The Board object in Johnny-Five acts as the central hub for communication between your JavaScript code and the hardware. When you initialize a new Board instance, it establishes a connection with the microcontroller (such as an Arduino) and manages the configuration of various pins.

Key Features of the Board Object:

- **Initialization:** The Board object initializes the connection to the hardware upon creation. You can configure options, such as the port, which allows you to specify which board to connect to.
- **Event Handling:** The Board object emits events that you can listen to. For instance, you can respond to the "ready" event, which indicates that the board is successfully connected and ready for interaction.
- **Pin Management:** The Board object manages the digital and analog pins of the microcontroller, allowing you to control various components like motors, sensors, and LEDs.
- **Plugin Support:** The Board object can load additional IO plugins to support a wider range of hardware interfaces, enhancing its versatility.

Example of Board Initialization:

```javascript
Copy code
const { Board } = require("johnny-five");
const board = new Board({
```

```
port: "COM3" // Change this to your board's port
});

board.on("ready", () => {
console.log("Board is ready!");
});
```

3.6.2 Input/Output (IO) Plugins

J ohnny-Five supports various IO plugins, which expand the functionality of the framework and allow communication with specific hardware components. These plugins abstract the complexities of interfacing with different devices, making it easier for developers to focus on building their applications.

Common IO Plugins:

- **Firmata:** The Firmata protocol allows you to control Arduino boards from your JavaScript application without writing any Arduino code. Johnny-Five comes with built-in support for Firmata, making it easier to interact with Arduino.
- **Raspberry Pi:** The Raspberry Pi plugin allows you to use Johnny-Five with Raspberry Pi boards. This plugin supports GPIO pins, PWM, and I2C interfaces.
- **BeagleBone:** The BeagleBone plugin provides similar functionality for BeagleBone boards, enabling you to interact with its GPIO and other interfaces.

Example of Using an IO Plugin:

To use the Firmata protocol, you only need to install the Firmata library on your Arduino. The following code demonstrates how to initialize a board with Firmata:

javascript

Copy code

```javascript
const { Board } = require("johnny-five");
const board = new Board({
io: new Firmata()
});

board.on("ready", function() {
console.log("Connected to Arduino via Firmata!");
});
```

Conclusion

In this chapter, we delved into the Johnny-Five framework, a powerful tool for building robotic applications using JavaScript. We explored the core concepts of Johnny-Five, including its architecture, the Board object, and the various IO plugins that facilitate communication with hardware components.

We also covered how to install Johnny-Five, set up hardware requirements, and build a basic robot, providing hands-on experience in working with motors and sensors. This foundation will enable you to create more complex robotic systems and projects.

As you progress, the understanding of the Board object and IO plugins will be invaluable as you integrate additional sensors, actuators, and communication protocols into your robotic applications. In the next chapter, we will further enhance our projects by exploring advanced robotics components and their integration within the Johnny-Five framework.

4.1 Introduction to Sensors in Robotics

S ensors play a crucial role in robotics, serving as the primary means through which robots perceive and interact with their environment. They gather data about various physical phenomena, allowing robots to make informed decisions and perform tasks autonomously. In this section, we'll explore the different types of sensors commonly used in robotic applications and how they integrate with JavaScript through the Johnny-Five framework.

4.1.1 Types of Sensors

Robotic systems can incorporate a variety of sensors, each designed to detect specific environmental conditions or objects. Here are some of the most common types of sensors used in robotics:

- **Proximity Sensors:** These sensors detect the presence of nearby objects without physical contact. Common types include ultrasonic and infrared sensors. Proximity sensors are essential for obstacle detection and avoidance in mobile robots.
- **Light Sensors:** Light sensors, or photoresistors, measure ambient light levels. They can be used in projects that require light-following behavior or environmental monitoring.
- **Temperature Sensors:** Temperature sensors, such as thermistors and thermocouples, provide data on ambient temperature. These sensors are crucial for applications in environmental monitoring and climate control.
- **Humidity Sensors:** Humidity sensors measure moisture levels in the air. They are often used in weather stations and agricultural applications to monitor environmental conditions.
- **Accelerometers and Gyroscopes:** These sensors measure acceleration and angular velocity, respectively. They are vital for robotics applications requiring orientation and movement detection, such as drones and mobile robots.
- **Cameras:** Camera modules enable visual perception, allowing robots to recognize and interpret visual data. They are widely used in computer

vision applications, including object detection and facial recognition.

4.1.2 Integrating Sensors with Johnny-Five

The Johnny-Five framework simplifies the integration of sensors into JavaScript-based robotics projects. Each sensor type has its corresponding class in Johnny-Five, making it straightforward to read data and implement logic based on sensor inputs.

Example: Using an Ultrasonic Sensor

The ultrasonic sensor is commonly used for measuring distance and detecting obstacles. It emits sound waves and measures the time it takes for the waves to return after hitting an object. Here's a simple example of using an ultrasonic sensor with Johnny-Five:

```javascript
Copy code
const { Board, Proximity } = require("johnny-five");

const board = new Board();

board.on("ready", () => {
  const proximity = new Proximity({
  pin: "A0", // Connect the ultrasonic sensor to analog pin A0
  freq: 500 // Frequency of reading in milliseconds
  });

proximity.on("data", () => {
```

```
console.log(`Distance: ${this.cm} cm`);
});
});
```

In this code:

- We initialize the Board and create a Proximity instance, specifying the pin to which the sensor is connected.
- The data event is used to retrieve distance measurements from the ultrasonic sensor continuously.

4.1.3 Practical Applications of Sensors in Robotics

Sensors enable a wide range of applications in robotics, including:

- **Obstacle Avoidance:** Robots equipped with proximity sensors can navigate through environments without colliding with objects. This capability is essential for autonomous vehicles and drones.
- **Environmental Monitoring:** Temperature and humidity sensors are utilized in agricultural robots and weather stations to collect data about the environment.
- **Robotic Vision:** Integrating cameras with computer vision algorithms allows robots to identify and interact with objects in their surroundings, enhancing their functionality in various tasks, such as sorting and navigation.
- **Feedback Control:** Sensors provide real-time data that can be used for feedback control in robotic systems. For example, feedback from accelerometers can help maintain balance in humanoid robots.

Summary

I n this section, we introduced the essential role of sensors in robotics and their various types, including proximity, light, temperature, humidity sensors, accelerometers, gyroscopes, and cameras. We also highlighted how the Johnny-Five framework facilitates sensor integration through simple JavaScript code, allowing developers to easily implement sensor functionality in their robotic applications.

4.2 Working with Motors and Actuators

I n robotics, motors and actuators are essential components that enable movement and control of robotic systems. While sensors provide data about the environment, motors and actuators convert electrical energy into mechanical motion, allowing robots to interact with their surroundings. This section explores the various types of motors and actuators used in robotics, their integration with JavaScript through the Johnny-Five framework, and practical applications in robotic projects.

4.2.1 Types of Motors and Actuators

There are several types of motors and actuators commonly used in robotic applications, each suited for different tasks:

- **DC Motors:** Direct current (DC) motors are the most basic type of motor, providing continuous rotation. They are widely used in mobile robots and simple robotic arms due to their simplicity and ease of control. Speed and direction can be easily modified by adjusting the voltage applied to the motor.
    - **Servo Motors:** Servo motors are specialized DC motors designed for precise control of angular position. They typically include a feedback mechanism, allowing for accurate positioning and control. Servo motors are commonly used in applications requiring precise movements, such as robotic arms and pan-tilt camera systems.
    - **Stepper Motors:** Stepper motors divide a full rotation into discrete steps, providing precise control over angular position. They are often used in 3D printers and CNC machines where accurate positioning is crucial. Stepper motors can be controlled to move a specific number of steps in either direction.
    - **Linear Actuators:** Linear actuators convert rotary motion into linear motion, enabling straight-line movements. They are commonly used in applications requiring lifting or pushing actions, such as robotic arms and automated drawer systems.

4.2.2 Integrating Motors and Actuators with Johnny-Five

The Johnny-Five framework provides classes for controlling different types of motors and actuators. Below, we will cover how to work with DC motors, servo motors, and stepper motors.

Example: Controlling a DC Motor

To control a DC motor, we can use the Motor class provided by Johnny-Five. Here's an example of how to set up and control a DC motor:

```javascript
Copy code
const { Board, Motor } = require("johnny-five");

const board = new Board();

board.on("ready", () => {
  const motor = new Motor({
  pin: 9 // Connect the DC motor to digital pin 9
  });

// Start the motor at full speed
  motor.start(255);

// Reverse the motor after 3 seconds
  setTimeout(() => {
```

```
motor.reverse();
}, 3000);

// Stop the motor after 6 seconds
setTimeout(() => {
motor.stop();
}, 6000);
});
```

In this example:

- We initialize the Board and create a Motor instance connected to digital pin 9.
- The motor starts at full speed (255) for 3 seconds, reverses direction, and then stops after another 3 seconds.

Example: Controlling a Servo Motor

Servo motors are controlled using angles rather than speed. Here's an example of how to control a servo motor:

```
javascript
Copy code
const { Board, Servo } = require("johnny-five");

const board = new Board();

board.on("ready", () => {
const servo = new Servo(10); // Connect the servo to digital pin 10

// Move the servo to 0 degrees
servo.to(0);

// Move the servo to 90 degrees after 2 seconds
setTimeout(() => {
servo.to(90);
```

```
}, 2000);
```

```
// Move the servo to 180 degrees after 4 seconds
  setTimeout(() => {
  servo.to(180);
  }, 4000);
  });
```

In this example:

- We create a Servo instance connected to digital pin 10 and move it to specific angles over time.

Example: Controlling a Stepper Motor

Stepper motors require more complex control than DC or servo motors. Here's an example of using the Stepper class to control a stepper motor:

```
javascript
Copy code
const { Board, Stepper } = require("johnny-five");
```

```
const board = new Board();
```

```
board.on("ready", () => {
  const stepper = new Stepper({
  type: Stepper.TYPE.DRIVER,
  stepsPerRev: 200, // Specify the number of steps per revolution
  pin1: 8, // Connect to digital pin 8
  pin2: 9, // Connect to digital pin 9
  });
```

```
// Step 100 steps forward
  stepper.step(100, () => {
  console.log("Stepped 100 steps forward");
  });
```

```
});
```

In this code:

- We create a Stepper instance and specify its configuration, including the number of steps per revolution and the pins used.
- The step() method is called to move the stepper motor forward by 100 steps.

4.2.3 Practical Applications of Motors and Actuators in Robotics

The ability to control motors and actuators opens up a world of possibilities in robotic applications, including:

- **Mobile Robots:** DC motors are often used to drive wheels, allowing robots to move across various terrains. Combining sensors and motors enables obstacle avoidance and path following.
- **Robotic Arms:** Servo motors provide the precision needed for robotic arms, enabling them to perform tasks such as picking and placing objects with high accuracy.
- **Automated Systems:** Linear actuators can be used in applications such as conveyor belts, automated doors, and adjustable furniture, where straight-line motion is required.
- **3D Printing and CNC Machines:** Stepper motors are essential in 3D printers and CNC machines, where precise movements are critical for creating accurate parts.

Summary

I n this section, we explored the various types of motors and actuators used in robotics, including DC motors, servo motors, stepper motors, and linear actuators. We discussed how to integrate these components into JavaScript-based robotics projects using the Johnny-Five framework, providing practical examples of controlling each type of motor.

As we move forward, we will delve deeper into specific motor and actuator applications, including building projects that combine sensors, motors, and JavaScript to create fully functional robotic systems. Understanding how to effectively utilize motors and actuators is fundamental to building intelligent robots that can navigate and interact with their environments.

4.3 Using LEDs and Displays for Feedback

I n robotic systems, providing feedback to the user or indicating the robot's status is crucial for effective interaction and operation. LEDs (Light Emitting Diodes) and displays are commonly used components for feedback in robotics projects. This section explores how to integrate LEDs and displays into robotic systems using JavaScript and the Johnny-Five framework, along with practical examples and applications.

4.3.1 Understanding LEDs in Robotics

LEDs are simple electronic components that emit light when an electric current passes through them. They are widely used in robotics for various purposes:

- **Status Indicators:** LEDs can indicate the operational status of a robot (e.g., power on/off, running, error states).
- **User Feedback:** LEDs can provide visual feedback based on sensor readings, user inputs, or environmental conditions.
- **Communication Signals:** In some applications, LEDs can signal other devices or robots about specific conditions or events.

Types of LEDs:

- **Single-Color LEDs:** Emit light in one color (e.g., red, green, blue).
- **RGB LEDs:** Can produce multiple colors by combining red, green, and blue light. They are versatile for indicating different states or modes.

4.3.2 Integrating LEDs with Johnny-Five

The Johnny-Five framework provides an easy way to control LEDs. Below are examples of how to set up and control both single-color and RGB LEDs.

Example: Controlling a Single-Color LED

To control a single-color LED, we can use the Led class in Johnny-Five. Here's an example:

```javascript
Copy code
const { Board, Led } = require("johnny-five");

const board = new Board();

board.on("ready", () => {
  const led = new Led(13); // Connect the LED to digital pin 13

// Turn on the LED
  led.on();

// Turn off the LED after 2 seconds
  setTimeout(() => {
  led.off();
  }, 2000);
});
```

In this example:

- We initialize the Board and create an instance of Led connected to digital pin 13.
- The LED turns on immediately and turns off after 2 seconds.

Example: Controlling an RGB LED

RGB LEDs can be controlled to display various colors. Here's how to set up an RGB LED:

```javascript
Copy code
const { Board, Led } = require("johnny-five");

const board = new Board();

board.on("ready", () => {
  const rgb = new Led.RGB([9, 10, 11]); // Connect the RGB LED to digital pins 9, 10, and 11

  // Set the RGB LED to red
  rgb.color("red");

  // Change the color to green after 2 seconds
  setTimeout(() => {
    rgb.color("green");
  }, 2000);

  // Change the color to blue after 4 seconds
  setTimeout(() => {
    rgb.color("blue");
  }, 4000);
});
```

In this example:

- We create an instance of Led.RGB connected to three digital pins.

- The RGB LED changes color every two seconds, demonstrating its ability to represent different states visually.

4.3.3 Using Displays for User Interaction

D isplays provide a more sophisticated way to give feedback to users. They can present more detailed information compared to LEDs, making them ideal for various applications.

Common Types of Displays in Robotics:

- **LCD Displays:** Liquid Crystal Displays (LCDs) are commonly used in robotics for displaying text and simple graphics. They can show information such as sensor readings, status messages, or menus.
- **OLED Displays:** Organic Light Emitting Diodes (OLEDs) are more advanced displays that provide better contrast and color. They are suitable for more complex graphics and detailed user interfaces.

Example: Using an LCD Display

Here's how to use an LCD display with Johnny-Five:

javascript

Copy code

```
const { Board, LCD } = require("johnny-five");

const board = new Board();

board.on("ready", () => {
  const lcd = new LCD({
  controller: "PCF8574", // Specify the controller type for the LCD
  });
```

```javascript
// Display a message
  lcd.print("Hello, Robot!");
```

```javascript
// After 2 seconds, clear the display
  setTimeout(() => {
  lcd.clear();
  }, 2000);
  });
```

In this example:

- We create an instance of LCD and display a message on the screen. The message clears after 2 seconds.

Example: Using an OLED Display

For an OLED display, you might use a library like oled-display. Here's a simple example:

```javascript
javascript
Copy code
const { Board } = require("johnny-five");
const OLED = require("oled-i2c-bus");
```

```javascript
const board = new Board();
```

```javascript
board.on("ready", () => {
  const oled = new OLED({ width: 128, height: 64, address: 0x3c });
```

```javascript
// Clear the display
  oled.clearDisplay();
```

```javascript
// Set text size and color
  oled.setCursor(1, 1);
  oled.writeString(null, 1, "Hello, World!", 1, true);
  });
```

In this example:

- We initialize an OLED display and write a string to the display, showcasing how to present text in a more visually appealing format.

4.3.4 Practical Applications of LEDs and Displays in Robotics

Integrating LEDs and displays in robotics allows for effective user interaction and feedback. Some practical applications include:

- **Status Indicators:** Use LEDs to indicate power status, operational states, or error conditions in robots.
- **User Interfaces:** Employ LCD or OLED displays to create user interfaces for configuring robot settings or displaying sensor data.
- **Interactive Feedback:** Use RGB LEDs and displays to provide interactive feedback in educational robots, making them more engaging for users.

Summary

In this section, we explored how to use LEDs and displays for providing feedback in robotic systems. We discussed the integration of single-color and RGB LEDs using the Johnny-Five framework, along with practical examples for each. Additionally, we covered the use of LCD and OLED displays for presenting more complex information to users.

The effective use of LEDs and displays enhances the usability and functionality of robotic systems, enabling better interaction and user experience. As we continue our journey in robotic development, we will further explore how to combine sensors, motors, LEDs, and displays to create more sophisticated robotic applications.

4.4 Integrating Cameras and Vision Systems

C ameras and vision systems are essential components in modern robotics, enabling robots to perceive their environment and make informed decisions based on visual input. This section will discuss how to integrate cameras into robotic projects using JavaScript, explore the key concepts of computer vision, and provide examples of how to utilize vision systems with the Johnny-Five framework.

4.4.1 Importance of Vision Systems in Robotics

V ision systems allow robots to "see" and interpret their surroundings, which is crucial for tasks such as navigation, object recognition, and interaction with humans. Some common applications of vision systems in robotics include:

- **Object Detection and Recognition:** Identifying and classifying objects in the robot's environment.
- **Facial Recognition:** Recognizing human faces for security or interactive applications.
- **Navigation and Pathfinding:** Using visual cues to navigate through complex environments.
- **Gesture Recognition:** Interpreting human gestures for interactive control of robots.

4.4.2 Types of Cameras Used in Robotics

D ifferent types of cameras can be used in robotic applications, each suited to specific tasks:

• **Webcams:** Simple and widely available, suitable for basic image capture and streaming.

• **Raspberry Pi Camera Module:** A small, high-quality camera specifically designed for the Raspberry Pi, ideal for embedded robotics.

• **USB Cameras:** Plug-and-play cameras that can easily connect to computers or single-board computers for image processing.

• **Depth Cameras:** Such as the Intel RealSense, which can capture 3D information and is useful for tasks that require depth perception.

4.4.3 Integrating a Camera with Johnny-Five

To integrate a camera into a robotic project, you can use libraries that handle image capture and processing. Below, we explore how to use a simple webcam with Johnny-Five and Node.js to capture and display images.

Example: Capturing Images from a Webcam

In this example, we will use the node-webcam library to capture images from a webcam and display them on the console.

1. **Install the Required Packages:**

bash
Copy code
npm install johnny-five node-webcam

1. **Capture Images from the Webcam:**

Here's a simple example demonstrating how to capture and display an image:

```javascript
Copy code
const { Board } = require("johnny-five");
const NodeWebcam = require("node-webcam");
```

```
const board = new Board();

board.on("ready", () => {
  console.log("Board is ready!");

const opts = {
  width: 1280,
  height: 720,
  quality: 100,
  output: "jpeg",
  device: false,
  callbackReturn: "location",
  };

const Webcam = NodeWebcam.create(opts);

// Capture an image every 5 seconds
  setInterval(() => {
  Webcam.capture("image", (err, data) => {
  if (err) {
  console.error("Error capturing image:", err);
  } else {
  console.log("Image captured:", data);
  }
  });
  }, 5000);
  });
```

In this example:

- We set up a webcam with specific dimensions and output format using the node-webcam library.
- The program captures an image every 5 seconds and logs the file location to the console.

4.4.4 Processing Images with Computer Vision Libraries

After capturing images, you can use computer vision libraries to analyze and process the images. One popular library is opencv4nodejs, which provides bindings for OpenCV in Node.js. OpenCV is a powerful computer vision library that can perform various image processing tasks, such as edge detection, filtering, and object recognition.

Example: Basic Image Processing with OpenCV

1. **Install the Required Packages:**

bash
   Copy code
   npm install opencv4nodejs

1. **Perform Image Processing:**

Here's an example of how to use OpenCV to convert an image to grayscale:
   javascript
   Copy code
   const cv = require("opencv4nodejs");
   const fs = require("fs");

const imagePath = "image.jpg"; // Path to the captured image

```
// Load the image
  const image = cv.imread(imagePath);

// Convert to grayscale
  const grayImage = image.bgrToGray();

// Save the processed image
  cv.imwrite("gray_image.jpg", grayImage);

console.log("Grayscale image saved as gray_image.jpg");
```
  In this example:

- We load the captured image using OpenCV, convert it to grayscale, and save the processed image.

4.4.5 Using Pre-trained Models for Object Detection

For more advanced vision tasks, you can utilize pre-trained models for object detection. Libraries such as TensorFlow.js allow you to run machine learning models in the browser or Node.js, enabling real-time object detection.

Example: Object Detection with TensorFlow.js

You can use a pre-trained model like COCO-SSD (Single Shot Detector) for detecting objects in images. Below is an outline of how to set this up:

1. **Install TensorFlow.js:**

bash
Copy code
npm install @tensorflow/tfjs @tensorflow-models/coco-ssd

1. **Detect Objects in Images:**

Here's a simplified example of how to detect objects in an image:
javascript
Copy code
const tf = require("@tensorflow/tfjs-node");
const cocoSsd = require("@tensorflow-models/coco-ssd");
const Jimp = require("jimp");

```
async function detectObjects(imagePath) {
    const image = await Jimp.read(imagePath);
    const tensor = tf.node.decodeImage(image.bitmap.data);
    const model = await cocoSsd.load();

const predictions = await model.detect(tensor);

predictions.forEach(prediction => {
    console.log(`Detected ${prediction.class} with confidence ${prediction.scor
e}`);
    });
    }

// Call the function with the path to the image
    detectObjects("image.jpg");
    In this example:
```

- We load an image, convert it into a tensor, and use a pre-trained COCO-SSD model to detect objects, logging the results to the console.

Summary

I n this section, we explored the integration of cameras and vision systems into robotic projects. We discussed the importance of vision systems for tasks such as object detection and navigation, and highlighted different types of cameras suitable for robotics. Through practical examples, we demonstrated how to capture images using webcams, process them with computer vision libraries like OpenCV, and utilize pre-trained models for object detection.

The ability to integrate vision systems significantly enhances a robot's capabilities, enabling it to perceive and respond to its environment in real time. As we move forward in our exploration of robotic development, we will continue to build on these concepts to create more sophisticated robotic applications that leverage visual data for intelligent decision-making.

4.5 Understanding Servos and Stepper Motors

Servos and stepper motors are vital components in robotics, providing precise control over movement and positioning. This section will delve into the characteristics, applications, and programming of servos and stepper motors, helping you understand how to effectively use them in your robotic projects.

4.5.1 Introduction to Servos

4.5.1.1 What is a Servo Motor?

A servo motor is a rotary actuator that allows for precise control of angular position, velocity, and acceleration. Servos are typically used in applications where accurate position control is required, such as robotic arms, remote-controlled vehicles, and robotic joints.

4.5.1.2 Types of Servo Motors

There are primarily three types of servo motors:

- **Standard Servos:** These have a limited range of motion (typically 0 to 180 degrees) and are commonly used in hobby robotics.
- **Continuous Rotation Servos:** Unlike standard servos, these can rotate continuously in either direction, allowing for more dynamic movement. However, they do not provide positional feedback.
- **Digital Servos:** These offer improved performance over analog servos, providing faster response times and greater torque. They often come with built-in feedback systems for more precise control.

4.5.2 Introduction to Stepper Motors

4.5.2.1 What is a Stepper Motor?

A stepper motor is a type of DC motor that divides a full rotation into a large number of steps, allowing for precise positioning and repeatability. Stepper motors are ideal for applications that require accurate control of rotation and positioning, such as 3D printers, CNC machines, and robotics.

4.5.2.2 Types of Stepper Motors

There are several types of stepper motors, including:

- **Permanent Magnet Stepper Motors:** These use permanent magnets in their rotor and are known for their good torque at low speeds.
- **Variable Reluctance Stepper Motors:** These have a simple construction and are typically used in applications requiring lower torque.
- **Hybrid Stepper Motors:** These combine features of both permanent magnet and variable reluctance motors, offering improved performance and precision.

4.5.3 Applications of Servos and Stepper Motors in Robotics

- **Robotic Arms:** Servos are often used in robotic arms for precise joint control, enabling accurate positioning of the arm.
- **Wheeled Robots:** Continuous rotation servos are used for movement, allowing robots to navigate their environment.
- **3D Printing:** Stepper motors are essential for the accurate movement of print heads and platforms in 3D printers.
- **CNC Machines:** Stepper motors provide precise control over cutting tools, enabling intricate designs and patterns.

4.5.4 Connecting and Controlling Servos with Johnny-Five

To control servo motors with Johnny-Five, you'll first need to connect them to your microcontroller (like Arduino). The following example demonstrates how to control a standard servo using Johnny-Five.

Example: Controlling a Servo Motor

1. **Hardware Setup:**

- Connect the servo motor's control wire to a digital pin on the microcontroller (e.g., pin 10).
- Connect the power wire (typically red) to the positive voltage (5V).
- Connect the ground wire (typically black or brown) to the ground.

1. **Install Johnny-Five:** Ensure you have Johnny-Five installed:

bash
Copy code
npm install johnny-five

1. **Control the Servo:**

Here's a simple example to demonstrate how to control a servo motor:
javascript

Copy code

```
const { Board, Servo } = require("johnny-five");
const board = new Board();

board.on("ready", () => {
    // Create a new Servo on pin 10
    const servo = new Servo(10);

// Sweep the servo back and forth
    servo.sweep();

// Stop sweeping after 5 seconds
    board.wait(5000, () => {
    servo.stop();
    servo.to(90); // Set the servo to the middle position
    });
    });
```

In this example:

- We initialize a servo motor connected to pin 10 and make it sweep back and forth.
- After 5 seconds, the servo stops and moves to the middle position (90 degrees).

4.5.5 Controlling Stepper Motors with Johnny-Five

To control stepper motors, you can use the johnny-five library in conjunction with a stepper motor driver, such as the A4988 or DRV8825.

Example: Controlling a Stepper Motor

1. **Hardware Setup:**

- Connect the stepper motor to a stepper motor driver.
- Connect the driver to your microcontroller according to the manufacturer's instructions.

1. **Install Johnny-Five:** Ensure you have Johnny-Five installed:

bash
Copy code
npm install johnny-five

1. **Control the Stepper Motor:**

Here's a simple example to control a stepper motor:
javascript
Copy code

```javascript
const { Board, Stepper } = require("johnny-five");
const board = new Board();

board.on("ready", () => {
  const stepper = new Stepper({
  type: Stepper.TYPE.DRIVER,
  stepsPerRev: 200, // Number of steps per revolution for your motor
  pins: {
  step: 3, // Connect step pin to digital pin 3
  dir: 4 // Connect direction pin to digital pin 4
  }
  });

// Move the stepper motor 1 revolution forward
  stepper.step(200, 1, () => {
  console.log("Completed one revolution forward");

// Move the stepper motor 1 revolution backward
  stepper.step(200, -1, () => {
  console.log("Completed one revolution backward");
  });
  });
  });
```

In this example:

- We initialize a stepper motor with specified pins and steps per revolution.
- The stepper motor moves one revolution forward and then one revolution backward.

Summary

In this section, we explored servos and stepper motors, essential components for robotic movement and control. We learned about their types, applications, and how to integrate them into robotic projects using the Johnny-Five framework.

By understanding the characteristics of servos and stepper motors, you can effectively choose the right components for your robotic applications, ensuring precise control and reliable performance. In the following sections, we will continue to explore more advanced components and concepts in robotic development, building upon the foundation laid in this chapter.

4.6 Connecting Bluetooth and Wi-Fi Modules

In modern robotics, communication between the robot and external devices or systems is critical. Bluetooth and Wi-Fi modules provide the ability to control robots remotely, send and receive data in real-time, and integrate with IoT ecosystems. In this section, we'll explore the hardware and software required to add wireless communication capabilities to your JavaScript-powered robot.

1. Introduction to Bluetooth and Wi-Fi Modules

Bluetooth and Wi-Fi modules are hardware components that enable wireless communication for robots. These modules allow robots to connect to other devices (smartphones, computers, or other robots) for control, monitoring, and data sharing.

1.1 Bluetooth Modules

- **Common Bluetooth Modules:** Popular Bluetooth modules include the HC-05 and HC-06, which are low-cost and easy to interface with microcontrollers.
- **Range:** Bluetooth generally has a shorter range (up to 10 meters) but is ideal for close-range communication between devices.
- **Applications:** Bluetooth is commonly used for controlling robots via mobile apps or for pairing multiple devices in a local area.

1.2 Wi-Fi Modules

- **Common Wi-Fi Modules:** The ESP8266 and ESP32 are popular Wi-Fi modules that can be integrated into robotic systems for Internet connectivity.
- **Range:** Wi-Fi modules provide a much longer range than Bluetooth, typically up to 100 meters or more, depending on the network setup.
- **Applications:** Wi-Fi is used in applications where remote control,

real-time monitoring, and cloud integration are necessary, such as IoT robotics.

2. Connecting Bluetooth Modules to a Robot

2.1 Setting Up the Hardware

To add Bluetooth functionality to your robot, you'll need a Bluetooth module (e.g., HC-05) connected to your microcontroller (such as Arduino or Raspberry Pi). The key pins are:

- **TX (Transmit)**: Connects to the RX pin of the microcontroller.
- **RX (Receive)**: Connects to the TX pin of the microcontroller.
- **VCC**: Connects to the 5V or 3.3V power source.
- **GND**: Connects to the ground.

2.2 Example: Controlling a Robot with Bluetooth

Here's a basic example of how to control a robot using the Johnny-Five framework and a Bluetooth module:

1. **Hardware Setup:**

- Connect the Bluetooth module to the microcontroller.
- Ensure proper TX-RX connections between the Bluetooth module and the microcontroller.

1. **Control the Robot via Bluetooth:**

javascript

```
Copy code
const { Board, Servo } = require("johnny-five");
const SerialPort = require("serialport");
const Readline = require("@serialport/parser-readline");

const board = new Board();
const port = new SerialPort("/dev/tty.HC-05-DevB", { baudRate: 9600 });
const parser = new Readline();
port.pipe(parser);

board.on("ready", () => {
const servo = new Servo(10); // Assuming the servo is on pin 10

parser.on("data", (data) => {
if (data.trim() === "left") {
servo.to(45); // Move the servo to 45 degrees
} else if (data.trim() === "right") {
servo.to(135); // Move the servo to 135 degrees
}
});
});
```

In this example:

- The robot is equipped with a servo motor.
- Commands are sent over Bluetooth (using an HC-05 module) to move the servo based on the received data.

3. Connecting Wi-Fi Modules to a Robot

3.1 Setting Up the Hardware

To add Wi-Fi functionality, you can use an ESP8266 or ESP32 module. These modules can be connected to your microcontroller or even serve as standalone controllers due to their onboard processing power.

The key connections are similar to Bluetooth modules:

- **TX**: Connects to RX of the microcontroller.
- **RX**: Connects to TX of the microcontroller.
- **VCC**: Connects to the power source (3.3V for ESP8266/ESP32).
- **GND**: Connects to the ground.

3.2 Example: Controlling a Robot via Wi-Fi

1. **Hardware Setup:**

- Connect the ESP8266 or ESP32 module to your microcontroller.
- Configure the module to connect to a Wi-Fi network.

1. **Control the Robot over Wi-Fi:**

Here's a simple Johnny-Five example to control a robot over Wi-Fi using the ESP8266 module:

javascript
Copy code

```
const { Board, Servo } = require("johnny-five");
const express = require("express");
const app = express();

const board = new Board();

board.on("ready", () => {
  const servo = new Servo(10); // Servo connected to pin 10

app.get("/move/:direction", (req, res) => {
  const { direction } = req.params;

if (direction === "left") {
  servo.to(45);
  } else if (direction === "right") {
  servo.to(135);
  }

res.send('Moved ${direction}');
  });

app.listen(3000, () => {
  console.log("Robot server running on port 3000");
  });
  });
```
In this example:

- The robot is controlled via a web server hosted on the ESP8266 or connected to an external Node.js server.
- HTTP requests control the movement of the servo, allowing for real-time robot control over Wi-Fi.

4. Bluetooth vs. Wi-Fi for Robotics

When deciding between Bluetooth and Wi-Fi for your robotics project, consider the following factors:

- **Bluetooth** is best for close-range control using mobile devices or other nearby controllers.
- **Wi-Fi** is ideal for long-range, internet-based control, real-time data streaming, and cloud-based applications.

Conclusion

C hapter 4 provided an in-depth exploration of various hardware components essential for robotic systems, focusing on sensors, motors, LEDs, cameras, and wireless communication modules like Bluetooth and Wi-Fi. Understanding these components and their integration into your JavaScript-powered robotic projects is crucial for building sophisticated and responsive systems.

- **Sensors** play a key role in perceiving the environment, allowing robots to interact intelligently.
- **Motors and actuators** enable movement and action, with precise control offered by servos and stepper motors.
- **Feedback components** like LEDs and displays provide real-time information to both the robot and the user.
- **Vision systems** are critical for advanced robotic perception, enabling tasks like object recognition and tracking.
- **Bluetooth and Wi-Fi modules** add wireless communication capabilities, allowing for remote control and integration with IoT ecosystems.

By understanding the different hardware components and how to interface them with JavaScript frameworks like Johnny-Five, you now have the foundation to build and control intelligent robotic systems. The next chapters will build on this knowledge by delving into more advanced topics such as control algorithms, machine learning for robotics, and autonomous systems.

CHAPTER 5: DEVELOPING DECENTRALIZED APPLICATIONS (DAPPS)

5.1 What are DApps?

Decentralized Applications, commonly known as DApps, represent a new paradigm in software development. Unlike traditional applications that rely on centralized servers and databases, DApps operate on decentralized networks, offering users enhanced security, transparency, and control over their data. This section will explore the fundamental characteristics of DApps, their architecture, and the benefits they provide.

Defining DApps

At their core, DApps are applications that run on a peer-to-peer network of computers instead of a single server. They utilize blockchain technology to store data and execute logic, ensuring that no single entity has control over the application. DApps can be built on various blockchain platforms, including Ethereum, Hyperledger, and Corda.

Key Characteristics of DApps

1. **Decentralization**: DApps operate on a decentralized network, where no central authority governs them. This characteristic ensures that no single party can control or manipulate the application.
2. **Open Source**: Most DApps are open source, allowing developers to inspect, modify, and enhance the code. This transparency fosters trust within the community and encourages collaboration.

3. **Blockchain-Based**: DApps use blockchain technology for data storage and transaction processing. This feature guarantees immutability, transparency, and security of data.

4. **Incentives and Tokens**: Many DApps incorporate a native cryptocurrency or token, which serves as an incentive for users to participate in the network. Tokens can be used for governance, transaction fees, or rewarding users for their contributions.

5. **Smart Contracts**: DApps rely on smart contracts to execute predefined logic automatically. These contracts run on the blockchain and facilitate trustless interactions between users.

Types of DApps

DApps can be classified into three main categories based on their functionalities:

1. **Type I DApps**: These are entirely decentralized applications built on their own blockchain. An example is Bitcoin, which serves as a cryptocurrency and a payment network.

2. **Type II DApps**: These DApps are built on existing blockchains and leverage their infrastructure. For example, Ethereum-based DApps utilize the Ethereum network for executing smart contracts and managing transactions.

3. **Type III DApps**: These are applications that integrate both blockchain and traditional technologies. They may use a blockchain for specific features, such as transaction verification, while relying on centralized components for other functionalities.

Benefits of DApps

1. **Censorship Resistance**: DApps cannot be easily censored or shut down, as they operate on a distributed network. This feature is particularly valuable in regions with oppressive governments or strict regulations.

2. **Enhanced Security**: DApps benefit from the security of blockchain

technology, making them less vulnerable to hacking and data breaches compared to centralized applications.

3. **User Control**: Users have full control over their data and transactions, minimizing the risks of data exploitation by centralized entities.

4. **Increased Transparency**: All interactions within a DApp are recorded on the blockchain, providing transparency and auditability. This characteristic fosters trust among users.

5. **Lower Costs**: By eliminating intermediaries, DApps can reduce transaction costs and fees associated with traditional applications.

Challenges in DApp Development

While DApps offer numerous advantages, they also face challenges, including:

- **Scalability**: Many blockchains struggle with scalability, leading to slow transaction times and high fees during peak usage.
- **User Experience**: DApps often have a steeper learning curve for users unfamiliar with blockchain technology and wallets, affecting adoption.
- **Interoperability**: Ensuring that DApps can communicate across different blockchain platforms remains a significant challenge.

Summary

Decentralized Applications (DApps) are at the forefront of the blockchain revolution, offering a new approach to application development that prioritizes decentralization, security, and user empowerment. As we delve deeper into this chapter, we will explore the architecture of DApps, how to connect them to the Ethereum blockchain using Web3.js, and build a simple DApp step by step. Understanding the foundational concepts of DApps will pave the way for creating robust and innovative blockchain solutions that harness the full potential of decentralized technology.

5.2 Architecture of a DApp: Frontend, Smart Contract, and Blockchain

Understanding the architecture of a Decentralized Application (DApp) is crucial for developers seeking to build robust and efficient applications on blockchain technology. A DApp typically consists of three main components: the frontend, the smart contract, and the underlying blockchain. This section will delve into each of these components, their roles, and how they interact with one another.

1. Frontend

The frontend of a DApp is the user interface that interacts with users. It is responsible for presenting data, accepting user input, and facilitating interactions with the underlying smart contracts. The frontend can be developed using popular web technologies such as HTML, CSS, and JavaScript frameworks like React, Angular, or Vue.js.

Key Features of the Frontend:

- **User Experience (UX)**: A well-designed frontend enhances user experience, making the DApp more accessible and user-friendly. It should provide intuitive navigation, clear instructions, and easy access to features.
- **Interaction with Smart Contracts**: The frontend communicates with smart contracts using libraries like Web3.js or Ethers.js. These libraries allow the frontend to send transactions, call smart contract functions, and listen for events emitted by the contracts.
- **Wallet Integration**: DApps often integrate with cryptocurrency wallets, such as MetaMask, to manage user accounts and handle transactions. This integration allows users to sign transactions securely and interact with the blockchain directly from the frontend.

2. Smart Contract

Smart contracts are self-executing contracts with the terms of the agreement directly written into code. They run on the blockchain and automate processes without the need for intermediaries. Smart contracts play a pivotal role in the functionality of DApps.

Key Features of Smart Contracts:

- **Automation**: Smart contracts execute predefined actions when specific conditions are met. For example, in a token sale DApp, a smart contract can automatically distribute tokens to users when they send Ether.
- **Immutability**: Once deployed on the blockchain, smart contracts cannot be altered. This immutability ensures that the rules governing the DApp remain consistent and transparent.
- **Transparency**: The code and transactions of smart contracts are visible on the blockchain, allowing users to verify the contract's logic and its execution history.
- **Gas Fees**: Interacting with smart contracts incurs gas fees, which are paid in the blockchain's native cryptocurrency (e.g., Ether for Ethereum). These fees compensate miners or validators for processing transactions and executing contract code.

3. Blockchain

The blockchain serves as the underlying infrastructure for DApps, providing a distributed ledger that records all transactions and states associated with the DApp. It ensures the integrity, security, and availability of data.

Key Features of the Blockchain:

- **Decentralization**: The blockchain is maintained by a network of nodes, which work together to validate and record transactions. This decentralization eliminates the need for a central authority.
- **Consensus Mechanisms**: Blockchains use consensus mechanisms, such as Proof of Work (PoW) or Proof of Stake (PoS), to agree on the validity of transactions. This process ensures that all participants in the network have a consistent view of the blockchain.
- **Data Integrity**: Once data is recorded on the blockchain, it cannot be altered or deleted, ensuring a permanent and tamper-proof history of all interactions.
- **Interoperability**: Some blockchains allow DApps to communicate with other blockchains or external systems, enabling cross-chain functionality and enhancing the capabilities of the DApp.

Interaction Between Components

The frontend, smart contract, and blockchain interact in a seamless flow to deliver the functionality of a DApp:

1. **User Interaction**: Users interact with the frontend by inputting data, signing transactions, or executing actions.
2. **Calling Smart Contracts**: The frontend sends requests to the smart contracts through Web3.js or Ethers.js, invoking specific functions and passing necessary parameters.
3. **Transaction Processing**: The smart contract processes the request and interacts with the blockchain to record the transaction or change the state.
4. **Feedback to Frontend**: The blockchain responds with the transaction result, which is then displayed on the frontend, providing feedback to the user.

Summary

The architecture of a Decentralized Application (DApp) comprises three critical components: the frontend, smart contracts, and the blockchain. Each component plays a unique role in ensuring the DApp functions effectively, providing users with a seamless experience while leveraging the benefits of blockchain technology. Understanding this architecture is essential for developers looking to create innovative DApps that can transform industries and empower users through decentralization. In the upcoming sections, we will explore how to connect the frontend to the Ethereum blockchain using Web3.js and build a simple DApp step by step.

5.3 Connecting JavaScript Frontend with Ethereum using Web3.js

Connecting your JavaScript frontend to the Ethereum blockchain is a crucial step in developing Decentralized Applications (DApps). Web3.js is a powerful JavaScript library that enables developers to interact with the Ethereum blockchain and its smart contracts from the frontend. This section will guide you through the process of setting up Web3.js, connecting it to the Ethereum network, and performing basic operations.

1. Setting Up Web3.js

To get started with Web3.js, you first need to install the library in your project. You can do this using npm (Node Package Manager). Open your terminal and run the following command in your project directory:

bash

Copy code

npm install web3

Alternatively, if you are using a CDN, you can include Web3.js directly in your HTML file:

html

Copy code

```
<script src="https://cdnjs.cloudflare.com/ajax/libs/web3/1.6.0/web3.min.js"></script>
```

2. Connecting to the Ethereum Network

Web3.js can connect to various Ethereum networks, including the mainnet, testnets (such as Ropsten, Kovan, and Rinkeby), and local development networks like Ganache. For this example, we will connect to a local Ganache instance.

Using Ganache:

1. **Install Ganache**: If you haven't already, download and install Ganache from the Truffle Suite website.
2. **Start Ganache**: Launch Ganache, and it will create a local Ethereum blockchain, providing you with a set of accounts, private keys, and gas limits.
3. **Connect to Ganache**: In your JavaScript code, create a Web3 instance and connect it to the Ganache provider:

javascript

Copy code

```
// Import Web3.js (if using ES6 modules)
import Web3 from 'web3';
```

```
// Create a Web3 instance
const web3 = new Web3(new Web3.providers.HttpProvider('http://127.0.
0.1:7545'));
```

Using MetaMask:

If you prefer to connect your DApp to the Ethereum mainnet or a testnet using MetaMask, you can use the following code:

javascript

Copy code

```
// Check if MetaMask is installed
if (typeof window.ethereum !== 'undefined') {
// Create a Web3 instance with MetaMask provider
const web3 = new Web3(window.ethereum);

// Request account access
window.ethereum.request({ method: 'eth_requestAccounts' })
.then(accounts => {
console.log('Connected account:', accounts[0]);
})
.catch(error => {
console.error('User denied account access:', error);
});
} else {
console.error('Please install MetaMask!');
}
```

3. Interacting with Smart Contracts

Once you have established a connection to the Ethereum network, you can interact with smart contracts. This involves creating a contract instance and calling its methods. Here's how to do it:

Creating a Contract Instance:

Assuming you have deployed a smart contract and have its ABI (Application Binary Interface) and address, you can create a contract instance as follows:

javascript

Copy code

// Define the ABI and address of the deployed contract

const contractABI = [...] // Replace with your contract's ABI

const contractAddress = '0xYourContractAddress'; // Replace with your contract's address

// Create a contract instance

const contract = new web3.eth.Contract(contractABI, contractAddress);

Calling Smart Contract Methods:

You can call both constant (view) and non-constant (state-changing) methods on the smart contract.

Calling a View Function:

To call a view function, you can use the call() method, which does not alter the state of the blockchain:

javascript

Copy code

```
// Call a view function
contract.methods.yourViewFunction().call()
.then(result => {
console.log('Result from view function:', result);
})
.catch(error => {
console.error('Error calling view function:', error);
});
```

Sending a Transaction:

To send a transaction to a state-changing function, you will need to specify the sender's address and the method parameters:

javascript

Copy code

```
// Send a transaction to a state-changing function
const account = '0xYourAccountAddress'; // Replace with the user's account address
```

contract.methods.yourStateChangingFunction(arg1, arg2).send({ from:

```
account })
  .then(receipt => {
  console.log('Transaction receipt:', receipt);
  })
  .catch(error => {
  console.error('Error sending transaction:', error);
  });
```

4. Listening for Events

Web3.js also allows you to listen for events emitted by smart contracts, which is useful for updating the frontend based on blockchain events:

```javascript
Copy code
// Listening for an event
contract.events.YourEventName({
filter: { /* optional filter options */ },
fromBlock: 'latest'
}, (error, event) => {
if (error) {
console.error('Error listening for event:', error);
} else {
console.log('Event received:', event);
}
});
```

Summary

Connecting your JavaScript frontend to the Ethereum blockchain using Web3.js is an essential step in building a Decentralized Application (DApp). By setting up Web3.js and establishing a connection to the Ethereum network, you can interact with smart contracts, call functions, send transactions, and listen for events. This integration enables you to create dynamic and responsive user interfaces that leverage the power of blockchain technology. In the next section, we will build a simple DApp step-by-step, applying the concepts learned in this chapter.

5.4 Building a Simple DApp: Step-by-Step Example

In this section, we will build a simple Decentralized Application (DApp) that allows users to store and retrieve messages on the Ethereum blockchain. This DApp will demonstrate key concepts such as smart contract interactions, front-end development with JavaScript, and the integration of Web3.js. We will use the following components:

- **Smart Contract**: To handle message storage and retrieval.
- **Frontend**: A simple HTML/CSS/JavaScript interface to interact with the smart contract.

Step 1: Setting Up the Environment

Before we start coding, ensure you have the following tools installed:

1. **Node.js**: To run the JavaScript code.
2. **Ganache**: A local Ethereum blockchain for testing.
3. **Truffle**: A development framework for Ethereum smart contracts.
4. **MetaMask**: A browser extension to manage Ethereum accounts.

After installing the required tools, create a new directory for your DApp and navigate to it:

bash
Copy code
mkdir simple-dapp
cd simple-dapp

Next, initialize a new Truffle project:

bash
Copy code
truffle init

Step 2: Writing the Smart Contract

Create a new Solidity file for the smart contract. In the contracts directory, create a file named MessageStorage.sol:

solidity
Copy code

```
// SPDX-License-Identifier: MIT
pragma solidity ^0.8.0;

contract MessageStorage {
  string private message;

// Store a message
  function setMessage(string memory _message) public {
  message = _message;
  }


// Retrieve the stored message
  function getMessage() public view returns (string memory) {
  return message;
  }
  }
```

Step 3: Compiling and Deploying the Smart Contract

Now, we need to compile and deploy our smart contract to Ganache. In your terminal, run the following command to compile the contract:

bash

Copy code

truffle compile

Next, create a migration script in the migrations directory to deploy the contract. Create a new file named 2_deploy_contracts.js:

javascript

Copy code

```
const MessageStorage = artifacts.require("MessageStorage");

module.exports = function(deployer) {
  deployer.deploy(MessageStorage);
  };
```

Finally, make sure Ganache is running and deploy the contract using:

bash

Copy code

truffle migrate

Step 4: Building the Frontend

Create an index.html file in the root directory of your project with the following content:

html

Copy code

```
<!DOCTYPE html>
<html lang="en">
<head>
<meta charset="UTF-8">
<meta name="viewport" content="width=device-width, initial-scale=1.0">
<title>Simple DApp</title>
<script src="https://cdnjs.cloudflare.com/ajax/libs/web3/1.6.0/web3.min.js"></script>
<script src="app.js" defer></script>
</head>
<body>
<h1>Simple DApp</h1>
<input type="text" id="message" placeholder="Enter your message">
<button id="setMessageButton">Set Message</button>
<button id="getMessageButton">Get Message</button>
<p id="output"></p>
</body>
</html>
```

Next, create a app.js file to handle user interactions and smart contract interactions:

javascript

Copy code

```
// Import Web3.js (if using ES6 modules)
// import Web3 from 'web3';

let web3;
```

```
let contract;

const contractAddress = 'OxYourContractAddress'; // Replace with your
deployed contract address
    const contractABI = [ /* ABI array here */ ]; // Replace with your contract's
ABI

window.addEventListener('load', async () => {
    // Check if MetaMask is installed
    if (typeof window.ethereum !== 'undefined') {
    web3 = new Web3(window.ethereum);
    await window.ethereum.request({ method: 'eth_requestAccounts' });

// Create contract instance
    contract = new web3.eth.Contract(contractABI, contractAddress);

// Setup button click handlers
    document.getElementById('setMessageButton').onclick = setMessage;
    document.getElementById('getMessageButton').onclick = getMessage;
    } else {
    console.error('Please install MetaMask!');
    }
    });

async function setMessage() {
    const accounts = await web3.eth.getAccounts();
    const message = document.getElementById('message').value;

try {
    await contract.methods.setMessage(message).send({ from: accounts[0] });
    alert('Message set successfully!');
    } catch (error) {
    console.error('Error setting message:', error);
```

```
    }
  }

async function getMessage() {
  try {
    const message = await contract.methods.getMessage().call();
    document.getElementById('output').innerText = 'Stored Message: ' +
message;
  } catch (error) {
    console.error('Error getting message:', error);
  }
}
```

Step 5: Running the DApp

Now that you have everything set up, you can run your DApp:

1. Open the index.html file in a web browser (preferably Chrome with MetaMask).
2. Ensure MetaMask is connected to the same network as Ganache (e.g., the local network).
3. Enter a message in the input field and click on the "Set Message" button to store the message in the blockchain.
4. Click on the "Get Message" button to retrieve and display the stored message.

Summary

In this section, we successfully built a simple Decentralized Application (DApp) that allows users to store and retrieve messages on the Ethereum blockchain. By creating a smart contract, deploying it to a local Ethereum network, and developing a user-friendly frontend, we demonstrated the fundamental principles of DApp development. This step-by-step example highlights the power of combining blockchain technology with JavaScript, enabling developers to create innovative and decentralized solutions. In the next section, we will discuss user authentication with MetaMask, which is crucial for securing DApps and managing user accounts.

5.5 User Authentication with MetaMask

User authentication is a critical aspect of decentralized applications (DApps), as it ensures that users can securely access and interact with blockchain resources. MetaMask, a popular browser extension wallet, simplifies this process by allowing users to manage their Ethereum accounts and sign transactions. In this section, we will explore how to implement user authentication using MetaMask in our DApp.

Step 1: Understanding MetaMask Integration

MetaMask serves as a bridge between a user's browser and the Ethereum blockchain. By integrating MetaMask into our DApp, we can:

- Prompt users to log in using their Ethereum account.
- Access their account addresses and balances.
- Sign transactions securely without exposing private keys.

Step 2: Checking for MetaMask

Before implementing user authentication, we need to ensure that Meta-Mask is installed and accessible. We'll update our app.js to include a check for MetaMask's presence:

```javascript
Copy code
window.addEventListener('load', async () => {
// Check if MetaMask is installed
if (typeof window.ethereum !== 'undefined') {
web3 = new Web3(window.ethereum);
await window.ethereum.request({ method: 'eth_requestAccounts' });

// Create contract instance
contract = new web3.eth.Contract(contractABI, contractAddress);

// Setup button click handlers
document.getElementById('setMessageButton').onclick = setMessage;
```

```
document.getElementById('getMessageButton').onclick = getMessage;
```

// Display connected account
```
    displayAccount();
    } else {
    console.error('Please install MetaMask!');
    document.getElementById('output').innerText = 'Please install Meta-
Mask!';
    }
    });
```

```
async function displayAccount() {
    const accounts = await web3.eth.getAccounts();
    const account = accounts[0];
    document.getElementById('output').innerText = 'Connected account: ' +
account;
    }
```

This modification ensures that when MetaMask is available, the user will be prompted to connect their account, and their connected account will be displayed.

Step 3: Handling Account Changes and Network Changes

MetaMask allows users to switch accounts and networks. It is essential to handle these changes in our DApp to maintain a seamless user experience. We can listen for account and network changes with the following code:

```
javascript
Copy code
window.ethereum.on('accountsChanged', (accounts) => {
displayAccount(); // Update the displayed account
});
```

```
window.ethereum.on('networkChanged', (networkId) => {
    // Optionally, you can reload the page or update the contract instance
    console.log('Network changed to:', networkId);
```

alert('Network changed! Please refresh the page.');

});

This code ensures that whenever the user switches their account or the network, the DApp updates accordingly.

Step 4: Improving User Experience with Alerts

To enhance user experience, we can add alerts to notify users when they are successfully logged in or if there are any issues. We can modify our existing functions to include alert messages:

javascript

Copy code

```
async function setMessage() {
const accounts = await web3.eth.getAccounts();
const message = document.getElementById('message').value;

try {
    await contract.methods.setMessage(message).send({ from: accounts[0] });
    alert('Message set successfully!');
    } catch (error) {
    console.error('Error setting message:', error);
    alert('Error setting message: ' + error.message);
    }
}

async function getMessage() {
    try {
    const message = await contract.methods.getMessage().call();
    document.getElementById('output').innerText = 'Stored Message: ' + message;
    } catch (error) {
    console.error('Error getting message:', error);
    alert('Error getting message: ' + error.message);
    }
}
```

Step 5: Testing User Authentication

To test the user authentication flow:

1. Open your DApp in a web browser with MetaMask installed.
2. Make sure MetaMask is connected to the same network as your Ganache instance.
3. Once the page loads, you should see your connected Ethereum account.
4. Enter a message and click "Set Message" to store it in the smart contract. You should receive a success alert.
5. Click "Get Message" to retrieve the stored message.

If you switch accounts in MetaMask or change the network, you should see appropriate alerts or updates in the DApp.

Summary

In this section, we successfully implemented user authentication in our DApp using MetaMask. By allowing users to connect their Ethereum accounts and handling account changes, we ensured a secure and user-friendly experience. This integration is essential for any DApp, as it not only provides a means of authentication but also facilitates secure transaction signing. With user authentication in place, we can now focus on deploying our DApp to the Ethereum network, ensuring that our application is accessible to a broader audience. In the next section, we will cover how to deploy our DApp effectively.

5.6 Deploying a DApp to the Ethereum Network

Once you've developed your decentralized application (DApp) and thoroughly tested it, the next crucial step is deployment to the Ethereum network. This process makes your DApp available to users and allows it to interact with the Ethereum blockchain. In this section, we will walk through the steps to deploy our DApp and its associated smart contracts.

Step 1: Preparing for Deployment

Before deploying, ensure that your DApp's code is optimized, and all smart contracts are thoroughly tested. Use the following checklist to prepare:

- **Test Contracts:** Make sure all smart contracts have been tested on a test network like Ropsten or Rinkeby.
- **Optimize Gas Usage:** Review and optimize your smart contracts to minimize gas costs during deployment.
- **Front-End Setup:** Ensure that your front-end code is ready and integrates correctly with your smart contracts.

Step 2: Deploying Smart Contracts

To deploy your smart contracts to the Ethereum network, follow these steps:

1. **Configure Truffle for Deployment:** Update your truffle-config.js file to include the configuration for the Ethereum network. You can use services like Infura or Alchemy to connect to the Ethereum network.

javascript

```
Copy code
const HDWalletProvider = require('@truffle/hdwallet-provider');
const Web3 = require('web3');
const provider = new HDWalletProvider(
'YOUR_MNEMONIC',
'https://mainnet.infura.io/v3/YOUR_INFURA_PROJECT_ID'
);
```

```
const web3 = new Web3(provider);
```

```
module.exports = {
  networks: {
  mainnet: {
  provider: () => provider,
  network_id: 1, // Ethereum mainnet
  gas: 5000000, // Gas limit
  gasPrice: Web3.utils.toWei('50', 'gwei'), // Gas price
```

```
},
ropsten: {
provider: () => new HDWalletProvider('YOUR_MNEMONIC', 'https://ro
psten.infura.io/v3/YOUR_INFURA_PROJECT_ID'),
network_id: 3,
gas: 5000000,
gasPrice: Web3.utils.toWei('20', 'gwei'),
},
},
};
```

1. **Deploy the Contracts:** Use Truffle's migration feature to deploy your contracts. Run the following command in your terminal:

bash
Copy code
truffle migrate —network mainnet
or for Ropsten:
bash
Copy code
truffle migrate —network ropsten

This command will compile your contracts, deploy them to the specified network, and provide you with the contract addresses.

1. **Verify Deployment:** After deployment, verify that your contracts are successfully deployed by checking the addresses on an Ethereum block explorer like Etherscan or Ropsten Etherscan.

Step 3: Deploying the Frontend

Once your smart contracts are deployed, the next step is to host your frontend application. You can deploy your DApp's frontend to various hosting services, such as:

- **GitHub Pages:** Ideal for static sites.
- **Netlify:** Easy deployment for static and serverless functions.
- **Vercel:** Offers serverless functions and optimized performance for static sites.
- **AWS S3:** Great for hosting static files with scalability.

To deploy your frontend on GitHub Pages, for example:

1. **Create a GitHub Repository:** Initialize a new repository on GitHub and push your front-end code.
2. **Deploy to GitHub Pages:** Use GitHub Pages to host your application. You can configure it in your repository settings.
3. **Update Frontend Configuration:** Ensure your front-end code points to the correct Ethereum network and uses the deployed smart contract addresses.

javascript
Copy code

```
const contractAddress = 'DEPLOYED_CONTRACT_ADDRESS';
const contractABI = [/* ABI array */];
const contract = new web3.eth.Contract(contractABI, contractAddress);
```

Step 4: Final Testing and Launch

After deploying both your smart contracts and front end, conduct thorough testing to ensure everything works as expected:

- **Test User Interactions:** Ensure users can interact with the DApp without issues.
- **Monitor Gas Costs:** Keep an eye on transaction costs and optimize if necessary.

Once testing is complete and you are confident in your DApp's functionality, you can officially launch it to the public!

Conclusion for Chapter 5

In this chapter, we explored the essential aspects of developing decentralized applications (DApps) on the Ethereum blockchain. We began by understanding what DApps are and the architecture that underpins them. Then, we delved into the technical details of connecting our JavaScript frontend to Ethereum using the Web3.js library.

We also discussed user authentication using MetaMask, enabling secure and seamless interaction for users. Finally, we covered the critical steps involved in deploying both our smart contracts and frontend to the Ethereum network, ensuring that our DApp is ready for public use.

With a solid understanding of DApp development and deployment, you're now equipped to create and launch your own decentralized applications. In the next chapter, we will explore Hyperledger Fabric, focusing on building permissioned blockchain solutions and understanding how to leverage its features for enterprise applications.

CHAPTER 6: EXPLORING HYPERLEDGER FABRIC

6.1 Introduction to Hyperledger and Permissioned Blockchains

Hyperledger is an open-source collaborative effort hosted by the Linux Foundation, designed to advance cross-industry blockchain technologies. It provides a robust framework for building enterprise-grade blockchain solutions that can address specific use cases across various sectors. Unlike public blockchains, Hyperledger focuses on permissioned blockchains, which offer greater control over who can access the network and how data is shared.

Understanding Permissioned Blockchains

Permissioned blockchains are networks where participants must be granted permission to join, making them more suitable for enterprise use. This contrasts with public blockchains, like Bitcoin and Ethereum, where anyone can join and participate without restrictions.

Key characteristics of permissioned blockchains include:

- **Access Control:** Only authorized participants can join the network, which ensures that sensitive data is only accessible to those who need it.
- **Privacy and Confidentiality:** Permissioned blockchains can implement privacy features, allowing transactions to be visible only to specific participants.
- **Performance and Scalability:** These networks can achieve higher throughput and lower latency compared to public blockchains due to their controlled environment.

Hyperledger Frameworks

Hyperledger encompasses several projects, including:

- **Hyperledger Fabric:** A modular blockchain framework tailored for enterprise solutions, offering flexibility in terms of architecture and governance.
- **Hyperledger Sawtooth:** Designed for various use cases, including supply chain and IoT applications, with a focus on modularity.
- **Hyperledger Iroha:** A simple blockchain framework designed for mobile applications and targeting the needs of developers.
- **Hyperledger Indy:** Focused on decentralized identity solutions, enabling secure and private identities on the blockchain.

Among these projects, Hyperledger Fabric is one of the most widely adopted, known for its scalability, flexibility, and extensive features tailored for enterprise applications. In the following sections, we will delve deeper into Hyperledger Fabric, its architecture, and how to set up and develop applications using this framework.

Key Features of Hyperledger Fabric

Hyperledger Fabric provides several key features that make it attractive for enterprises:

- **Modular Architecture:** Fabric's architecture is composed of different components, allowing developers to plug in their preferred consensus mechanisms, identity management solutions, and data storage options.
- **Chaincode:** Fabric's smart contracts, called chaincode, can be written in multiple programming languages, such as Go, Java, and JavaScript.
- **Channels:** Fabric allows the creation of private channels, enabling specific groups of participants to transact confidentially while maintaining a shared ledger.
- **Endorsement Policies:** Participants can define policies to specify which members must endorse a transaction before it is considered valid.
- **Data Privacy:** By using private data collections, Hyperledger Fabric

ensures that sensitive information can be kept off the shared ledger, allowing for data confidentiality.

With these features, Hyperledger Fabric provides a robust environment for developing permissioned blockchain applications tailored to the specific needs of enterprises, from supply chain management to healthcare data sharing.

Summary

In this section, we introduced Hyperledger as a significant player in the blockchain ecosystem, particularly for enterprises seeking permissioned solutions. We explored the key features of Hyperledger Fabric, highlighting its modular architecture, privacy capabilities, and focus on performance. As we move forward in this chapter, we will delve into the specifics of setting up a Hyperledger Fabric network and developing chaincode, enabling you to leverage this powerful framework for your blockchain applications.

6.2 Key Features of Hyperledger Fabric

Hyperledger Fabric stands out as a versatile and robust framework designed for enterprise-grade blockchain solutions. Its modular architecture and extensive features cater to a wide range of applications, allowing organizations to build custom blockchain networks tailored to their specific needs. Below, we explore the key features of Hyperledger Fabric in detail.

1. Modular Architecture

Hyperledger Fabric's modular architecture is one of its most significant advantages. It allows developers to select and configure various components based on their application requirements, such as:

- **Consensus Mechanisms:** Fabric supports multiple consensus algorithms, enabling organizations to choose the best fit for their specific use case. This flexibility allows developers to implement consensus methods that align with their transaction volume, security requirements, and performance goals.
- **Chaincode Languages:** Developers can write chaincode (smart contracts) in different programming languages, including Go, Java, and

228

JavaScript. This flexibility ensures that teams can leverage their existing skills and resources to develop blockchain applications.

2. Permissioned Network

Hyperledger Fabric is inherently a permissioned blockchain framework, meaning that participants must be authenticated and authorized to join the network. This feature provides several benefits:

- **Controlled Access:** Organizations can define who can participate in the network and what permissions they have. This level of control is crucial for applications that require confidentiality and data privacy.
- **Improved Security:** By restricting access to only verified participants, Hyperledger Fabric reduces the risk of malicious actors compromising the network.

3. Channels

Fabric introduces the concept of channels, which allows subsets of participants to create private communication paths within the network. Key benefits of channels include:

- **Data Privacy:** Channels ensure that transactions and data shared within them are visible only to participants in that channel. This feature is essential for businesses that require confidentiality in their operations.
- **Flexibility:** Organizations can form channels based on specific projects, partnerships, or use cases, enabling tailored collaboration without exposing sensitive information to the entire network.

4. Endorsement Policies

Hyperledger Fabric allows organizations to define endorsement policies that specify the conditions under which a transaction is considered valid. These policies can vary for different transactions, offering flexibility in governance. Benefits include:

- **Custom Governance:** Organizations can establish rules that dictate how many and which members must endorse a transaction, enhancing security and accountability.
- **Tailored Solutions:** Different applications can have distinct endorsement requirements, allowing organizations to align their blockchain solutions with their business processes.

5. Data Privacy

Hyperledger Fabric offers advanced data privacy features, enabling organizations to protect sensitive information. Key aspects include:

- **Private Data Collections:** Organizations can create private data collections that are only accessible to authorized participants. This feature allows sensitive data to be stored and managed off the main ledger, maintaining confidentiality while still benefiting from the integrity of the blockchain.
- **Encryption:** Data exchanged between participants can be encrypted, ensuring that only authorized parties can access it.

6. Pluggable Components

Hyperledger Fabric's design promotes the use of pluggable components, allowing developers to integrate various technologies and tools. Key components include:

- **Membership Service Provider (MSP):** The MSP manages identities and roles within the network, ensuring secure and flexible identity management.
- **Transaction Validation:** Organizations can implement custom transaction validation logic, adapting the network to their specific business rules and compliance requirements.

7. Scalability and Performance

Hyperledger Fabric is designed to handle high transaction volumes efficiently, making it suitable for enterprise applications. Key performance features include:

- **Parallel Transaction Processing:** Fabric allows multiple transactions to be processed concurrently, improving throughput and reducing latency.
- **Efficient Data Management:** By separating transaction validation and consensus, Fabric optimizes resource utilization and enhances overall performance.

Summary

The key features of Hyperledger Fabric position it as a leading framework for enterprise blockchain solutions. Its modular architecture, permissioned network capabilities, and advanced privacy features allow organizations to develop tailored applications that meet their specific needs. In the following sections, we will explore how to set up a Hyperledger Fabric network, write chaincode, and integrate JavaScript with Fabric SDK, enabling you to leverage these powerful features for your blockchain development projects.

6.3 Setting Up a Hyperledger Network

Setting up a Hyperledger Fabric network involves several steps, including preparing the development environment, configuring the network components, and deploying the network. This section provides a comprehensive guide to help you establish your Hyperledger Fabric network efficiently.

1. Prerequisites

Before you begin, ensure that you have the following prerequisites installed on your development machine:

- **Docker:** Hyperledger Fabric uses Docker containers to run its components. Ensure that Docker is installed and running on your system.
- **Docker Compose:** This tool is used to define and manage multi-container Docker applications. You will need it to orchestrate your Fabric network.
- **Node.js and npm:** These are required for installing the Hyperledger Fabric SDK and for developing client applications.

- **Go Language:** Since Hyperledger Fabric is built using Go, having Go installed will be helpful for chaincode development.
- **Hyperledger Fabric Samples, Binaries, and Docker Images:** Download the Fabric samples, binaries, and Docker images using the following commands:

bash

Copy code

curl -sSL https://bit.ly/2ysbOFE | bash -s — 1.4.8 1.5.0

This command fetches the binaries and Docker images for the specified versions of Hyperledger Fabric.

2. Understanding the Network Components

A Hyperledger Fabric network consists of several components that work together to create a decentralized environment. Key components include:

- **Peers:** These nodes maintain the ledger and execute smart contracts (chaincode). They can be categorized into endorsing peers (which endorse transactions) and committing peers (which commit transactions to the ledger).
- **Orderers:** Orderer nodes are responsible for ordering transactions into blocks and ensuring consistency across the network.
- **Channels:** Channels are private communication paths that allow subsets of participants to transact confidentially. You can create multiple channels within a single network.
- **Certificate Authorities (CAs):** CAs manage identities and issue certificates for participants, ensuring secure access to the network.

3. Creating a Basic Network with Docker Compose

To create a simple Hyperledger Fabric network, follow these steps:

1. **Clone the Hyperledger Fabric Samples Repository:**

bash

Copy code
git clone https://github.com/hyperledger/fabric-samples.git
cd fabric-samples

1. **Navigate to the First Network Sample:**

The first-network sample provides a straightforward example for setting up a basic network.
bash
Copy code
cd first-network

1. **Start the Network:**

You can start the network using Docker Compose with the following command:
bash
Copy code
./start.sh
This script performs the following tasks:

- Starts the Docker containers for the peers, orderer, and CAs.
- Initializes the channel and deploys the chaincode.

1. **Verify the Network is Running:**

To check if your network is running correctly, use the following command:
bash
Copy code
./network.sh list
This command lists all the active components of your network.

4. Creating and Joining Channels
Once the network is up and running, you can create and join channels:

1. **Create a Channel:**

You can create a new channel using the following command:
bash
Copy code
./network.sh createChannel

1. **Join Peers to the Channel:**

After creating the channel, you can join peers to it:
bash
Copy code
./network.sh joinChannel

5. Deploying Chaincode

After setting up your network and creating a channel, you can deploy chaincode:

1. **Install Chaincode:**

Navigate to the chaincode directory and install your chaincode on the peers:
bash
Copy code
./network.sh installChaincode

1. **Instantiate Chaincode:**

After installation, instantiate the chaincode on the channel:
bash
Copy code
./network.sh instantiateChaincode

1. **Invoke Chaincode:**

You can invoke functions on the deployed chaincode:

bash

Copy code

./network.sh invokeChaincode

1. **Query Chaincode:**

To retrieve data from the ledger, use the query command:

bash

Copy code

./network.sh queryChaincode

6. Stopping and Cleaning Up the Network

To stop the network and remove all Docker containers and volumes, run:

bash

Copy code

./teardown.sh

Summary

Setting up a Hyperledger Fabric network involves a series of steps that require careful configuration of components, channels, and chaincode. By following this guide, you should now have a basic understanding of how to create and manage a Hyperledger Fabric network. In the next section, we will explore how to write smart contracts using Chaincode in Hyperledger Fabric, allowing you to develop your applications and leverage the powerful features of the framework.

6.4 Writing Smart Contracts in Hyperledger Fabric with Chaincode

Smart contracts in Hyperledger Fabric are written using **chaincode**, which is essentially the business logic governing transactions between participants in the blockchain network. Unlike Ethereum, where smart contracts are written in Solidity, Hyperledger Fabric allows chaincode to be written in multiple languages, including **Go, Java,** and **Node.js**. In this section, we will focus on writing chaincode in Go, which is the most widely used language for Hyperledger Fabric chaincode development.

1. Chaincode Overview

Chaincode is deployed on peer nodes and invoked during transaction execution. It interacts with the ledger's state database to retrieve, update, and delete data, ensuring all transactions follow predefined rules.

Key functions in chaincode include:

- **init**: Initializes the chaincode when it is instantiated on the network.
- **invoke**: Executes the business logic defined in the smart contract. It can handle multiple operations, such as creating, updating, or querying assets.

2. Structure of a Chaincode Application

Chaincode in Go follows a standard structure, consisting of:

- **The main package**: This contains the entry point of the chaincode.
- **Smart contract logic**: The business logic of the chaincode, with functions that define the rules for executing transactions.
- **Stub interface**: Used to interact with the ledger's state.

Here's a basic structure for a chaincode written in Go:

```go
Copy code
package main

import (
  "fmt"
  "github.com/hyperledger/fabric-contract-api-go/contractapi"
)

// SmartContract defines the structure of the chaincode
type SmartContract struct {
  contractapi.Contract
}
```

```go
// Asset represents a simple object in the ledger
   type Asset struct {
   ID string 'json:"id"'
   Value string 'json:"value"'
   }


// InitLedger initializes the ledger with some default assets
   func (s *SmartContract) InitLedger(ctx contractapi.TransactionContextInt
erface) error {
   assets := []Asset{
   {ID: "asset1", Value: "100"},
   {ID: "asset2", Value: "200"},
   }
   for _, asset := range assets {
   err := ctx.GetStub().PutState(asset.ID, []byte(asset.Value))
   if err != nil {
   return fmt.Errorf("failed to add asset: %s", asset.ID)
   }
   }
   return nil
   }


// QueryAsset allows querying the ledger for a specific asset
   func (s *SmartContract) QueryAsset(ctx contractapi.TransactionContextI
nterface, id string) (string, error) {
   value, err := ctx.GetStub().GetState(id)
   if err != nil {
   return "", fmt.Errorf("failed to read asset: %s", err)
   }
   if value == nil {
   return "", fmt.Errorf("asset not found: %s", id)
   }
   return string(value), nil
```

```
}


// CreateAsset allows adding a new asset to the ledger
func (s *SmartContract) CreateAsset(ctx contractapi.TransactionContextI
nterface, id string, value string) error {
    existingAsset, err := ctx.GetStub().GetState(id)
    if err != nil {
    return fmt.Errorf("failed to read asset: %s", err)
    }
    if existingAsset != nil {
    return fmt.Errorf("asset already exists: %s", id)
    }
    return ctx.GetStub().PutState(id, []byte(value))
    }


func main() {
    chaincode, err := contractapi.NewChaincode(new(SmartContract))
    if err != nil {
    fmt.Printf("Error creating chaincode: %s", err)
    }
    if err := chaincode.Start(); err != nil {
    fmt.Printf("Error starting chaincode: %s", err)
    }
    }
```

3. Key Chaincode Functions

- **InitLedger**: This function is called once during the chaincode's instanti-ation to initialize the ledger with default values. In the example above, it initializes two assets: asset1 and asset2.
- **QueryAsset**: Allows querying the ledger for an asset by its ID. It retrieves the asset's value stored in the ledger.
- **CreateAsset**: Adds a new asset to the ledger. It checks if the asset ID already exists before creating a new one, ensuring no duplicate IDs are

added.

4. Deploying the Chaincode

Once the chaincode is written, you will need to package, install, and instantiate it on the peers in your Hyperledger Fabric network. Here's how you can deploy it:

1. **Package the Chaincode**: In the fabric-samples directory, package your chaincode into a tar.gz file:

bash
Copy code
peer lifecycle chaincode package basic.tar.gz —path ./chaincode/go —label basic_1.0

1. **Install the Chaincode**: Install the chaincode on each peer:

bash
Copy code
peer lifecycle chaincode install basic.tar.gz

1. **Approve the Chaincode Definition**: Each organization must approve the chaincode definition:

bash
Copy code
peer lifecycle chaincode approveformyorg —orderer orderer.example.com:7050 —channelID mychannel —name basic —version 1.0 —package-id [PACKAGE_ID] —sequence 1 —tls —cafile $ORDERER_CA

1. **Commit the Chaincode**: Commit the chaincode to the channel:

bash

Copy code
peer lifecycle chaincode commit —channelID mychannel —name basic —version 1.0 —sequence 1 —tls —cafile $ORDERER_CA

1. **Invoke and Query the Chaincode**: Now that the chaincode is installed, you can invoke it or query the ledger:

bash
Copy code
peer chaincode invoke -o orderer.example.com:7050 —tls —cafile $OR-DERER_CA -C mychannel -n basic -c '{"Args":["CreateAsset","asset3","300"]}'
To query the ledger:
bash
Copy code
peer chaincode query -C mychannel -n basic -c '{"Args":["QueryAsset","asset3"]}'

5. Chaincode Best Practices

- **Validation and Error Handling**: Always validate inputs before writing to the ledger. Implement thorough error handling to prevent corrupt transactions.
- **Modularity**: Break your chaincode into modular functions to keep it organized and maintainable.
- **Efficient Data Storage**: Store minimal data on-chain to reduce transaction and storage costs. Use off-chain databases for large datasets and link them through hashes stored on-chain.

Summary

Chaincode is the backbone of business logic in Hyperledger Fabric. With the knowledge of Go and the chaincode structure, you can now define how assets are created, updated, and queried within your network. The process of deploying and interacting with chaincode enables you to build powerful and secure decentralized applications on permissioned blockchains. In the next section, we will delve into more advanced chaincode features, such as access control, querying rich data, and integrating off-chain storage solutions.

6.5 Deploying and Testing Chaincode

Deploying and testing chaincode in Hyperledger Fabric involves multiple steps to ensure the business logic operates as expected. This section outlines the process for deploying chaincode on the Hyperledger Fabric network and the best practices for testing it to ensure accuracy, performance, and security.

1. Preparing for Chaincode Deployment

Before deploying chaincode, you need to ensure that your Hyperledger Fabric network is set up correctly. The key prerequisites include:

- A running Hyperledger Fabric network with at least one channel.
- Chaincode packaged and ready for deployment.
- Peer nodes installed with the chaincode.

You will also need:

- **Certificate Authority (CA)** credentials.
- **Orderer** and **peer node** access.
- **CLI** tools for interacting with the network.

2. Packaging the Chaincode

Packaging the chaincode is the first step before installing it on the peer nodes. Chaincode is packaged into a compressed file (e.g., .tar.gz) which contains the code and associated metadata.

Here's how to package chaincode:

bash

Copy code

peer lifecycle chaincode package mychaincode.tar.gz —path ./chaincode/go —label mychaincode_1.0

In this command:

- —path specifies the location of your chaincode.

241

- —label is used to identify the version of the chaincode.

3. Installing Chaincode on Peer Nodes

After packaging, the next step is to install the chaincode on all the peer nodes that will execute it. Each organization in the network must install the chaincode on its peer nodes.

bash

Copy code

peer lifecycle chaincode install mychaincode.tar.gz

Once installed, the peer node will generate a **package ID**, which you'll use in the approval process.

To check if the installation was successful:

bash

Copy code

peer lifecycle chaincode queryinstalled

This command will display the list of installed chaincodes and their package IDs.

4. Approving the Chaincode for the Organization

Each organization must approve the chaincode before it can be committed to the network. Approval involves sending a request to the orderer to verify that the installed chaincode matches the packaged chaincode.

bash

Copy code

peer lifecycle chaincode approveformyorg \

—channelID mychannel \

—name mychaincode \

—version 1.0 \

—package-id <PACKAGE_ID> \

—sequence 1 \

—tls —cafile $ORDERER_CA

Here, <PACKAGE_ID> is the package ID obtained from the previous step, and —sequence is the chaincode sequence number, which increments each time the chaincode is updated.

5. Committing the Chaincode to the Channel

Once all organizations have approved the chaincode, it can be committed to the channel:

bash

Copy code

```
peer lifecycle chaincode commit \
—channelID mychannel \
—name mychaincode \
—version 1.0 \
—sequence 1 \
—tls —cafile $ORDERER_CA
```

The chaincode is now ready for use in the network. Peers can start invoking transactions and querying the ledger via the chaincode.

6. Invoking and Testing Chaincode

After deployment, testing is a crucial step to ensure that the chaincode behaves as expected. This can be done by invoking the chaincode's functions through the CLI or a client application.

Invoke a Chaincode Transaction

For example, to create a new asset using the chaincode:

bash

Copy code

```
peer chaincode invoke \
-o orderer.example.com:7050 \
—tls —cafile $ORDERER_CA \
-C mychannel -n mychaincode \
-c '{"Args":["CreateAsset","asset1","100"]}'
```

This command invokes the CreateAsset function, passing in asset1 with a value of 100. The transaction is processed by the peers, which update the ledger with the new asset.

Query the Chaincode

To verify that the asset has been created successfully:

bash

Copy code

peer chaincode query \
-C mychannel -n mychaincode \
-c '{"Args":["QueryAsset","asset1"]}'

The peer should return the value associated with asset1, confirming the chaincode's functionality.

7. Automating Tests for Chaincode

Manual testing is useful but can be time-consuming for large and complex chaincode logic. Automated testing frameworks, such as the Hyperledger Fabric Test Network or unit testing tools in Go, can help automate the testing process.

A basic automated test for chaincode in Go might look like this:

```go
Copy code
func TestCreateAsset(t *testing.T) {
contract := new(SmartContract)
ctx := new(contractapi.MockTransactionContext)
stub := new(contractapi.MockStub)

ctx.GetStubReturns(stub)
stub.GetStateReturns(nil, nil)

err := contract.CreateAsset(ctx, "asset1", "100")
if err != nil {
t.Fatalf("Failed to create asset: %v", err)
}
}
```

This test case ensures that the CreateAsset function works as expected when creating a new asset. More comprehensive tests can be written to check for edge cases, error handling, and performance.

8. Best Practices for Testing Chaincode

1. **Test Early and Often**: Conduct unit tests during development to catch errors early.

2. **Simulate Different Scenarios**: Test for all possible transaction outcomes, including invalid inputs and edge cases.
3. **Performance Testing**: Check how the chaincode performs under load, especially with a high volume of transactions.
4. **Security Testing**: Test for vulnerabilities like replay attacks or unauthorized access to chaincode functions.

9. Debugging Chaincode

Chaincode debugging can be done through logging or by running the peer in **development mode**. To log debug information, use the fmt package in Go to print messages to the peer logs:

```go
Copy code
fmt.Println("Debug: Creating asset with ID: asset1")
```

Logs can be viewed using the peer logs, which provide insight into the chaincode execution process:

```bash
Copy code
docker logs -f peer0.org1.example.com
```

If errors occur during chaincode invocation, the logs will help identify issues with input validation, state updates, or transaction handling.

Summary

Deploying and testing chaincode is an essential phase in the Hyperledger Fabric development lifecycle. By following the outlined steps, you ensure that your chaincode is installed correctly, performs as expected, and handles all necessary transactions securely. Testing—both manual and automated—helps ensure robustness and reliability, while best practices for debugging streamline the identification and resolution of potential issues. In the next chapter, we will explore advanced chaincode functionality, including accessing private data collections, querying rich data, and more.

6.6 Integrating JavaScript with Hyperledger Fabric SDK

The Hyperledger Fabric SDK for JavaScript allows developers to interact with a Hyperledger Fabric network using JavaScript applications. This integration is vital for building decentralized applications (DApps) that leverage the power of Hyperledger Fabric, enabling users to perform tasks such as invoking transactions, querying the blockchain, and managing identities within a familiar JavaScript environment.

1. Overview of Hyperledger Fabric SDK for JavaScript

The **Hyperledger Fabric SDK for JavaScript** provides a set of APIs that allow developers to interact with their blockchain network, connect to peers, submit transactions, and retrieve data. It is designed to simplify the process of building JavaScript-based client applications that can interface with the Hyperledger Fabric network.

Key capabilities include:

- **Connecting to the blockchain network**: Establish connections to the peers and orderers of the network.
- **Submitting transactions**: Invoke chaincode functions to modify the ledger.
- **Querying the blockchain**: Fetch ledger data through chaincode queries.
- **Identity management**: Handle user identities and permissions for secure transactions.

2. Setting Up the Fabric SDK in a JavaScript Project

To begin integrating the Fabric SDK into a JavaScript project, the following steps must be taken:

1. **Install the Fabric SDK**: The SDK can be installed via npm:

bash
Copy code
npm install fabric-network
This installs the fabric-network module, which contains the APIs needed to interact with the blockchain network.

1. **Import Required Modules**: In your JavaScript file, import the neces-

sary modules to interact with the Hyperledger Fabric network:

javascript
```
Copy code
const { Gateway, Wallets } = require('fabric-network');
const path = require('path');
const fs = require('fs');
```

1. **Establish a Network Connection**: The SDK uses a Gateway object to establish a connection with the Fabric network. To do this, load the network configuration (commonly in a connection.json file) and create a Gateway instance:

javascript
```
Copy code
async function connectToNetwork() {
const ccpPath = path.resolve(__dirname, 'connection.json');
const ccp = JSON.parse(fs.readFileSync(ccpPath, 'utf8'));

const walletPath = path.join(process.cwd(), 'wallet');
const wallet = await Wallets.newFileSystemWallet(walletPath);

const gateway = new Gateway();
await gateway.connect(ccp, { wallet, identity: 'user1', discovery: { enabled: true, asLocalhost: true } });

const network = await gateway.getNetwork('mychannel');
const contract = network.getContract('mychaincode');
return contract;
}
```
In this snippet:

- **ccpPath** points to the network connection profile, which contains details of the peers and orderers.

- **wallet** is used to manage identities for secure communication with the network.
- The **Gateway** object connects to the network, and getNetwork() fetches the specified channel (in this case, mychannel).

1. **Submitting Transactions**: Once connected, you can submit transactions to the blockchain using the submitTransaction() method:

javascript

```
Copy code
async function submitTransaction() {
const contract = await connectToNetwork();
await contract.submitTransaction('CreateAsset', 'asset1', '100');
console.log('Transaction has been submitted');
}
```

This code invokes the CreateAsset function in the chaincode, passing in arguments asset1 and 100.

1. **Querying the Blockchain**: You can also query the ledger using evaluateTransaction():

javascript

```
Copy code
async function queryTransaction() {
const contract = await connectToNetwork();
const result = await contract.evaluateTransaction('QueryAsset', 'asset1');
console.log('Transaction result: ${result.toString()}');
}
```

This queries the state of asset1 and returns the result from the ledger.

3. Managing User Identities with the SDK

Identity management is a crucial part of interacting with Hyperledger Fabric. The SDK allows developers to manage user identities using a wallet system, which stores user certificates and keys.

To add a new identity to the wallet:

javascript

Copy code

```
const identity = {
credentials: {
certificate: userCert,
privateKey: userPrivateKey,
},
mspId: 'Org1MSP',
type: 'X.509',
};


await wallet.put('user1', identity);
```

This stores the user's credentials in the wallet, enabling them to authenticate with the network for transactions and queries.

4. Error Handling and Debugging

Proper error handling is critical when interacting with the blockchain. Common issues include transaction failures, connectivity problems, and identity mismatches. It's important to wrap SDK calls in try-catch blocks to handle these errors gracefully:

javascript

Copy code

```
try {
await contract.submitTransaction('CreateAsset', 'asset1', '100');
console.log('Transaction successfully submitted');
} catch (error) {
console.error('Failed to submit transaction: ${error}');
}
```

5. Best Practices for Integrating JavaScript with Hyperledger Fabric

1. **Use Asynchronous Code**: Blockchain interactions are time-consuming operations. Use async/await or Promises to handle these operations

without blocking the main thread.

2. **Identity Management**: Properly manage user identities and permissions, ensuring each identity has the correct access rights.

3. **Security**: Always encrypt sensitive information like certificates and private keys, and store them securely.

4. **Error Handling**: Implement robust error handling to manage connectivity issues, transaction failures, and other potential errors.

Integrating JavaScript with Hyperledger Fabric SDK is a powerful way to build scalable, secure applications that can interact with the Hyperledger blockchain. The SDK allows developers to easily connect to the network, invoke transactions, query data, and manage identities, all within a JavaScript-based environment. By following best practices for identity management, error handling, and security, developers can create robust decentralized applications using Hyperledger Fabric and JavaScript.

Conclusion

Chapter 6 provided an in-depth exploration of **Hyperledger Fabric**, one of the most prominent permissioned blockchain platforms for enterprise use. We began by understanding the architecture and key features of Fabric, including its modular design and support for private transactions through channels. We then delved into setting up a Fabric network, writing and deploying smart contracts (chaincode), and testing them to ensure proper functionality.

A significant highlight of the chapter was the **integration of JavaScript with Hyperledger Fabric SDK**, which allows developers to build decentralized applications using JavaScript, providing a seamless way to interact with the Fabric network, submit transactions, and query the blockchain. This flexibility makes it easier to develop enterprise blockchain solutions tailored to specific business needs.

CHAPTER 7: BUILDING BLOCKCHAIN SOLUTIONS WITH HYPERLEDGER

I n this chapter, we will explore how to build robust permissioned blockchain solutions using the **Hyperledger** framework. Permissioned blockchains, like those created with Hyperledger, provide privacy, security, and control, making them ideal for enterprises that require trust and transparency across distributed parties. This chapter focuses on practical steps to design and develop a permissioned blockchain application.

7.1 Building a Permissioned Blockchain Application

A permissioned blockchain is a type of blockchain where only a specific group of known participants is allowed to join the network. Unlike public blockchains (such as Ethereum or Bitcoin), which are open to anyone, permissioned blockchains restrict access to a predefined set of participants, offering higher security, privacy, and scalability. These qualities make permissioned blockchains well-suited for industries like finance, healthcare, and supply chain management.

This section will guide you through the process of building a permissioned blockchain application using **Hyperledger Fabric**.

1. Designing the Application

The first step in building a permissioned blockchain application is designing the solution architecture. Key components to consider include:

- **Participants**: Identify the organizations or users who will participate in the network. For instance, in a supply chain application, participants might include manufacturers, distributors, retailers, and regulators.

- **Assets**: Define the assets that will be managed on the blockchain. In a financial application, this might include digital currencies or bonds. In a healthcare app, it could be patient records or medical equipment.
- **Transactions**: Outline the key transactions that participants will perform. In a real estate application, transactions could include buying, selling, and transferring property ownership. Ensure that each transaction is secure and verifiable.
- **Chaincode (Smart Contracts)**: Write chaincode (smart contracts) to define the business logic and rules governing how transactions should occur on the blockchain. These contracts ensure that transactions follow the predefined rules.

2. Setting Up the Hyperledger Fabric Network

After designing the application, the next step is to set up the **Hyperledger Fabric** network. This process involves configuring the necessary components, such as peers, orderers, and channels.

- **Peers**: These nodes maintain the ledger, execute smart contracts (chaincode), and validate transactions. Each participant in the network usually operates its own peer node.
- **Orderers**: The orderer node ensures that transactions are processed in the correct sequence and that all participants see the same ledger.
- **Channels**: Channels provide a way to isolate communication between a subset of participants. This feature is critical for ensuring data privacy in permissioned blockchains, as only channel members can see the transactions that occur within the channel.

To set up the network, follow these steps:

1. **Download and Install the Fabric Binaries**: Hyperledger Fabric provides a pre-configured Docker Compose file to quickly set up a test network.

bash

Copy code

curl -sSL https://bit.ly/2ysbOFE | bash -s

This script will download the necessary Fabric binaries and Docker images.

1. **Set Up the Network Configuration**: Use the cryptogen tool to generate cryptographic materials for your network participants (such as certificates and keys).
2. **Start the Network**: After configuring the network, you can start it using Docker Compose:

bash

Copy code

./startFabric.sh

This command initializes the peers, orderers, and channels necessary for the blockchain network.

3. Writing Chaincode (Smart Contracts)

The core of any blockchain application is the **chaincode** or **smart contract** that defines the business logic. In Hyperledger Fabric, chaincode can be written in several programming languages, including Go, Java, and JavaScript (using Node.js).

Here's a basic example of how to write chaincode to manage assets (e.g., property records):

javascript

Copy code

```javascript
const { Contract } = require('fabric-contract-api');

class AssetContract extends Contract {

async createAsset(ctx, assetId, owner, value) {
  const asset = {
  owner,
  value,
```

```
};
await ctx.stub.putState(assetId, Buffer.from(JSON.stringify(asset)));
return 'Asset ${assetId} created successfully';
}

async transferAsset(ctx, assetId, newOwner) {
  const assetBytes = await ctx.stub.getState(assetId);
  if (!assetBytes || assetBytes.length === 0) {
  throw new Error('Asset ${assetId} does not exist');
  }
  const asset = JSON.parse(assetBytes.toString());
  asset.owner = newOwner;
  await ctx.stub.putState(assetId, Buffer.from(JSON.stringify(asset)));
  return 'Asset ${assetId} transferred to ${newOwner}';
  }

async queryAsset(ctx, assetId) {
  const assetBytes = await ctx.stub.getState(assetId);
  if (!assetBytes || assetBytes.length === 0) {
  throw new Error('Asset ${assetId} does not exist');
  }
  return assetBytes.toString();
  }
  }

module.exports = AssetContract;
```

In this chaincode:

- **createAsset** allows participants to create a new asset on the blockchain.
- **transferAsset** enables the transfer of ownership from one participant to another.
- **queryAsset** retrieves information about an existing asset.

4. Deploying the Chaincode

Once the chaincode is written, it needs to be deployed to the Fabric network. This involves the following steps:

1. **Install the Chaincode**: Install the chaincode on all the peers that will execute it.

bash
Copy code
peer chaincode install -n assetContract -v 1.0 -p ./chaincode/

1. **Instantiate the Chaincode**: Instantiate the chaincode on the channel so that it can be invoked by participants.

bash
Copy code
peer chaincode instantiate -n assetContract -v 1.0 -C mychannel -c '{"Args":[""]}'

This makes the chaincode available for all peers on the specified channel (mychannel).

5. Building the Application Frontend

A blockchain application typically includes a user-friendly interface where participants can perform actions like creating, transferring, and querying assets. The frontend can be built using JavaScript frameworks like **React**, **Angular**, or **Vue**. The application will use the **Fabric SDK for JavaScript** to interact with the blockchain.

To integrate the frontend with the blockchain:

- Use the **Fabric SDK** to submit transactions and query the ledger.
- Use a **REST API** or **WebSocket** to communicate between the frontend and the backend that interacts with Hyperledger Fabric.

6. Testing and Deploying the Application

Before deploying the blockchain application to a production environment, it's important to thoroughly test it:

- **Unit Tests**: Test individual functions within the chaincode.
- **Integration Tests**: Ensure that the entire system, including the network, chaincode, and frontend, works as expected.
- **Security Testing**: Verify that access controls and identity management are correctly implemented.

Once testing is complete, deploy the network and application on a cloud platform or in an on-premises data center.

Conclusion of Section 7.1

Building a permissioned blockchain application with Hyperledger Fabric involves designing the architecture, setting up the network, writing smart contracts (chaincode), and developing a frontend that interacts with the blockchain. By using Hyperledger's modular framework and its rich set of tools, developers can build secure, private, and scalable blockchain solutions for enterprise use cases.

7.2 Hyperledger Fabric Transaction Flow

In Hyperledger Fabric, the transaction flow differs significantly from traditional blockchain platforms like Ethereum or Bitcoin, as it introduces a unique endorsement and validation process. This model enhances scalability, privacy, and performance, making it particularly suitable for permissioned blockchains. Understanding the transaction flow in Hyperledger Fabric is critical for developing enterprise-grade blockchain solutions.

In this section, we will break down the step-by-step process of how a transaction flows through the Hyperledger Fabric network, from proposal to validation and commitment.

1. Transaction Flow Overview

In Hyperledger Fabric, the transaction flow consists of three major phases:

1. **Proposal Phase**: The transaction proposal is sent by the client application to endorsing peers for validation.

2. **Endorsement Phase**: Endorsing peers simulate the transaction without updating the ledger and sign the result.
3. **Commitment Phase**: The transaction is validated by the ordering service and then committed to the ledger by peers.

Let's explore each phase in more detail.

2. Transaction Proposal Phase

The transaction begins with a client application sending a **transaction proposal** to a subset of network nodes called **endorsing peers**. Endorsing peers are selected based on an endorsement policy, which specifies which peers must approve the transaction for it to be considered valid.

- **Client Application**: This is the application that initiates the transaction. It can be a web application, mobile app, or backend system that interacts with the blockchain through a software development kit (SDK), such as the **Fabric SDK for JavaScript**.
- **Transaction Proposal**: The client application creates a proposal that includes the desired transaction details (e.g., asset transfer) and sends it to the endorsing peers. The proposal is sent without making any changes to the ledger at this point.

Here's how the transaction proposal phase works:

1. **Client Application Invokes Smart Contract**: The client application sends an invocation request (transaction proposal) to the relevant endorsing peers. This includes a specific function within the chaincode (smart contract), as well as arguments for the function (e.g., asset ID, new owner).
2. **Endorsing Peers Simulate the Transaction**: Endorsing peers receive the transaction proposal and simulate its execution based on the current state of the ledger. The simulation involves running the requested chaincode but **without** actually modifying the ledger.
3. **Proposal Response**: Each endorsing peer returns a **proposal response**

to the client application. This response includes the result of the simulated transaction and the **endorsement** (a signature from the peer indicating that the transaction was valid based on the peer's state).

At this point, the transaction has not yet been written to the ledger. The responses from endorsing peers must now be submitted to the next stage.

3. Endorsement Phase

The client application collects the responses from the endorsing peers. For the transaction to proceed, these responses must meet the criteria outlined in the **endorsement policy**.

- **Endorsement Policy**: This is a rule that specifies which peers (and how many) must endorse a transaction for it to be considered valid. For example, a policy might require that three out of five endorsing peers sign the transaction before it can be processed further.

Here's what happens during the endorsement phase:

1. **Client Application Collects Endorsements**: The client receives the signed responses from the endorsing peers and checks if the responses meet the endorsement policy. If the required number of peers have endorsed the transaction, the transaction can proceed to the next phase.
2. **Transaction Submission**: The client submits the transaction, along with the collected endorsements, to the **ordering service**. The ordering service is responsible for ordering transactions into blocks and ensuring consensus on the transaction order.

4. Ordering and Validation Phase

At this stage, the transaction is ordered and validated. Unlike traditional blockchain systems, where all peers participate in consensus, Hyperledger Fabric uses a more efficient ordering service to establish the final order of transactions.

- **Ordering Service**: The ordering service collects transactions from clients, orders them, and creates blocks of transactions. It does not execute or validate transactions; it merely ensures that transactions are ordered in a deterministic way, which is crucial for maintaining a consistent ledger state across all peers.

Here's what happens in the ordering and validation phase:

1. **Transaction Ordering**: The ordering service collects endorsed transactions from the network and orders them into blocks. This ensures that all peers receive transactions in the same sequence, which prevents inconsistencies.
2. **Block Creation**: The ordered transactions are grouped into a block, which is then distributed to all peers in the network (both endorsing and committing peers).

5. Commitment Phase

After receiving a block from the ordering service, each peer independently verifies and commits the transactions in the block.

- **Committer Peers**: All peers in the network participate in the commitment phase. They validate the block of transactions and ensure that the results match the endorsement policy and the current state of the ledger.
- **State Validation**: During this phase, peers check for potential issues, such as double-spending or invalid transactions, to ensure the integrity of the ledger.

The commitment phase involves the following steps:

1. **Transaction Validation**: Each peer independently validates the transactions within the block. This includes checking if the transactions meet the endorsement policy and ensuring that there are no conflicts with the current state (such as two transactions trying to modify the same

asset simultaneously).

2. **Ledger Update**: Once a transaction is validated, the peer commits the changes to its local copy of the ledger. The ledger consists of two components:

- **World State**: The current state of all assets on the blockchain.
- **Transaction Log**: A log of all transactions, which provides a complete history of asset transfers and state changes.

1. **Event Emission**: After committing a transaction, peers emit events that notify the client application about the status of the transaction (e.g., whether it was successfully committed).

6. Finalizing the Transaction

Once the transaction has been validated and committed by the peers, it becomes a permanent part of the blockchain ledger. The client application can now query the ledger to verify the result of the transaction or listen for transaction events to confirm its successful execution.

Summary

Hyperledger Fabric's transaction flow is designed for efficiency, privacy, and scalability. The separation of transaction endorsement, ordering, and validation allows for flexible governance and faster transaction processing, making it well-suited for enterprise applications. By understanding each phase of the transaction flow—proposal, endorsement, ordering, and commitment—developers can design robust and secure blockchain solutions using Hyperledger Fabric.

7.3 Querying and Invoking Transactions

In Hyperledger Fabric, interacting with the blockchain network involves two key actions: **querying** the ledger and **invoking** transactions. Querying allows participants to read data from the ledger, while invoking transactions enables them to update the ledger by making changes to the blockchain's state.

Understanding how to query and invoke transactions is essential for building applications on Hyperledger Fabric. In this section, we will explore both operations in detail and demonstrate how they can be implemented using **Fabric SDKs** (such as the **JavaScript SDK**).

1. Querying the Ledger

Querying is the process of retrieving data from the blockchain ledger without modifying it. This is often used to read the current state of an asset or retrieve a historical record of transactions.

In Hyperledger Fabric, queries are executed against the **world state**, which stores the current state of all assets on the blockchain. Since querying does not affect the blockchain's state, it does not require endorsement or validation from peers.

Here's how querying works:

- **World State vs. Transaction Log**: The world state represents the latest snapshot of the blockchain, while the transaction log provides the history of all transactions. Queries are typically executed against the world state to retrieve the most up-to-date information.
- **Chaincode Functions for Querying**: Chaincode (smart contract) functions are written to handle querying requests. These functions can query specific data stored in the ledger (such as an asset's current value) and return the result to the client application.

Example: Querying the World State

Let's consider an example where a DApp needs to retrieve the current state of a particular asset (e.g., an asset with ID asset1). The following steps outline how to perform a query using Fabric SDK for JavaScript:

1. **Create a Client Application**: The client application sends a request to the blockchain network to query the state of the asset.
2. **Call the Chaincode Function**: The client application invokes the relevant chaincode function that is designed to query the world state.
3. **Retrieve and Return Data**: The chaincode executes the query on the world state and returns the current value of the asset to the client

application.

Here's a simplified example using **Fabric JavaScript SDK**:

```javascript
Copy code
async function queryAsset(assetId) {
const network = await gateway.getNetwork('mychannel'); // Connect to the network
const contract = network.getContract('mychaincode'); // Access chaincode
const result = await contract.evaluateTransaction('queryAsset', assetId); // Query the asset
console.log('Asset state: ${result.toString()}');
}
```

In this example:

- The queryAsset function is called to retrieve the current state of the asset with the provided assetId.
- The evaluateTransaction method is used for queries since it does not alter the state of the blockchain.

2. Invoking Transactions

While querying is used to read data, invoking a transaction is used to update the ledger by modifying the state of assets or creating new records. Invoking a transaction requires several steps, including proposal submission, endorsement, ordering, and commitment, as described in the **transaction flow** section.

Invoking a transaction follows this flow:

1. **Client Application Proposes a Transaction**: The client application sends a transaction proposal to endorsing peers.
2. **Endorsing Peers Simulate the Transaction**: Endorsing peers simulate the transaction, verify its correctness, and return an endorsement to the client.

3. **Transaction Submission**: The client collects the endorsements and submits the transaction to the ordering service.

4. **Transaction Commitment**: The transaction is validated by the ordering service and committed to the ledger by peers.

Example: Invoking a Transaction to Update Asset Ownership

Consider an example where a DApp needs to transfer ownership of an asset. The following example demonstrates how to invoke a transaction using the Fabric JavaScript SDK:

```javascript
Copy code
async function transferAsset(assetId, newOwner) {
const network = await gateway.getNetwork('mychannel'); // Connect to the network
const contract = network.getContract('mychaincode'); // Access chaincode
await contract.submitTransaction('transferAsset', assetId, newOwner); // Invoke transaction
console.log('Asset ${assetId} ownership transferred to ${newOwner}');
}
```

In this example:

- The submitTransaction method is used to invoke the transferAsset function in the chaincode.
- The submitTransaction method requires an endorsement from peers and will modify the state of the asset (ownership).

After the transaction is successfully submitted and committed to the ledger, the asset's ownership is updated, and the new state is reflected in the world state.

3. Common Scenarios for Querying and Invoking Transactions

Here are some common scenarios where querying and invoking transactions come into play in a Hyperledger Fabric network:

1. **Asset Transfer**:

- **Query**: A client queries the ledger to check the current owner of an asset.
- **Invoke**: The client invokes a transaction to transfer the asset to a new owner.

1. **Supply Chain Tracking**:

- **Query**: A client queries the current location and status of goods in the supply chain.
- **Invoke**: A transaction is invoked to update the location and status of the goods as they move through the supply chain.

1. **Financial Services**:

- **Query**: A client queries an account's balance or transaction history.
- **Invoke**: A transaction is invoked to perform a transfer between accounts.

4. Query vs. Invoke: Key Differences
Summary

Querying and invoking transactions are the core operations for interacting with the Hyperledger Fabric blockchain. While querying allows for reading data without modifying the blockchain, invoking transactions enables updates and changes to the ledger. Understanding when and how to query or invoke transactions is crucial for building robust blockchain applications.

7.4 Access Control and Identity Management in Hyperledger

In Hyperledger Fabric, access control and identity management are essential components that ensure only authorized participants can interact with the blockchain network. Since Hyperledger is a **permissioned blockchain**, meaning that participants need permission to join and perform actions, the system employs robust mechanisms for managing identities, enforcing access control, and maintaining security across the network.

In this section, we will explore how Hyperledger manages identities and implements access control through key features such as **Membership Service Providers (MSPs), certificates**, and **policies**.

1. Membership Service Providers (MSP)

In Hyperledger Fabric, **Membership Service Providers (MSPs)** play a central role in identity management. An MSP is responsible for defining the set of identities or organizations that are allowed to participate in the network. It verifies the identities of participants and ensures that only those with valid credentials can access the network.

Each participant (such as an organization, peer, or client) has its own MSP, which contains the information needed to identify members. MSPs manage digital certificates, which are used to prove the identity of users and enforce access control.

Key Functions of MSPs:

- **Identifying Network Participants**: MSPs identify which organizations or users are part of the network and what roles they play (e.g., peer, orderer, client).
- **Handling Certificates**: MSPs manage digital certificates issued by a **Certificate Authority (CA)**, which provides a secure way to authenticate participants.
- **Enforcing Policies**: MSPs enforce policies that dictate what actions participants are allowed to take on the blockchain (e.g., who can endorse transactions or write data).

Certificate Authorities (CA):

Hyperledger Fabric uses **Certificate Authorities** to issue digital certificates for identity verification. These certificates are based on **Public Key Infrastructure (PKI)**, where each user or organization receives a unique private key (used for signing transactions) and a public key (used for identity verification).

2. Types of Identities in Hyperledger Fabric

Hyperledger Fabric manages different types of identities depending on the role of the participant. Here are the most common identity types:

- **Client Identity**: Represents an end user or application that interacts with the network to submit transactions or query data. This identity typically resides on the client side (e.g., JavaScript application).
- **Peer Identity**: Represents a peer node in the network. Peers validate transactions and maintain the ledger's state.
- **Orderer Identity**: Represents the orderer node, which is responsible for ordering transactions and broadcasting them to peers.
- **Admin Identity**: Represents an administrative user with higher-level privileges for managing the network.

Each identity is tied to a unique digital certificate issued by a Certificate Authority.

3. Access Control through Policies

Hyperledger Fabric uses **access control policies** to determine what actions participants can take. Policies are associated with various parts of the network (channels, chaincode, etc.) and are enforced by the Membership Service Provider (MSP). These policies specify the conditions under which a participant can read, write, or endorse transactions.

Common Policy Types:

- **Endorsement Policies**: Determine which participants (usually peers) must endorse a transaction before it is considered valid. For example, a policy might require endorsements from two different organizations.
- **Access Control Policies**: Define which users can perform certain actions, such as invoking chaincode, querying the ledger, or creating new channels.
- **Channel Policies**: Control access to channels and who can add peers, install chaincode, or modify channel configurations.

Each policy is typically defined as a set of rules (e.g., requiring signatures from specific organizations), and it must be met for the transaction or action to be valid.

4. Managing Identities with Fabric CA

Fabric CA is the default Certificate Authority provided by Hyperledger Fabric. It is responsible for issuing, revoking, and renewing certificates. Fabric CA plays a critical role in identity management by ensuring that only authorized participants can access the blockchain network.

Steps for Managing Identities Using Fabric CA:

1. **Registration**: When a new participant (user or organization) needs to join the network, it must first be registered with Fabric CA. This step includes defining the participant's role (e.g., peer, client, admin).
2. **Enrollment**: After registration, the participant requests enrollment, which involves generating cryptographic keys (public and private) and receiving a digital certificate signed by Fabric CA.
3. **Re-enrollment and Revocation**: Fabric CA can also re-issue or revoke certificates based on policy changes or security requirements.

Certificates issued by Fabric CA are critical for establishing trust within the network. Every transaction submitted to the blockchain is signed with a participant's private key and verified using the corresponding public key.

5. Implementing Access Control in Chaincode

Access control can also be implemented directly within **chaincode** (smart contracts). Developers can include logic in the chaincode to enforce specific rules on who can execute certain functions or update specific assets.

Example: Access Control in Chaincode

Here's an example of how access control can be enforced in chaincode using the **Client Identity** library in Fabric SDK:

```javascript
Copy code
async function transferAsset(ctx, assetId, newOwner) {
const clientIdentity = ctx.clientIdentity.getID(); // Get the client ID (certificate)

// Ensure the current user is authorized to transfer the asset
if (clientIdentity !== 'Org1MSP') {
```

```
throw new Error('Access denied. Only Org1 can transfer assets.');
}
```

```
// Perform the asset transfer logic
await ctx.stub.putState(assetId, Buffer.from(newOwner));
}
```

In this example:

- The chaincode retrieves the client's identity (clientIdentity) and checks if they belong to a specific organization (Org1).
- If the client is not authorized, an error is thrown, preventing unauthorized users from transferring the asset.

6. Identity and Access Control in Multi-Organization Networks

In networks with multiple organizations, managing identities and enforcing access control becomes more complex. Hyperledger Fabric allows each organization to have its own Membership Service Provider (MSP) and Certificate Authority (CA), ensuring that organizations can independently manage their participants' identities while maintaining trust across the network.

Inter-Organization Trust:

Trust between organizations is established through **cross-signing certificates** and **endorsement policies**. For example, a policy might require signatures from peers in both Organization A and Organization B for a transaction to be valid. This ensures that no single organization can dominate the network.

Summary

Access control and identity management are critical to the secure operation of a permissioned blockchain network like Hyperledger Fabric. The Membership Service Provider (MSP) and Certificate Authority (CA) manage the identities of participants and enforce access control policies that determine who can read, write, and endorse transactions.

7.5 Hyperledger Composer: Simplifying Development

Hyperledger Composer is a development framework that simplifies building blockchain applications on **Hyperledger Fabric**. It provides a suite of tools that make it easier for developers to model, develop, and deploy business networks without needing to dive into the lower-level complexities of Fabric itself. Composer abstracts much of the underlying blockchain infrastructure, allowing developers to focus on the logic and functionality of their applications.

In this section, we'll explore the key components of Hyperledger Composer, how it simplifies blockchain development, and its role in rapidly building and deploying blockchain solutions.

1. Key Features of Hyperledger Composer

Hyperledger Composer offers several features that make it attractive for developers:

- **Business Network Definition**: With Composer, developers can define entire business networks, including assets, participants, and transactions, using a high-level modeling language.
- **High-Level Abstraction**: Composer abstracts many complex aspects of Hyperledger Fabric, such as identity management, transactions, and access control, making development faster and more efficient.
- **Integration with Web and Enterprise Systems**: Composer allows easy integration of blockchain solutions with existing web applications and enterprise systems via REST APIs and JavaScript SDKs.
- **Rapid Prototyping**: The framework is well-suited for quickly creating prototypes and proofs of concept, allowing organizations to validate blockchain use cases before committing to full-scale development.
- **Modularity**: Composer uses modular components, which makes it easier to modify or extend specific functionalities without needing to overhaul the entire application.

2. Key Components of Hyperledger Composer

Composer provides a range of tools that work together to streamline the development of blockchain applications. Below are the key components:

- **Business Network Model**: Defines the structure of the business network, including the assets, participants, and transactions. This model is written using **Composer Modeling Language** (a high-level domain-specific language).

Example of a business network model:

```
text
Copy code
asset Car identified by vin {
o String vin
o String make
o String model
o Double mileage
—> Person owner
}

participant Person identified by personId {
o String personId
o String firstName
o String lastName
}

transaction TransferOwnership {
—> Car car
—> Person newOwner
}
```

In this example:

- **Car** is an asset with attributes like vin, make, and model.
- **Person** is a participant with a unique personId.
- **TransferOwnership** is a transaction that transfers the ownership of a Car from one participant to another.
- **Transaction Logic**: Contains the business rules and logic that define

how transactions will be processed. This logic is written in JavaScript, making it familiar for many developers.

Example of transaction logic in Composer:

```javascript
Copy code
/**
* Transfer the ownership of a car to a new owner
* @param {org.example.mynetwork.TransferOwnership} tx - the transaction object
* @transaction
*/
async function transferOwnership(tx) {
tx.car.owner = tx.newOwner;
const assetRegistry = await getAssetRegistry('org.example.mynetwork.Car'
);
await assetRegistry.update(tx.car);
}
```

In this example, the transaction logic updates the owner of the Car asset in the asset registry.

- **Access Control Language (ACL)**: Defines who can access or modify assets, participants, and transactions. ACL files allow you to specify granular permissions based on roles.

Example ACL:

```text
Copy code
rule OnlyOwnerCanTransferCar {
description: "Only the current owner of the car can transfer ownership"
participant(p): "org.example.mynetwork.Person"
operation: ALL
resource(r): "org.example.mynetwork.Car"
```

```
condition: (r.owner == p)
action: ALLOW
}
```

This rule ensures that only the current owner of the car can transfer its ownership.

- **REST API Generator**: Composer automatically generates REST APIs for your business network, allowing developers to integrate blockchain functionality into external applications easily.

Example: If you have defined a Car asset and a TransferOwnership transaction, Composer will generate endpoints like:

- POST /api/Car to create a new car.
- POST /api/TransferOwnership to transfer a car's ownership.
- **Playground**: Hyperledger Composer includes a **Playground** environment, which is a web-based tool that allows developers to model, deploy, and test business networks quickly. It provides an easy-to-use graphical interface for creating blockchain applications without needing to write code directly in a text editor or set up complex development environments.

3. Workflow of Developing Blockchain Applications with Hyperledger Composer

Developing a blockchain application with Composer involves the following steps:

1. **Define the Business Network**:

- Use Composer Modeling Language to define the assets, participants, and transactions in your business network. This high-level abstraction allows you to focus on the business logic rather than the low-level blockchain implementation.

1. **Write Transaction Logic**:

- Write JavaScript functions that implement the transaction logic for your application. These functions handle the business rules and operations, such as transferring ownership of assets.

1. **Set Access Controls**:

- Define access control rules using Composer's ACL language to specify which participants can perform certain actions on assets, transactions, and participants.

1. **Deploy the Business Network**:

- Deploy your business network definition to a Hyperledger Fabric instance. Composer automates the deployment process, making it easy to get your business logic running on the blockchain.

1. **Test the Network**:

- Use the Composer Playground to interact with the blockchain network by testing transactions, querying data, and verifying that the application works as expected.

1. **Generate REST APIs**:

- Use the built-in REST API generator to create RESTful endpoints for your application, enabling easy integration with frontend applications, mobile apps, or other enterprise systems.

4. Benefits of Using Hyperledger Composer

- **Ease of Use**: Composer simplifies the development process by abstracting the complexities of Hyperledger Fabric, making it accessible to developers who may not have extensive blockchain experience.

- **Faster Development Cycle**: The high-level modeling language and tools like Playground allow for rapid prototyping, reducing the time it takes to go from concept to implementation.
- **Interoperability**: With built-in support for REST API generation, Composer makes it easy to integrate blockchain applications with existing systems, such as enterprise databases or web platforms.
- **Enterprise-Grade Security**: Composer leverages the robust security features of Hyperledger Fabric, including permissioned access and identity management, ensuring that blockchain applications meet enterprise security requirements.
- **Extensibility**: Composer is modular, meaning developers can easily extend or modify specific parts of their applications without affecting the entire network.

5. Hyperledger Composer vs. Hyperledger Fabric SDK

While both Composer and the **Hyperledger Fabric SDK** can be used to develop blockchain applications, they serve different purposes:

- **Composer** is aimed at simplifying and speeding up development, especially for rapid prototyping and business-oriented use cases. It abstracts many low-level details and is ideal for developers looking for a high-level approach to building blockchain applications.
- **Fabric SDK** provides a lower-level interface for interacting directly with the Hyperledger Fabric network. It offers more fine-grained control over the blockchain but requires more in-depth knowledge of Hyperledger Fabric's architecture and functionality.

6. Transition to Other Tools

As of 2021, Hyperledger Composer's development has slowed, and the Hyperledger community has shifted focus to using **Hyperledger Fabric SDK** and other tools for production-level applications. While Composer remains a useful tool for prototyping and learning, it's recommended to transition to using Fabric SDK for larger, more complex deployments.

Summary

Hyperledger Composer is a powerful tool that simplifies the development of blockchain applications on Hyperledger Fabric. By abstracting many of the complexities of Fabric, it enables developers to focus on business logic rather than the underlying blockchain infrastructure. Its rapid prototyping capabilities, easy integration with external systems, and high-level modeling language make it an excellent choice for those looking to quickly build and test blockchain applications.

7.6 Real-World Use Case: Supply Chain Solution with Hyperledger

The supply chain industry is one of the most promising fields for blockchain adoption, particularly permissioned blockchain solutions like **Hyperledger Fabric**. In this section, we'll walk through a real-world use case of a supply chain management system built on **Hyperledger**. This will illustrate how Hyperledger's features, such as transparency, immutability, and decentralization, provide significant advantages in managing the complexities of supply chains.

1. Overview of Supply Chain Challenges

Supply chains are complex networks that involve multiple stakeholders—manufacturers, suppliers, logistics providers, retailers, and customers. Some of the challenges faced by supply chains include:

- **Lack of transparency**: It's difficult to track the movement of goods across various stages, from raw materials to finished products.
- **Inefficient record-keeping**: Many supply chains rely on outdated, manual methods of tracking inventory, leading to discrepancies and delays.
- **Counterfeiting**: In industries like pharmaceuticals and luxury goods, counterfeit products can infiltrate the supply chain, damaging brand reputation and endangering consumers.
- **Disputes**: Disagreements between supply chain participants over prod-

uct quality, delivery times, and payments often arise, requiring third-party intervention.

By implementing blockchain, many of these challenges can be addressed with features such as real-time tracking, tamper-proof records, and automated smart contracts.

2. Blockchain-Based Supply Chain Solution

A supply chain solution built on Hyperledger Fabric would typically involve the following components:

- **Participants**: These would include manufacturers, suppliers, logistics companies, retailers, and auditors, each with specific roles and permissions in the blockchain network.
- **Assets**: Products or goods would be tracked as blockchain assets, with information about their origin, production, and movement recorded at each stage.
- **Smart Contracts**: Business logic, such as quality checks, payment processing, and delivery confirmations, would be implemented as chaincode (smart contracts) on Hyperledger Fabric.
- **Transactions**: Each movement of goods or change in status would be recorded as a transaction on the blockchain, ensuring an immutable and transparent audit trail.

3. Supply Chain Example: Tracking Food Products

Consider a food supply chain where the stakeholders include farmers, food processors, distributors, retailers, and consumers. A blockchain solution could ensure that every step—from farm to fork—is recorded on a shared, decentralized ledger. Here's how Hyperledger Fabric would address key challenges:

- **Traceability**: Every batch of produce is tracked from the farm, through processing, to retail shelves. Each actor (farmer, processor, distributor) logs relevant information on the blockchain, such as the date of harvest, processing methods, and storage conditions.

- **Quality Control**: Smart contracts can be used to enforce quality control standards at each step of the chain. For example, if food is stored above a certain temperature during transport, the smart contract could flag the issue, preventing the product from being delivered to retailers.
- **Transparency**: Consumers can scan QR codes on food packaging to view the complete history of the product, from the farm where it was grown to the store where it's sold. This enhances trust in product quality and provenance.
- **Dispute Resolution**: If there are disputes over delivery times or product quality, the immutable records on the blockchain provide a clear, tamper-proof history of events, making it easier to resolve disagreements.

4. Architecture of the Supply Chain Solution

A blockchain-based supply chain solution built with Hyperledger Fabric would be composed of the following key elements:

- **Chaincode (Smart Contracts)**: The core business logic for the supply chain is implemented as chaincode, which governs actions such as transfers of ownership, quality checks, and payments.
- **Ledger**: Every transaction, such as the transfer of goods from one participant to another, is recorded on the Hyperledger Fabric ledger, creating a transparent and immutable audit trail.
- **Access Control**: Hyperledger Fabric's permissioned network ensures that only authorized participants can access specific types of information. For example, while auditors may have access to the full history of goods, end consumers may only see limited product details.
- **Peer Nodes and Ordering Service**: Peer nodes maintain a copy of the ledger and execute chaincode. The ordering service manages the consensus process and ensures that transactions are ordered and validated before being appended to the blockchain.

5. Benefits of Using Hyperledger for Supply Chain Solutions

- **Increased Transparency**: By having all stakeholders record data on a shared, tamper-proof ledger, transparency across the supply chain is greatly enhanced.
- **Real-Time Tracking**: Stakeholders can monitor the location and condition of goods in real-time, reducing the likelihood of loss, theft, or damage.
- **Reduced Fraud and Counterfeiting**: Hyperledger Fabric's immutability ensures that once data is recorded, it cannot be altered, making it easier to detect fraudulent activity or counterfeit goods.
- **Improved Efficiency**: Automating transactions, such as payments and deliveries, through smart contracts can reduce delays and improve overall efficiency.
- **Simplified Compliance**: Regulatory authorities or auditors can access real-time data and historical records on the blockchain, reducing the burden of manual reporting and ensuring compliance with regulations.

6. Real-World Example: Walmart's Blockchain for Food Safety

One of the most well-known blockchain implementations in supply chain management is **Walmart's food safety blockchain**, developed in collaboration with IBM and based on **Hyperledger Fabric**. Walmart uses this system to track the origins of food products, from farm to shelf, ensuring quick identification of contaminated products in the case of a foodborne illness outbreak.

With blockchain, Walmart was able to reduce the time it takes to trace a product's origin from days or weeks to just a few seconds. This not only improves food safety but also reduces waste and enhances consumer trust in the products they purchase.

Conclusion

In this chapter, we explored how Hyperledger Fabric can be used to build permissioned blockchain applications, focusing on both the technical architecture and the practical use cases. We began by discussing how to build a permissioned blockchain application and moved on to explore the transaction flow in Hyperledger Fabric, access control, and identity management.

We also introduced **Hyperledger Composer**, a high-level framework for quickly building and deploying blockchain applications, and its role in simplifying development. Lastly, we examined a real-world use case of using Hyperledger Fabric for supply chain management, illustrating how blockchain can improve transparency, efficiency, and traceability across complex supply chains.

With its modular architecture, permissioned network model, and support for smart contracts, Hyperledger Fabric is well-suited for industries that require high levels of security, privacy, and control.

CHAPTER 8: INTRODUCTION TO CORDA BLOCKCHAIN

8.1 What is Corda? Unique Features of Corda

Corda is a blockchain platform designed specifically for businesses to manage complex transactions while ensuring privacy and scalability. Unlike many traditional blockchain platforms like Ethereum or Bitcoin, Corda focuses on providing solutions that cater to real-world business needs, particularly in industries where privacy, efficiency, and legal certainty are essential.

While Corda is often described as a blockchain, it is technically a **distributed ledger technology (DLT)** platform. One of its defining features is its approach to privacy and data sharing, where transactions are only shared with the parties involved, rather than broadcasting them across the entire network, as in other blockchains.

1. Overview of Corda

Corda was originally developed by **R3**, a consortium of more than 200 financial institutions, as a blockchain solution that could address the unique challenges faced by businesses, particularly in regulated industries like finance, healthcare, supply chains, and insurance. Over time, Corda has evolved into a multi-purpose platform suitable for a wide range of industries.

Corda aims to combine the best of both worlds: the transparency and immutability of blockchain with the privacy and scalability required for enterprise-level applications. It allows organizations to transact directly with one another with high trust, eliminating the need for costly intermediaries, while ensuring that sensitive data remains private and secure.

2. Unique Features of Corda

Corda's design addresses several limitations of traditional blockchain platforms, making it a popular choice for businesses. Some of its unique features include:

a) Privacy and Selective Data Sharing

One of the standout features of Corda is its focus on privacy. Unlike many blockchains where transactions are visible to all participants, Corda uses a **point-to-point communication model**. This means that only the parties involved in a transaction and those who need to verify it have access to the relevant data.

- **Private Transactions**: Data related to a transaction is only shared with parties directly involved. This ensures that sensitive business information, such as transaction terms or amounts, is not exposed to the entire network.
- **Notary Service**: To prevent double-spending and maintain consensus across the network, Corda uses a **Notary** service. The Notary ensures the uniqueness of transactions without revealing their details to the entire network.

b) Legal Certainty

Corda is designed to support **legally binding agreements** and contracts, which is crucial for regulated industries. It focuses on aligning blockchain transactions with real-world legal agreements through **smart contracts**, known in Corda as **CorDapps** (Corda Distributed Applications).

- **Contract States**: Corda represents real-world agreements as **states** on the ledger. These states can be shared, updated, or transferred between parties, with all changes being legally enforceable.
- **Legal Prose Binding**: Corda's smart contracts often have associated legal prose, meaning that the digital contract can be tied to a traditional legal document, ensuring that it complies with relevant regulations and

can be enforced in courts of law.

c) Scalability and High Throughput

Corda was built to handle the demands of large enterprises, which often require high throughput for processing thousands or even millions of transactions per day. Its **directed acyclic graph (DAG)** structure and **sharding** capabilities make it more scalable than traditional blockchain systems.

- **Efficient Data Handling**: Because Corda does not require broadcasting transactions to the entire network, it significantly reduces network congestion and allows for higher transaction throughput.
- **Parallel Processing**: The platform supports the parallel execution of transactions, allowing it to scale and meet the performance requirements of businesses with high-volume transactional needs.

d) Interoperability and Flexibility

Corda was designed with interoperability in mind, allowing it to work alongside other blockchain platforms and legacy systems. It supports integrations with existing enterprise systems, making it easier for businesses to adopt blockchain technology without having to overhaul their existing infrastructure.

- **Integration with Legacy Systems**: Corda allows businesses to integrate blockchain technology into their existing operations. This is especially beneficial for industries like finance, where businesses often rely on decades-old systems that are difficult to replace.
- **Cross-Platform Transactions**: Corda also supports interoperability between different blockchain platforms, allowing assets or data to move across multiple blockchains.

e) Permissioned Blockchain

Like Hyperledger Fabric, Corda operates on a **permissioned network**.

This means that only authorized participants can join the network and view specific data, which is crucial for businesses operating in regulated environments. The permissioned model ensures that data privacy and security are maintained at all times, making it an ideal choice for industries like finance and healthcare, where compliance with regulations such as **GDPR** or **HIPAA** is mandatory.

f) Consensus via Notaries

Corda uses a unique consensus mechanism based on **Notary nodes**, which act as validators for transactions. Notaries in Corda can be **single** or **distributed**, providing flexibility depending on the needs of the network.

- **Single Notary**: A single notary service ensures the uniqueness and validity of transactions but can be a point of centralization.
- **Distributed Notaries**: To address the issue of centralization, Corda allows for distributed notaries, where a group of notaries collectively validate transactions. This ensures greater decentralization while still maintaining the security and efficiency required for enterprise solutions.

3. Real-World Applications of Corda

Corda is being actively used in several industries for various real-world applications, including:

- **Finance**: Corda is heavily used in the financial sector for applications such as trade finance, payment settlements, and insurance claim processing. Its privacy features and legal enforceability make it ideal for industries where regulations and compliance are crucial.
- **Healthcare**: Corda is used in healthcare for secure patient data sharing, medical records management, and tracking the supply chain for pharmaceutical products.
- **Supply Chain**: Similar to Hyperledger Fabric, Corda has been implemented in supply chain management to enhance transparency, traceability, and efficiency in the movement of goods.
- **Energy**: In the energy sector, Corda is being used to manage decen-

tralized energy grids, where energy producers and consumers can trade energy directly with one another in a trustless environment.

Summary

Corda is a unique and powerful platform designed specifically for businesses, offering features that address the complex requirements of privacy, scalability, and legal certainty. Its selective data-sharing model, legal enforceability of contracts, and high transaction throughput make it an attractive choice for enterprises in finance, healthcare, supply chain, and more.

8.2 Corda vs. Ethereum and Hyperledger

When it comes to blockchain and distributed ledger technologies, Corda, Ethereum, and Hyperledger serve distinct purposes and address different needs within the business landscape. Understanding their differences is essential for selecting the right platform for your specific use case. In this section, we will explore the key differences and similarities among these three prominent blockchain platforms.

1. Purpose and Target Audience

Corda:

Corda was specifically designed for businesses and enterprises that require a secure and private environment for transactions. Its focus on permissioned access and legal certainty makes it suitable for industries like finance, healthcare, and supply chain management. Corda targets organizations looking to enhance transaction efficiency while maintaining compliance with regulations.

Ethereum:

Ethereum, in contrast, was developed as a public blockchain platform primarily for decentralized applications (DApps) and smart contracts. Its broad audience includes developers and enterprises looking to leverage blockchain for various applications, including finance (DeFi), gaming, and identity management. Ethereum is known for its openness and community-driven approach, which encourages innovation.

Hyperledger:

Hyperledger, which is a consortium of open-source projects, targets enterprises needing modular blockchain solutions. Unlike Corda and Ethereum, Hyperledger offers multiple frameworks (like Fabric, Sawtooth, and Indy) that can be tailored to specific business requirements. It emphasizes privacy, scalability, and interoperability, making it suitable for various industries, including finance, healthcare, and manufacturing.

2. Consensus Mechanism

Corda:

Corda employs a unique consensus mechanism involving **Notary nodes** that validate transactions. This system allows for greater privacy since only the parties involved in a transaction share relevant data with each other and the Notary, which prevents double-spending and ensures validity without broadcasting all information to the network.

Ethereum:

Ethereum primarily uses the **Proof of Stake (PoS)** consensus mechanism (after its transition from Proof of Work). This mechanism relies on validators who propose and confirm blocks based on their stake in the network. While PoS allows for decentralization and security, it can lead to public visibility of transactions, which may not be suitable for businesses requiring confidentiality.

Hyperledger:

Hyperledger supports various consensus mechanisms depending on the specific framework used. For instance, Hyperledger Fabric allows organizations to define their consensus protocol based on their needs, supporting models like **Practical Byzantine Fault Tolerance (PBFT)** and others. This flexibility enables enterprises to implement a consensus mechanism that aligns with their privacy and performance requirements.

3. Privacy and Data Sharing

Corda:

Corda's design prioritizes privacy, allowing data to be shared only with relevant parties involved in a transaction. This selective data-sharing model helps protect sensitive business information, making it ideal for regulated industries where confidentiality is paramount.

Ethereum:

In Ethereum, all transactions are visible to all network participants, which can raise privacy concerns for businesses dealing with sensitive data. While there are privacy-enhancing solutions being developed (like zk-SNARKs), the core Ethereum architecture is not inherently designed for confidentiality.

Hyperledger:

Hyperledger frameworks, particularly Hyperledger Fabric, are built for privacy and permissioned access. Participants in a Hyperledger network can define access controls for data sharing, ensuring that only authorized users can view specific information. This model aligns well with enterprise needs for secure transactions and compliance.

4. Smart Contracts and Development Language

Corda:

Smart contracts in Corda, referred to as **CorDapps**, are written in Java or Kotlin. They can be directly tied to legal agreements, allowing organizations to create contracts that are both executable on the blockchain and enforceable in a legal context. Corda's approach to smart contracts focuses on integrating business logic with legal frameworks.

Ethereum:

Ethereum popularized smart contracts, which are written in **Solidity**. These contracts can automate a wide range of functions and support a vibrant ecosystem of decentralized applications. However, Ethereum's flexibility comes at the cost of complexity, which may pose challenges for traditional enterprises transitioning to blockchain technology.

Hyperledger:

Hyperledger Fabric supports smart contracts written in several programming languages, including Go, Java, and JavaScript. This flexibility allows developers to use familiar languages and frameworks, making it easier to build and deploy applications. Smart contracts in Hyperledger are modular and can be tailored to specific business logic.

5. Ecosystem and Community

Corda:

Corda is supported by the R3 consortium, which includes a broad range of financial institutions and enterprises. This backing ensures that Corda evolves in response to the needs of its users and focuses on delivering practical solutions for real-world problems. However, its ecosystem is more centralized compared to open-source projects.

Ethereum:

Ethereum boasts one of the largest and most active developer communities in the blockchain space. Its open-source nature and extensive documentation have fostered a vibrant ecosystem of DApps and tools. The Ethereum community continuously works on improvements, such as scaling solutions and interoperability, enhancing the platform's functionality.

Hyperledger:

Hyperledger is governed by the Linux Foundation, with multiple open-source projects under its umbrella. This approach promotes collaboration among various industries and encourages contributions from a diverse set of stakeholders. Each Hyperledger project benefits from a community-driven approach, allowing for rapid development and innovation.

Summary

Corda, Ethereum, and Hyperledger cater to different needs within the blockchain landscape. Corda focuses on providing privacy and legal certainty for enterprise solutions, making it suitable for regulated industries. Ethereum emphasizes decentralization and openness, fostering innovation through a vast ecosystem of DApps. Hyperledger offers flexibility through various frameworks, enabling organizations to customize their blockchain solutions.

Choosing the right platform depends on your specific use case, regulatory requirements, and business goals. In the next sections, we will explore setting up a Corda network and developing applications tailored to your business needs.

8.3 Corda Network Architecture

Understanding the architecture of the Corda network is crucial for developers and enterprises looking to build applications on this platform. Corda's unique approach to blockchain architecture combines elements of traditional distributed systems with the specific needs of business applications. In this section, we will explore the components that make up the Corda network architecture and how they interact to facilitate secure, efficient transactions.

1. Key Components of Corda Architecture

1.1 Nodes

At the core of the Corda network are **nodes**, which represent individual participants in the network. Each node operates a Corda instance and is responsible for maintaining its ledger, processing transactions, and executing smart contracts (CorDapps). There are two main types of nodes in Corda:

- **Notary Nodes**: These nodes provide transaction validation and prevent double-spending by uniquely identifying transactions. Notary nodes maintain a single source of truth for transaction validity, ensuring that the same transaction cannot be executed multiple times across different nodes.
- **Regular Nodes**: These nodes represent organizations or participants involved in transactions. Regular nodes maintain their ledger copies and manage the execution of smart contracts. They communicate with other nodes to initiate and complete transactions.

1.2 Flows

In Corda, **flows** are the processes that dictate how transactions are created, signed, and finalized among nodes. Flows manage the sequence of steps required to execute a transaction, including communication with other nodes and handling approvals. Corda uses a programming model that allows developers to define custom flows that meet their business requirements.

1.3 State and Contracts

Corda utilizes a concept known as **state** to represent the current status of a business object. States are immutable data objects that capture essential information about a transaction. Each state can be linked to a specific smart contract, which enforces rules and logic governing the state. When a state is updated through a transaction, a new state is created, preserving the historical record.

1.4 Corda Ledger

Corda operates on a **distributed ledger** that is unique to each node. Instead of a global ledger shared by all participants (as in traditional blockchains), each node maintains its private ledger that contains only the states and transactions relevant to that node. This architecture enhances privacy, as sensitive information is not exposed to the entire network.

2. Communication Mechanism

Corda's architecture relies on a robust communication mechanism that enables nodes to exchange information securely. Key elements of this communication framework include:

2.1 Message Passing

Nodes in Corda communicate using **message passing**, allowing them to send and receive transaction proposals and responses asynchronously. This design enables efficient interaction without requiring all nodes to be online simultaneously.

2.2 Session and Counterparties

When a flow is initiated between two nodes, a **session** is established, allowing them to communicate securely. Each node identifies its counterparties (the nodes involved in the transaction) and sends messages that follow a defined protocol. This approach allows for privacy, as only the involved parties receive the transaction details.

2.3 Network Parameters

Corda nodes are governed by a set of **network parameters** that define the rules and configurations for the network. These parameters include consensus algorithms, notary details, and transaction validity criteria. Network parameters can be updated over time to accommodate changes in business requirements.

3. Security Features

Corda's architecture incorporates several security features to protect sensitive information and maintain transaction integrity:

3.1 Identity Management

Each node in the Corda network has a unique identity, established through public key infrastructure (PKI). This identity allows nodes to authenticate each other and verify transaction signatures, ensuring that only authorized participants can execute transactions.

3.2 Privacy and Confidentiality

Corda's architecture is designed to maintain privacy through selective data sharing. Only the parties involved in a transaction have access to the relevant states and information. This approach minimizes the risk of data exposure while maintaining transparency for the involved parties.

3.3 Auditing and Compliance

Corda's ledger structure allows for easy auditing and compliance tracking. Each transaction is recorded with cryptographic proofs, enabling organizations to maintain a transparent record of all activities. This feature is essential for industries subject to regulatory oversight.

Summary

The architecture of the Corda network is tailored to meet the needs of businesses requiring secure, private, and efficient transactions. By utilizing nodes, flows, states, and a distributed ledger, Corda creates an environment conducive to building enterprise-grade applications. Understanding this architecture is critical for developers as they design solutions that leverage Corda's unique capabilities. In the following sections, we will delve deeper into how to set up a Corda network and create applications that utilize its architecture effectively.

8.4 Understanding CorDapps: Corda's Decentralized Applications

CorDapps (Corda Distributed Applications) are the applications built on the Corda platform that utilize its unique architecture to provide efficient, secure, and private solutions for businesses. In this section, we will explore the characteristics of CorDapps, their structure, and how they differ from traditional decentralized applications (DApps) found on platforms like Ethereum.

1. What is a CorDapp?

A **CorDapp** is a type of decentralized application specifically designed to run on the Corda blockchain. It leverages Corda's capabilities to facilitate complex business processes through smart contracts, enabling organizations to automate and streamline their operations while ensuring data integrity and privacy.

Key Characteristics of CorDapps:

- **Business-Centric**: CorDapps are designed with specific business processes in mind, making them highly relevant to industries such as finance, supply chain, healthcare, and more.
- **Privacy-First Approach**: Unlike traditional blockchains where data is shared across all nodes, CorDapps focus on sharing information only with relevant parties. This selective sharing is critical for businesses that handle sensitive data.
- **Interoperability**: CorDapps can interact with other CorDapps and external systems, enabling seamless integration and collaboration across different business networks.

2. Structure of a CorDapp

A typical CorDapp consists of several key components:

2.1 States

States represent the essential data structures that capture the current status of business objects within the application. For example, in a supply chain CorDapp, a state could represent the current status of a shipment.

- **Immutable**: States are immutable; once created, they cannot be changed. Instead, new states are generated for updates.

2.2 Contracts

Contracts define the rules and logic that govern how states can be created, updated, or consumed. Each state is associated with a specific contract, ensuring that all transactions conform to business rules.

- **Smart Contracts**: In Corda, contracts are written in Kotlin or Java, allowing developers to use familiar programming languages while implementing business logic.

2.3 Flows

Flows are the executable processes that dictate how transactions are conducted between nodes. They handle the interaction logic, including message passing and managing transaction signatures.

- **Asynchronous Communication**: Flows allow for asynchronous communication between parties, making it easier to manage complex interactions.

2.4 Notary Services

CorDapps utilize notary services to ensure transaction uniqueness and prevent double-spending. Notaries verify the integrity of transactions and provide a timestamp to establish a reliable record.

3. Developing CorDapps

Building a CorDapp involves several steps:

3.1 Setting Up the Development Environment

Developers must set up their development environment, which includes installing the Corda framework, setting up a build tool (e.g., Gradle), and configuring necessary dependencies.

3.2 Writing States, Contracts, and Flows

Developers create the states, contracts, and flows that define the CorDapp's functionality. This process includes writing Kotlin or Java code to implement the business logic and interactions.

3.3 Testing the CorDapp

Testing is crucial for ensuring the functionality and security of the CorDapp. Developers can use Corda's built-in testing framework to simulate various scenarios and validate the behavior of the application.

3.4 Deployment

Once the CorDapp is developed and tested, it can be deployed on the Corda network. Deployment involves installing the CorDapp on the nodes that will participate in the application, ensuring that they have the necessary configurations and access to relevant data.

4. CorDapps vs. Traditional DApps

While both CorDapps and traditional DApps operate on decentralized platforms, there are key differences between them:

4.1 Data Privacy

- **CorDapps**: Focus on privacy by only sharing data with relevant participants.
- **Traditional DApps**: Often have open access to all data on the blockchain, which may not be suitable for business applications.

4.2 Business Logic

- **CorDapps**: Tailored to specific business processes and regulations, providing a higher degree of customization.
- **Traditional DApps**: More general-purpose and may not address specific industry needs effectively.

4.3 Programming Languages

- **CorDapps**: Developed using Java or Kotlin, enabling integration with existing enterprise systems.
- **Traditional DApps**: Often built with JavaScript, Solidity, or other languages specific to the platform.

Summary

CorDapps represent a powerful approach to building decentralized applications that prioritize privacy, security, and business relevance. By leveraging Corda's unique architecture, developers can create applications that streamline processes and enhance collaboration while maintaining the integrity of sensitive data. As we move forward, we will explore how to implement CorDapps effectively, ensuring they meet the needs of modern enterprises in various industries.

8.5 Writing Contracts and States in Corda

In Corda, writing contracts and states is a fundamental aspect of developing CorDapps. This section will guide you through the process of defining states that represent data structures in your application and writing contracts that enforce the business logic governing those states.

1. Understanding States in Corda

States are immutable data structures that encapsulate the current state of a business object. They hold the data relevant to a transaction and define the attributes that describe it.

1.1 Defining a State

To define a state in Corda, you need to create a class that implements the ContractState interface. This class will include all the necessary attributes and methods. For example, consider a simple CarState representing a car in a vehicle registry.

kotlin

Copy code

```
import net.corda.core.contracts.ContractState
import net.corda.core.identity.AbstractParty

data class CarState(
    val vin: String,
    val owner: AbstractParty,
    val model: String,
    val year: Int
) : ContractState {
    override val participants: List<AbstractParty> = listOf(owner)
}
```

Key Components of a State:

- **Attributes**: Define the characteristics of the state, such as vin, owner, model, and year in our example.
- **Participants**: The participants property lists the parties involved in the state, which is essential for transaction verification.

2. Writing Contracts in Corda

Contracts in Corda enforce the rules governing the states and define how they can be manipulated. A contract specifies conditions under which states can be created, updated, or consumed.

2.1 Defining a Contract

To write a contract, you need to create a class that implements the Contract interface. This class includes the contract code and any necessary methods to validate transactions.

Here's an example of a CarContract:

kotlin

Copy code

```kotlin
import net.corda.core.contracts.Contract
import net.corda.core.contracts.Requirements.using
import net.corda.core.transactions.LedgerTransaction

class CarContract : Contract {
  companion object {
  const val ID = "com.example.contracts.CarContract"
  }

override fun verify(tx: LedgerTransaction) {
  require(tx.inputs.isNotEmpty()) { "Transaction must have input states." }
  require(tx.outputs.size == 1) { "Transaction must have one output state." }

val output = tx.outputsOfType<CarState>().single()
  require(output.year > 1885) { "Year must be greater than 1885." }
  }
}
```

Key Components of a Contract:

- **ID**: A unique identifier for the contract.
- **verify**: This method contains the logic to check that the transaction complies with the rules set by the contract. It uses require statements to enforce these rules.

3. Creating and Consuming States

When working with states and contracts, you'll typically want to create and consume states as part of a transaction.

3.1 Creating a State

To create a new state, you need to instantiate your state class and use a flow to perform the transaction. Here's an example of creating a new CarState:

kotlin

Copy code

```
val carState = CarState(vin = "1HGCM82633A123456", owner = ourIdentity, model = "Honda Accord", year = 2020)
val command = Command(CarContract.Commands.Create(), listOf(ourIdentity.owningKey))
```

3.2 Consuming a State

To consume a state, you need to specify the input state in your transaction. The verify method in your contract will check that the state is valid for consumption.

4. Best Practices for Writing States and Contracts

- **Clarity**: Clearly define the attributes and requirements of your states and contracts. This will make your code easier to understand and maintain.
- **Immutability**: Remember that states are immutable. When updating a state, create a new state instead of modifying the existing one.
- **Testing**: Write comprehensive tests for your contracts to ensure they behave as expected. Utilize Corda's testing framework to simulate transactions and validate logic.

Summary

Writing states and contracts is a crucial step in developing CorDapps on the Corda platform. By defining states that accurately represent your business objects and contracts that enforce the rules governing them, you can create robust and reliable blockchain applications. As you become more familiar with these concepts, you'll be better equipped to implement complex business logic and ensure the integrity of your applications. In the next section, we will explore how to deploy and test your CorDapps effectively.

8.6 Setting Up a Corda Development Environment

Setting up a development environment for Corda is essential for building and testing your CorDapps efficiently. This section will guide you through the steps required to create a robust Corda development environment, enabling you to develop, test, and deploy your applications seamlessly.

1. Prerequisites

Before setting up your Corda development environment, ensure you have the following installed:

- **Java Development Kit (JDK)**: Corda requires JDK 11 or higher. You can download it from the AdoptOpenJDK or Oracle's official website.
- **Apache Maven**: Corda uses Maven for building projects. Install Maven by following the instructions on the Maven website.
- **Integrated Development Environment (IDE)**: A good IDE can greatly enhance your productivity. Popular choices include IntelliJ IDEA (recommended) or Eclipse. Ensure that your IDE has the Kotlin plugin installed, as Corda is built using Kotlin.

2. Setting Up Corda

2.1 Downloading Corda

Download the latest version of Corda from the Corda website. You can choose either the open-source version or the enterprise version, depending on your project requirements.

2.2 Creating a New Corda Project

You can create a new Corda project using the Corda Gradle plugin. Open your terminal or command prompt and follow these steps:

1. Create a new directory for your project:

bash
```
Copy code
mkdir MyCordaProject
cd MyCordaProject
```

1. Use the Gradle wrapper to initialize a new Corda project:

bash
```
Copy code
gradle init —type basic
```

1. Modify your build.gradle file to include the necessary Corda dependencies. Here's an example configuration:

groovy
```
Copy code
plugins {
id 'net.corda.plugins.cordformation' version '5.0'
id 'net.corda.plugins.cordformation' version '5.0'
}
```

```
dependencies {
cordapp "net.corda:corda-core:5.0"
cordapp "net.corda:corda-finance:5.0"
}
```

3. Running Corda Nodes

Once your project is set up, you can run Corda nodes locally for development and testing.

3.1 Configuring Nodes

Create a configuration file for each node in your project directory. A sample node.conf might look like this:

hocon
```
Copy code
dataDir = "C:\\corda\\node"
p2pPort = 10002
rpcSettings {
address = "localhost:10003"
}
```

3.2 Starting the Node

To start a node, use the following command:

bash

Copy code

gradle runCordapp

This command compiles your CorDapp, creates a node, and starts it. You can run multiple nodes by creating additional configurations.

4. Testing Your CorDapp

Corda provides testing utilities that help simulate transactions and validate your CorDapp's logic. Use the cordunit library to write unit tests for your states, contracts, and flows.

1. Create a test class and use JUnit annotations to define test cases.
2. Use the MockNetwork class to simulate nodes and perform transactions.

Example test setup:

kotlin

Copy code

```
class CarStateTest : ContractInterfaceTest() {
private val network = MockNetwork()

@Test
fun 'test car state creation'() {
// Implement test logic here
}
}
```

Conclusion

Setting up a Corda development environment is a crucial step in building efficient and effective CorDapps. By ensuring you have the necessary tools and frameworks in place, you can focus on developing innovative blockchain solutions. As you progress, remember that Corda's flexibility allows you to create applications tailored to specific business needs, from finance to supply chain management. With your environment configured, you are now ready to delve deeper into developing complex decentralized applications with Corda.

This concludes Chapter 8, providing you with the knowledge to set up your Corda development environment and effectively create decentralized applications. In the following chapters, we will explore advanced concepts and practical applications to further enhance your skills in blockchain development.

CHAPTER 9: DEVELOPING CORDAPPS WITH JAVASCRIPT

9.1 Key Components of a CorDapp

A CorDapp (Corda Decentralized Application) is composed of several crucial components that define its structure and functionality. Understanding these components is essential for developing efficient and secure blockchain applications on the Corda platform.

1. Contracts

- **Definition**: Contracts define the rules for what constitutes a valid transaction in a CorDapp. They ensure that any state changes follow the predefined rules of the application.
- **Functionality**: Contracts in Corda are written in Kotlin or Java and are deployed alongside the application.

Example structure:

```kotlin
Copy code
class CarContract : Contract {
override fun verify(tx: LedgerTransaction) {
// Contract verification logic
}
}
```

2. States

- **Definition**: States represent the data stored on the blockchain at a specific point in time. Each state is immutable and can only be changed through a transaction.
- **Usage**: States in Corda hold details such as asset ownership or the current status of an agreement.

Example state structure:

```kotlin
Copy code
data class CarState(val owner: Party, val model: String, val price: Int) : ContractState {
override val participants: List<AbstractParty> = listOf(owner)
}
```

3. Flows

- **Definition**: Flows manage the communication between different nodes during a transaction. They automate the process of state creation, modification, and verification.
- **Functionality**: Flows are written in Kotlin or Java and execute the business logic behind each transaction.

Example of a flow:

```kotlin
Copy code
@InitiatingFlow
@StartableByRPC
class CarPurchaseFlow(val carState: CarState) : FlowLogic<SignedTransaction>() {
@Suspendable
override fun call(): SignedTransaction {
// Flow logic
}
}
```

4. Nodes

- **Definition**: Nodes in a Corda network are responsible for maintaining a ledger, executing flows, and validating transactions. Each node operates independently but can communicate with other nodes via peer-to-peer networking.
- **Components**: A node includes a vault (for storing states), a flow engine (for running flows), and RPC interfaces for external communication.

5. Contracts and States in CorDapps

Contracts and states are the backbone of any CorDapp, as they define the data and rules governing the blockchain's transactions.

- **Contracts**: Enforce business rules within a CorDapp. They ensure that every transaction follows the rules specified in the contract.
- **States**: Store information about the current state of a particular asset or agreement.

Example contract verification:

```kotlin
Copy code
class ContractVerification {
override fun verify(tx: LedgerTransaction) {
// Verifies that the transaction follows the rules
}
}
```

6. Testing CorDapps

Testing is an essential part of CorDapp development. Corda offers tools like MockNetwork to simulate transactions and verify flows in a controlled environment. This helps ensure the correctness of your contracts, states, and flows before deploying them on a live network.

- **Unit Testing**: You can test individual components like states and contracts using JUnit.

- **Integration Testing**: Test the interaction between flows, contracts, and states using mock networks.

Example of a test case:

```kotlin
kotlin
Copy code
@Test
fun 'test contract validation'() {
val tx = TransactionBuilder(notary)
// Add inputs, outputs, and commands
contract.verify(tx.toLedgerTransaction(serviceHub))
}
```

Summary

The key components of a CorDapp—contracts, states, flows, and nodes—form the foundation for building decentralized applications on the Corda platform. These elements work together to ensure data integrity, secure transactions, and efficient execution of business logic in a permissioned environment. Understanding each component's role and functionality is essential for any developer looking to create robust blockchain solutions with Corda. In the following sections, we will explore how to leverage JavaScript to interact with and enhance CorDapp development.

9.2 Writing JavaScript-Based CorDapps

CorDapps (Corda Decentralized Applications) are traditionally written in Kotlin or Java, but developers can also integrate JavaScript for various purposes, such as interacting with the Corda node and building frontend applications that communicate with the backend Corda services. While the core components like contracts, states, and flows are primarily written in Java/Kotlin, JavaScript plays an essential role in frontend development and API integration.

1. JavaScript in CorDapps: An Overview

In the context of CorDapps, JavaScript is commonly used for:

- **Building Frontend Interfaces**: JavaScript frameworks such as React, Angular, or Vue can be used to create user interfaces that interact with Corda.
- **Interacting with the Corda Node via RPC**: JavaScript can be used to interact with Corda nodes using REST APIs or RPC calls, allowing external applications to query the ledger or initiate transactions.
- **Handling Data and Events**: JavaScript can process the data received from the Corda node and manage event-driven updates in the application.

2. Setting Up JavaScript for CorDapp Development

To integrate JavaScript with Corda for building CorDapps, you'll need a typical JavaScript development environment, which includes:

- **Node.js**: A runtime for executing JavaScript on the server-side. It allows for the development of APIs that interact with the Corda backend.
- **npm or Yarn**: Package managers for installing dependencies required in the JavaScript application.
- **Frontend Framework**: React, Angular, or Vue for building the user interface.

Example of setting up a Node.js project:

```bash
Copy code
mkdir cordapp-js
cd cordapp-js
npm init -y
npm install express body-parser axios
```

3. Connecting to the Corda Node using RPC or REST APIs

To interact with a Corda node from a JavaScript-based frontend, you can use either REST APIs or RPC (Remote Procedure Call) interfaces. Below are the steps for setting up both methods:

a. Using RPC in JavaScript

Corda nodes provide an RPC interface that allows external applications to

305

communicate with the node. In a JavaScript application, you can use an RPC client to send requests to the Corda node.

Example of using JavaScript with Corda's RPC client:

javascript

Copy code

```
const { Client } = require('rpc-websockets');

const client = new Client('ws://localhost:10006/ws/rpc');

client.on('open', () => {
  client.call('startFlow', ['flowName', { param1: 'value' }])
    .then(result => console.log('Flow result:', result))
    .catch(error => console.error('Error:', error));
});
```

This allows JavaScript-based applications to trigger Corda flows, fetch data from the ledger, and interact with the node.

b. Using REST APIs in JavaScript

For simpler integration, you can expose a Corda node's services via REST APIs. These APIs can then be consumed by a JavaScript frontend using libraries like axios or fetch.

Example of making an API call to a Corda node using axios:

javascript

Copy code

```
const axios = require('axios');

axios.post('http://localhost:10050/api/startFlow', {
  flowName: 'com.example.MyFlow',
  param1: 'value'
})
  .then(response => {
    console.log('Flow started:', response.data);
  })
  .catch(error => {
```

```
console.error('Error starting flow:', error);
});
```

By setting up a REST API interface, JavaScript applications can seamlessly interact with the Corda network, manage transactions, and fetch ledger data.

4. Building the Frontend for a CorDapp

For the frontend, JavaScript frameworks like **React** or **Vue** are well-suited for building interactive DApp interfaces. These frameworks allow the creation of dynamic, single-page applications that provide a smooth user experience while communicating with the Corda backend.

Example of integrating a frontend with Corda using React:

javascript

Copy code

```
import React, { useState, useEffect } from 'react';
import axios from 'axios';

function CorDappInterface() {
  const [data, setData] = useState(null);

useEffect(() => {
  axios.get('http://localhost:10050/api/getLedgerData')
  .then(response => setData(response.data))
  .catch(error => console.error('Error fetching ledger data:', error));
  }, []);

return (
  <div>
  <h1>Ledger Data</h1>
  {data ? (
  <ul>
  {data.map(item => (
  <li key={item.id}>{item.details}</li>
  ))}
  </ul>
```

```
) : (
<p>Loading...</p>
)}
</div>
);
}
```

export default CorDappInterface;

This code sets up a simple React component that fetches data from the Corda node via a REST API and displays it in a list. It can be expanded with more functionality, such as starting flows, handling user authentication, and managing blockchain transactions.

5. Testing and Debugging JavaScript-Based CorDapps

Testing JavaScript-based CorDapps requires thorough validation of both the backend (Corda node) and the frontend logic. Tools and techniques include:

- **Unit Testing**: Testing individual JavaScript functions using testing frameworks like Mocha or Jest.
- **Integration Testing**: Ensuring that the JavaScript frontend correctly communicates with the Corda backend by simulating API calls and checking responses.
- **End-to-End Testing**: Testing the entire flow from the user's interaction with the frontend to the backend's processing and blockchain transaction execution.

Example of a simple unit test with Mocha:

```
javascript
Copy code
const assert = require('assert');
const getTransactionData = require('./api');

describe('Transaction API', () => {
```

```
it('should return transaction data', async () => {
const data = await getTransactionData();
assert.equal(data.success, true);
});
});
```

Summary

JavaScript plays an integral role in enhancing CorDapp development, particularly for building frontend interfaces and integrating with the Corda backend. By using JavaScript in combination with Corda's RPC and REST APIs, developers can create intuitive user interfaces that facilitate seamless interactions with the blockchain. Whether you're building simple dashboard applications or fully-featured decentralized apps, JavaScript offers the flexibility and functionality needed to bring your CorDapp to life. In the following sections, we will explore more advanced topics, such as smart contract execution and integration with blockchain networks using JavaScript.

9.3 Communicating with the Corda Node from JavaScript

One of the key aspects of building CorDapps is enabling communication between the frontend (typically built using JavaScript) and the Corda node. The frontend application needs to communicate with the Corda node to interact with the blockchain, initiate flows, retrieve ledger data, and perform various other operations. This interaction can be achieved through **RPC** (Remote Procedure Call) and **REST APIs**.

In this section, we'll explore how JavaScript applications can communicate with the Corda node using these two methods, with practical examples.

1. Using RPC to Communicate with Corda Nodes

Corda provides an RPC interface that allows external applications to call flows on a Corda node. RPC is useful for invoking flows and retrieving real-time data from the ledger in a secure and efficient manner. Here's how you can set up communication using JavaScript:

a. Setting up a WebSocket RPC Client

Corda RPC typically works over WebSockets, allowing a persistent connection between the JavaScript application and the Corda node. You'll need to use a WebSocket client in JavaScript to establish communication.

1. Install the necessary WebSocket client package:

bash
    Copy code
    npm install rpc-websockets

1. Connect to the Corda node via RPC and call a flow:

javascript
    Copy code
    const { Client } = require('rpc-websockets');

```
// Connect to the Corda node's RPC WebSocket interface
    const client = new Client('ws://localhost:10006/ws/rpc');

// Wait for the connection to open
    client.on('open', () => {
    console.log('Connected to Corda RPC');

// Call a flow on the Corda node (e.g., MyFlow)
    client.call('startFlow', ['com.example.MyFlow', { param1: 'value' }])
    .then(response => {
    console.log('Flow Result:', response);
    })
    .catch(error => {
    console.error('Error starting flow:', error);
    });
    });
```

This example demonstrates how you can initiate a flow from a JavaScript-based client using RPC. Once connected, you can invoke any flow by passing its name and the required parameters.

b. Subscribing to Node Updates

Another benefit of using WebSockets is that you can subscribe to node updates, such as new transactions or ledger changes, and automatically update the frontend in real-time.

javascript

Copy code

```
client.on('flowUpdate', (update) => {
console.log('New flow update:', update);
});
```

This allows the frontend to stay up to date with the latest blockchain events and data.

2. Using REST APIs to Communicate with Corda Nodes

Another common approach for JavaScript applications to communicate with Corda nodes is by using REST APIs. REST APIs provide a simpler, stateless method to interact with Corda nodes, and can be easily integrated with any JavaScript framework using tools like axios or fetch.

a. Setting Up REST APIs on the Corda Node

To communicate with Corda nodes via REST, the node must expose endpoints through a web server. This is typically achieved using Spring Boot or other frameworks to wrap the Corda node's flows and data access in a REST interface.

Once the REST API is set up, you can use JavaScript to send requests to the Corda node. For example:

b. Making API Calls with JavaScript

1. Install axios or use the built-in fetch API in JavaScript:

bash

Copy code

npm install axios

1. Example of calling a REST API to initiate a flow:

javascript

Copy code

```
const axios = require('axios');

// POST request to start a flow on the Corda node
axios.post('http://localhost:8080/api/startFlow', {
flowName: 'com.example.MyFlow',
param1: 'value'
})
.then(response => {
console.log('Flow started:', response.data);
})
.catch(error => {
console.error('Error starting flow:', error);
});
```

In this example, the JavaScript application makes a POST request to start a flow on the Corda node. You can also make GET requests to retrieve ledger data or check the status of a transaction.

c. Retrieving Ledger Data

In addition to starting flows, you'll likely need to fetch data from the ledger to display on the frontend. Here's an example of a GET request to fetch ledger data:

javascript

Copy code

```
axios.get('http://localhost:8080/api/getLedgerData')
.then(response => {
console.log('Ledger Data:', response.data);
})
.catch(error => {
console.error('Error fetching ledger data:', error);
});
```

This approach allows you to display ledger entries or transaction details within the JavaScript frontend.

3. Security Considerations for Node Communication

When building a JavaScript application that communicates with a Corda node, it is important to secure the connection and data. Some security best practices include:

- **Authentication and Authorization**: Use OAuth or JWT tokens to authenticate API requests to the Corda node and ensure that only authorized users can interact with the node.
- **Secure Communication (HTTPS)**: Always use HTTPS instead of HTTP to secure the communication between the JavaScript frontend and the Corda node, especially when using REST APIs.
- **Error Handling**: Ensure robust error handling in the JavaScript code to manage failed RPC or REST requests gracefully.

4. Example: Frontend Interaction with Corda Node

Here's a simplified example of a JavaScript frontend interacting with a Corda node. It uses both RPC (for starting a flow) and REST (for retrieving ledger data):

```javascript
Copy code
import React, { useState, useEffect } from 'react';
import axios from 'axios';
const { Client } = require('rpc-websockets');

function CordaInteraction() {
  const [ledgerData, setLedgerData] = useState(null);

// RPC call to start a flow
  const startFlow = () => {
  const client = new Client('ws://localhost:10006/ws/rpc');
  client.on('open', () => {
  client.call('startFlow', ['com.example.MyFlow', { param1: 'value' }])
  .then(result => {
```

```javascript
console.log('Flow started:', result);
})
.catch(error => {
console.error('Error starting flow:', error);
});
});
};

// REST call to fetch ledger data
useEffect(() => {
axios.get('http://localhost:8080/api/getLedgerData')
.then(response => {
setLedgerData(response.data);
})
.catch(error => {
console.error('Error fetching ledger data:', error);
});
}, []);

return (
<div>
<button onClick={startFlow}>Start Flow</button>
<h2>Ledger Data</h2>
{ledgerData ? (
<ul>
{ledgerData.map(item => (
<li key={item.id}>{item.details}</li>
))}
</ul>
) : (
<p>Loading ledger data...</p>
)}
</div>
```

```
);
}
```

export default CordaInteraction;

This React component demonstrates how to trigger a flow using WebSockets (RPC) and retrieve ledger data using a REST API.

Summary

In CorDapp development, communication between the frontend (built with JavaScript) and the backend Corda node is crucial for a smooth and interactive user experience. Using RPC via WebSockets or REST APIs, JavaScript applications can initiate flows, query ledger data, and provide real-time updates to users. Whether you're using RPC for real-time communication or REST for simpler integration, JavaScript offers a powerful toolset to interact with Corda nodes and bring decentralized applications to life.

9.4 Deploying CorDapps to the Corda Network

Once you've developed and tested your CorDapp (Corda Decentralized Application), the next step is to deploy it to the Corda network. This process involves several important steps, from packaging your CorDapp to ensuring it runs on the network's nodes. Corda's deployment process is slightly different from that of other blockchain platforms, primarily due to its permissioned, enterprise-focused nature.

In this section, we'll go through the essential steps for deploying CorDapps, covering both **Corda Testnet** and **Corda Mainnet**.

1. Preparing Your CorDapp for Deployment

Before deploying a CorDapp, you need to ensure it's fully packaged and ready to be run on Corda nodes. This includes ensuring that all contracts, states, and flows have been written, tested, and debugged.

a. Packaging Your CorDapp

The CorDapp must be packaged into a **JAR (Java ARchive)** file that contains all the necessary code for the smart contracts, flows, states, and any additional dependencies.

1. **Gradle Setup**: Corda uses **Gradle** to manage dependencies and build

the CorDapp. To build your CorDapp, you will need to configure your build.gradle file with the necessary details:

gradle

```
Copy code
task deployNodes(type: net.corda.plugins.Cordform, dependsOn: ['jar']) {
nodeDefaults {
projectCordapp {
deploy = true
}
}
node {
name "PartyA"
rpcUsers = [[user: "user1", "password": "test", "permissions": ["ALL"]]]
}
node {
name "PartyB"
rpcUsers = [[user: "user1", "password": "test", "permissions": ["ALL"]]]
}
}
```

1. **Build the JAR File**: Once your build.gradle file is properly configured, you can use Gradle to build the CorDapp:

bash

```
Copy code
./gradlew clean deployNodes
```

This command compiles your project into a JAR file that can be deployed on the Corda node.

2. Deploying to the Corda Testnet

Corda Testnet is used to simulate real-world conditions for your CorDapp without the risks associated with deploying to a live production environment. The Testnet offers developers a sandbox environment to verify that their

CorDapp behaves as expected.

a. Register for Corda Testnet

To deploy to the Corda Testnet, you'll need to register for access by creating an account on the Corda Testnet platform. You'll get credentials that allow you to connect your CorDapp and nodes to the Testnet.

b. Configuring the Node for Testnet

Once you have your Testnet credentials, you need to configure your nodes to point to the Testnet. This can be done in the node.conf configuration file on each node:

```
conf
Copy code
myLegalName="O=PartyA, L=London, C=GB"
p2pAddress="corda-testnet:10003"
rpcSettings {
address="corda-testnet:10009"
adminAddress="corda-testnet:10049"
}
```

This configuration points your node to the Testnet, where you can interact with other participants in the network.

c. Deploying the CorDapp

To deploy the CorDapp, you'll upload the compiled JAR file to the Corda Testnet via the Testnet's deployment portal or by manually deploying it to the nodes:

1. Copy the JAR file to the cordapps directory on each node.
2. Restart the node so that it can recognize and deploy the new CorDapp.

Once the nodes are restarted, the CorDapp will be active on the Corda Testnet.

3. Deploying to the Corda Mainnet

After thoroughly testing on the Testnet, you're ready to deploy the CorDapp to the Corda Mainnet. The Mainnet is a live, permissioned network used for real-world transactions and applications. Deployment to the Mainnet involves stricter requirements to ensure the security, performance, and scalability of the application.

a. Register for Corda Network

To deploy on the Corda Mainnet, you need to register with the **Corda Network Foundation**. The foundation governs access to the network, ensuring compliance with legal and operational standards.

b. Obtain Legal Entity Identifier (LEI)

All nodes on the Corda Mainnet must be associated with an organization that has a **Legal Entity Identifier (LEI)**. An LEI is a global standard for identifying legal entities participating in financial transactions. You can apply for an LEI through official registration agencies.

c. Secure Your Nodes

Nodes on the Mainnet must meet strict security requirements, including the use of **TLS certificates** to secure communication between nodes. You can obtain a certificate from a trusted Certificate Authority (CA) and configure the node accordingly.

```
conf
Copy code
p2pAddress="your-mainnet-node:10003"
tlsCertPath="/path/to/cert.pem"
tlsKeyPath="/path/to/key.pem"
```

d. Uploading the CorDapp to Mainnet Nodes

Just like in the Testnet deployment, you'll need to copy your CorDapp's JAR file to the cordapps directory on each node and restart the node. The nodes will recognize the CorDapp and deploy it to the Corda Mainnet.

4. Monitoring and Maintaining Deployed CorDapps

Once your CorDapp is deployed to either the Testnet or Mainnet, monitoring its performance and maintaining the nodes becomes crucial. You'll need to ensure the nodes are always up-to-date, the flows are executing correctly, and you have adequate logging and alerting in place to catch any issues early.

a. Monitoring Nodes

You can monitor the health of your Corda nodes using monitoring tools such as **Prometheus** and **Grafana**, which can be configured to track key metrics like transaction throughput, node uptime, and flow execution times.

b. Debugging in Production

If issues arise in production, you can use Corda's built-in debugging tools, or rely on external tools such as **Splunk** or **Elastic Stack** for log aggregation and analysis.

c. Scaling CorDapps

As your CorDapp grows in usage, you may need to scale the infrastructure. This might involve adding more nodes to the network, or optimizing the smart contract flows and state management to handle higher volumes of transactions.

Summary

Deploying CorDapps to the Corda network, whether on the Testnet for development or the Mainnet for production, requires careful planning and a clear understanding of the deployment processes. From packaging your CorDapp into a JAR file to configuring nodes and adhering to security standards, successful deployment ensures that your application is accessible to participants on the network and ready for real-world usage. After deployment, it's essential to monitor your nodes and applications to maintain high availability, security, and performance as your CorDapp scales.

9.5 Testing and Debugging CorDapps

Once you have written your CorDapp, it's crucial to thoroughly test and debug it to ensure it functions as expected. Corda provides several tools and techniques to facilitate testing and debugging in a development environment, allowing you to simulate real-world scenarios and troubleshoot potential issues before deployment.

This section explores the best practices for testing and debugging CorDapps, covering unit testing, integration testing, and debugging tools available in the Corda ecosystem.

1. Unit Testing CorDapps

Unit tests in Corda focus on testing individual components of your CorDapp, such as states, contracts, and flows. These tests ensure that each unit of your application behaves as intended.

a. Writing Unit Tests for Contracts

Contracts in Corda define the rules for modifying states on the ledger. You can write unit tests to ensure that your contract logic is correct.

Here's an example of a basic unit test for a contract in Corda using **JUnit**:

kotlin

Copy code

```
class MyContractTests {

@Test
    fun 'contract should not allow zero value transactions'() {
    val ledgerServices = MockServices(listOf("com.example.contract"))
    val inputState = MyState(value = 0)
    ledgerServices.ledger {
    transaction {
    input(MyContract.ID, inputState)
    command(listOf(ALICE.publicKey), MyContract.Commands.Create())
    failsWith("Value cannot be zero.")
    }
    }
    }
}
```

In this example, the contract ensures that the value in a state cannot be zero. The test uses Corda's **MockServices** and **ledger** DSL to simulate a transaction and verify that it fails with the correct error message.

b. Writing Unit Tests for Flows

Flows are a critical part of CorDapps, as they define the processes that nodes follow when interacting with each other. You can test flows using **MockNetwork**, which simulates a network of Corda nodes.

kotlin

Copy code

```
class MyFlowTests {

private lateinit var mockNetwork: MockNetwork
    private lateinit var nodeA: StartedMockNode
    private lateinit var nodeB: StartedMockNode
```

```
@Before
  fun setup() {
  mockNetwork = MockNetwork(listOf("com.example.flow"))
  nodeA = mockNetwork.createNode()
  nodeB = mockNetwork.createNode()
  mockNetwork.runNetwork()
  }


@Test
  fun 'flow should be completed successfully'() {
  val future = nodeA.startFlow(MyFlow(nodeB.info.legalIdentities.first()))
  mockNetwork.runNetwork()
  val result = future.getOrThrow()
  assertEquals(result.transaction.tx.outputs.size, 1)
  }


@After
  fun tearDown() {
  mockNetwork.stopNodes()
  }
  }
```

This test sets up a **MockNetwork** and simulates a flow between two nodes, nodeA and nodeB. The flow result is then checked to ensure it has been completed successfully.

2. Integration Testing

While unit testing focuses on individual components, integration testing ensures that all parts of your CorDapp work together in a real environment. Corda provides tools such as the **Driver DSL** to spin up nodes and perform end-to-end integration tests.

a. Using the Driver DSL

The **Driver DSL** allows you to run a group of nodes in a controlled environment, testing how they interact with each other. Unlike **MockNetwork**, which simulates nodes in memory, the Driver DSL creates real nodes for more extensive testing.

```kotlin
Copy code
@Test
fun 'test flow using driver DSL'() {
driver {
val (partyA, partyB) = listOf(
startNode(providedName = CordaX500Name("PartyA", "London", "GB")),
startNode(providedName = CordaX500Name("PartyB", "New York", "US"))
).map { it.getOrThrow() }
```

val flowResult = partyA.rpc.startFlowDynamic(MyFlow::class.java, partyB.info.legalIdentities.first())
```kotlin
val result = flowResult.returnValue.getOrThrow()
```

```kotlin
assertEquals(result.transaction.tx.outputs.size, 1)
}
}
```

In this example, the Driver DSL starts two real nodes and runs a flow between them, verifying the result of the transaction.

3. Debugging CorDapps

Debugging in Corda involves identifying and resolving issues in your CorDapp. There are several tools and techniques that can help with debugging smart contracts, flows, and transactions.

a. Using Logs for Debugging

Corda nodes generate detailed logs, which can be invaluable for tracking down issues. You can use these logs to see how transactions and flows are processed in real-time.

To enable logging in your flows, you can use Corda's built-in **Logger**:

```kotlin
Copy code
class MyFlow : FlowLogic<SignedTransaction>() {
```

```
companion object {
  private val logger = LoggerFactory.getLogger(MyFlow::class.java)
  }
```

```
@Suspendable
  override fun call(): SignedTransaction {
  logger.info("Starting MyFlow…")
  // Flow logic here
  logger.info("Flow completed successfully.")
  return signedTransaction
  }
  }
```

These log messages will appear in the node's log files and can help you identify where a flow might be failing or taking an unexpected path.

b. Debugging in IDE

Most IDEs, such as **IntelliJ IDEA**, allow you to run and debug your CorDapps in a local development environment. By setting breakpoints in your contract or flow code, you can step through the execution process and inspect variable states.

To debug flows running on a node, ensure you are running the node in **debug mode** by configuring the node.conf:

```
conf
Copy code
devMode=true
```

With **devMode** enabled, the nodes will have additional debugging information that can help in troubleshooting.

4. Common Testing and Debugging Issues

Some common issues that arise during the testing and debugging process include:

a. Flow Timeouts

Flows can timeout if they take too long to execute. This is usually due to network latency or complex computations within the flow. To handle timeouts, ensure that your flows are designed to be efficient and consider splitting long-running tasks into smaller subflows.

b. Contract Verification Failures

When testing contracts, failures often occur because the transaction does not meet the conditions specified in the contract. Ensure that your test cases cover all possible transaction scenarios and that your contract logic is well-defined.

c. Misconfigured Nodes

During integration testing, node misconfigurations (e.g., incorrect port numbers or RPC settings) can prevent nodes from communicating with each other. Double-check your **node.conf** files and ensure all nodes are correctly configured before running tests.

Summary

Testing and debugging are essential steps in the development of CorDapps. By writing comprehensive unit and integration tests, and using tools such as **MockNetwork**, **Driver DSL**, and logging, you can ensure that your CorDapp behaves as expected before deployment. Debugging tools, especially the use of logs and IDE debuggers, are crucial for identifying and resolving issues during development. With rigorous testing and effective debugging strategies, you can build more reliable and secure applications on the Corda blockchain.

9.6 Use Case: Financial Services Application with Corda

Corda's unique features, such as privacy, scalability, and permissioned blockchain capabilities, make it an ideal platform for building financial services applications. In this section, we'll explore a practical use case: creating a financial services application that manages transactions between different parties in a secure, efficient, and private manner.

Overview of the Financial Services Use Case

In the financial services sector, various institutions such as banks, payment providers, and clearinghouses need to conduct transactions while maintaining confidentiality and compliance with regulatory requirements. Traditional systems rely heavily on intermediaries, which increase costs and delays. Corda can streamline this process by allowing direct transactions between parties, ensuring that only the relevant participants can see transaction details.

Key Features of the Corda Financial Services Application:

1. **Direct Transactions Between Banks**: The application facilitates secure, private, and direct transactions between banks without needing intermediaries.
2. **Smart Contracts for Transaction Rules**: Smart contracts enforce compliance with financial regulations and rules between parties.
3. **Real-Time Settlement**: Transactions are settled in real-time, improving liquidity management and reducing delays.
4. **Audit Trail and Privacy**: Corda's ledger ensures an immutable audit trail while maintaining the privacy of transaction details between parties.

Building the Application

To build a financial services application on Corda, the following components are typically implemented:

1. **Contracts and States**: Define the contract that governs how financial transactions (e.g., payments, loan disbursements) are executed between parties, and the state that represents the transaction on the ledger.

- **State**: Represents the financial transaction details, including the amount, currency, and the involved parties.
- **Contract**: Contains the rules that validate the transaction, ensuring compliance with regulatory standards.

1. **Flows**: Implement the flows that handle the creation, approval, and settlement of transactions between banks.

- **Transaction Initiation Flow**: A flow that initiates a transaction request between two parties (e.g., transferring funds between banks).
- **Transaction Approval Flow**: A flow that allows the receiving party to approve the transaction and settle the funds.

1. **Node Network Setup**: Set up the Corda nodes representing different banks or financial institutions involved in the network.

2. **Integration with Existing Systems**: Use Corda's REST API and RPC framework to integrate the blockchain system with existing banking infrastructure, enabling smooth communication between the blockchain and legacy systems.

Example Flow

An example of a flow for initiating and settling a payment transaction could look like this:

kotlin

Copy code

```
@InitiatingFlow
@StartableByRPC
class PaymentInitiationFlow(
private val amount: Amount<Currency>,
private val receiver: Party
) : FlowLogic<SignedTransaction>() {

@Suspendable
override fun call(): SignedTransaction {
// Build and sign the transaction
val notary = serviceHub.networkMapCache.notaryIdentities.first()
val txCommand = Command(PaymentContract.Commands.Create(),
ourIdentity.owningKey)
val txBuilder = TransactionBuilder(notary)
.addOutputState(PaymentState(amount, ourIdentity, receiver))
.addCommand(txCommand)

// Verify the transaction
txBuilder.verify(serviceHub)

// Collect signatures and finalize the transaction
val signedTx = serviceHub.signInitialTransaction(txBuilder)
val otherPartySession = initiateFlow(receiver)
```

```
val fullySignedTx = subFlow(CollectSignaturesFlow(signedTx, listOf(othe
rPartySession)))
```

```
return subFlow(FinalityFlow(fullySignedTx, listOf(otherPartySession)))
    }
}
```

In this flow:

- A bank initiates a payment transaction to another bank.
- The transaction is signed and sent to the other bank for approval.
- Once both parties sign the transaction, it is finalized on the ledger.

Testing the Application

To ensure the financial services application is secure and reliable, unit and integration tests can be written to validate the contract logic and flows. The **MockNetwork** and **Driver DSL** can be used to simulate the banking nodes and test transaction flows between them.

Conclusion

Chapter 9 has delved into the process of developing CorDapps (Corda decentralized applications) using JavaScript. We explored the key components of CorDapps, including states, contracts, and flows, and demonstrated how to build JavaScript-based CorDapps, communicate with Corda nodes, and deploy them on the Corda network.

Through practical examples and insights, you have learned how to:

- Write and deploy JavaScript-based CorDapps.
- Communicate with Corda nodes from JavaScript.
- Test and debug CorDapps to ensure they function as intended.
- Build real-world blockchain applications in Corda, including a financial services use case that demonstrates Corda's strengths in privacy and transaction finality.

With Corda's permissioned architecture and flexibility, developers can build applications that meet the specific needs of enterprise environments, especially in industries such as finance, supply chain, and healthcare. By understanding the concepts covered in this chapter, you are now well-equipped to build, deploy, and maintain robust CorDapps that bring the power of blockchain to real-world use cases.

CHAPTER 10: INTEGRATING BLOCKCHAIN WITH WEB TECHNOLOGIES

I n this chapter, we'll explore how blockchain applications can be integrated with web technologies, focusing on front-end frameworks and tools that help create seamless user experiences. A blockchain solution is not complete without a user interface that interacts with decentralized networks and smart contracts. We will begin by focusing on **React.js**, a popular JavaScript library for building user interfaces.

10.1 Using React.js for Blockchain Frontend Development

React.js is a powerful JavaScript library developed by Facebook, widely used for building single-page applications (SPAs) with dynamic and interactive user interfaces. React's component-based architecture makes it a perfect fit for developing blockchain applications, or **DApps** (Decentralized Applications), as it allows developers to build reusable components to interact with smart contracts and decentralized networks like Ethereum.

Why Use React.js for Blockchain Development?

1. **Component Reusability**: React's component-based system makes it easier to build modular, maintainable code, which is essential for scaling blockchain apps.

2. **State Management**: Blockchain interactions require real-time updates (such as transaction confirmations or balance updates). React's state management (often combined with libraries like Redux) provides an

effective way to handle these updates.

3. **Integration with Web3.js**: React can easily integrate with Web3.js, the Ethereum JavaScript API, allowing interaction with the Ethereum blockchain and smart contracts directly from the frontend.

4. **Developer Community and Tools**: React has a large ecosystem of tools, libraries, and a strong community, which accelerates development.

Setting Up React.js for Blockchain Development

To get started with React.js for blockchain development, we need to set up a React project and integrate it with **Web3.js** to communicate with the Ethereum network. Let's go through the steps to set up and integrate a simple React frontend for interacting with the blockchain.

Step 1: Install React.js

You can quickly create a React application using the **Create React App** tool:

bash

Copy code

```
npx create-react-app my-blockchain-app
cd my-blockchain-app
npm start
```

This will set up a basic React environment with everything you need to start developing.

Step 2: Install Web3.js

Next, install the **Web3.js** library, which provides an API to interact with the Ethereum blockchain.

bash

Copy code

```
npm install web3
```

Step 3: Connecting React to Ethereum via Web3

After installing Web3.js, you can set up your app to connect to an Ethereum network (such as Mainnet, Ropsten, or a local blockchain like Ganache). Here's how you can do it:

1. **Initialize Web3**: You need to initialize Web3 within your React component to connect to the blockchain.

```javascript
Copy code
import React, { useState, useEffect } from "react";
import Web3 from "web3";

function App() {
  const [account, setAccount] = useState("");

useEffect(() => {
  loadBlockchainData();
  }, []);

const loadBlockchainData = async () => {
  const web3 = new Web3(Web3.givenProvider || "http://localhost:8545");
  const accounts = await web3.eth.getAccounts();
  setAccount(accounts[0]);
  };

return (
  <div>
  <h1>Blockchain Frontend with React</h1>
  <p>Connected Account: {account}</p>
  </div>
  );
  }

export default App;
```

1. **Explaining the Code**:

- **Web3 Initialization**: Web3 is initialized using Web3.givenProvider (this is useful when connecting through MetaMask) or a local blockchain provider (like Ganache).
- **Getting User Accounts**: The web3.eth.getAccounts() function fetches the list of available accounts and sets it in the state using React's useState hook.

Step 4: Handling User Interactions

In blockchain applications, user interactions (such as submitting a transaction) require communication with the smart contract. Let's look at an example where a user interacts with a smart contract.

1. **Deploy a Simple Smart Contract**: First, you will need a smart contract. Here's an example of a simple contract that allows users to store a number:

solidity
```
Copy code
pragma solidity ^0.8.0;

contract SimpleStorage {
  uint public storedData;

function set(uint x) public {
  storedData = x;
  }

function get() public view returns (uint) {
  return storedData;
  }
  }
```

1. **React Integration with the Contract**: Now, let's interact with this

smart contract from your React frontend.

javascript

Copy code

```javascript
import React, { useState, useEffect } from "react";
import Web3 from "web3";
import SimpleStorage from "./contracts/SimpleStorage.json";

function App() {
  const [account, setAccount] = useState("");
  const [contract, setContract] = useState(null);
  const [storedValue, setStoredValue] = useState(0);

useEffect(() => {
  loadBlockchainData();
  }, []);

const loadBlockchainData = async () => {
  const web3 = new Web3(Web3.givenProvider || "http://localhost:8545");
  const accounts = await web3.eth.getAccounts();
  setAccount(accounts[0]);

const networkId = await web3.eth.net.getId();
  const networkData = SimpleStorage.networks[networkId];
  if (networkData) {
  const contract = new web3.eth.Contract(SimpleStorage.abi, networkData.address);
  setContract(contract);
  const value = await contract.methods.get().call();
  setStoredValue(value);
  } else {
  alert("Smart contract not deployed to the detected network.");
  }
```

```
};

const setNewValue = async (value) => {
    await contract.methods.set(value).send({ from: account });
    const newValue = await contract.methods.get().call();
    setStoredValue(newValue);
};

return (
    <div>
    <h1>Blockchain Frontend with React</h1>
    <p>Connected Account: {account}</p>
    <p>Stored Value: {storedValue}</p>
    <input
    type="number"
    placeholder="Enter new value"
    onChange={(e) => setNewValue(e.target.value)}
    />
    </div>
    );
    }

export default App;
```

Explanation:

- **Web3.js** is used to communicate with the blockchain and the deployed smart contract.
- The frontend interacts with the SimpleStorage contract, allowing users to set and retrieve the stored value.
- The current stored value is displayed on the page and updated in real time when the user submits a new value.

React.js provides a powerful, flexible way to build blockchain frontends, allowing seamless integration with Web3.js to interact with Ethereum smart contracts. By mastering this framework, developers can build robust, scalable decentralized applications (DApps) that bring blockchain to end users in a user-friendly and intuitive manner.

In the next sections, we will explore more advanced blockchain front-end integrations with frameworks and tools like Angular, Vue.js, and Web3 providers like MetaMask and WalletConnect.

10.2 Building Decentralized Web Applications with React and Web3.js

In this section, we will dive deeper into the process of building fully functional decentralized web applications (DApps) using **React** for the frontend and **Web3.js** for blockchain interactions. This combination is widely used in blockchain development, particularly in Ethereum-based projects, due to its flexibility, scalability, and ease of integration.

We will walk through the complete process of building a simple DApp, from setting up the development environment, creating a smart contract, interacting with the blockchain, and building a user-friendly React interface that connects to the smart contract using Web3.js.

What is a Decentralized Application (DApp)?

A **DApp** (Decentralized Application) is a web application that operates on a decentralized network, typically a blockchain. Unlike traditional web applications that rely on centralized servers, DApps interact with smart contracts deployed on a blockchain, such as Ethereum. They offer advantages like transparency, immutability, and decentralized control.

Key Components of a DApp:

- **Frontend (React)**: The user interface of the DApp, built with modern frontend frameworks such as React.js, Angular, or Vue.js.
- **Blockchain (Ethereum)**: The backend of the DApp, powered by a decentralized blockchain network.
- **Smart Contracts (Solidity)**: Self-executing contracts with predefined logic that run on the blockchain.
- **Web3.js**: A JavaScript library that enables interaction with the blockchain from the frontend.

Step-by-Step Example: Building a DApp with React and Web3.js

We will now go through the process of building a basic decentralized application that allows users to store and retrieve a number on the Ethereum blockchain. The application will consist of a smart contract deployed on the blockchain, and a React frontend that interacts with this smart contract.

Step 1: Setting Up the Development Environment

1. **Install Node.js**: Ensure that Node.js is installed on your machine, as it is required to run both React.js and Web3.js. You can download it from Node.js.
2. **Create a React App**: Use the create-react-app command to generate a new React project.

bash
Copy code
npx create-react-app my-dapp
cd my-dapp
npm start

This command creates a new React project and starts the development server.

1. **Install Web3.js**: Install the Web3.js library, which allows React to communicate with the Ethereum blockchain.

bash
Copy code
npm install web3

1. **Install MetaMask**: MetaMask is a browser extension that allows users to interact with Ethereum-based DApps. You will need MetaMask to connect to the Ethereum network and sign transactions. Install it from MetaMask.

Step 2: Creating the Smart Contract

We will create a simple smart contract in Solidity that stores a number on the blockchain. This contract will have two functions: one to set the number and another to get the stored number.

SimpleStorage.sol (Smart Contract):

solidity
Copy code
pragma solidity ^0.8.0;

```
contract SimpleStorage {
  uint public storedData;

function set(uint x) public {
  storedData = x;
  }

function get() public view returns (uint) {
  return storedData;
  }
  }
```

1. **Compile and Deploy the Contract**: Use a local Ethereum blockchain such as **Ganache** or deploy the contract on a test network like **Ropsten** using **Remix IDE** or **Truffle**.

Step 3: Connecting React with Web3.js

Once the smart contract is deployed, we need to connect the React frontend to interact with the contract using Web3.js.

1. **Initialize Web3 in React**: In the App.js file, initialize Web3.js to connect to the Ethereum network and interact with MetaMask.

javascript

```
Copy code
import React, { useState, useEffect } from "react";
import Web3 from "web3";
import SimpleStorage from "./contracts/SimpleStorage.json";

function App() {
  const [account, setAccount] = useState("");
  const [contract, setContract] = useState(null);
  const [storedValue, setStoredValue] = useState(0);
  const [inputValue, setInputValue] = useState("");

useEffect(() => {
  loadBlockchainData();
  }, []);

const loadBlockchainData = async () => {
  // Initialize Web3 instance
  const web3 = new Web3(Web3.givenProvider || "http://localhost:8545");
  const accounts = await web3.eth.getAccounts();
  setAccount(accounts[0]);

// Get network ID and contract instance
  const networkId = await web3.eth.net.getId();
  const networkData = SimpleStorage.networks[networkId];
  if (networkData) {
  const simpleStorage = new web3.eth.Contract(SimpleStorage.abi,
networkData.address);
  setContract(simpleStorage);
  const value = await simpleStorage.methods.get().call();
  setStoredValue(value);
  } else {
  alert("Smart contract not deployed to the detected network.");
  }
```

```
};

const handleInputChange = (e) => {
  setInputValue(e.target.value);
  };

const handleSet = async () => {
  await contract.methods.set(inputValue).send({ from: account });
  const newValue = await contract.methods.get().call();
  setStoredValue(newValue);
  };

return (
  <div>
  <h1>Decentralized Storage DApp</h1>
  <p>Connected Account: {account}</p>
  <p>Stored Value: {storedValue}</p>
  <input type="number" value={inputValue} onChange={handleInputChange}
/>
  <button onClick={handleSet}>Set Value</button>
  </div>
  );
  }


export default App;
```

Explanation:

- **Web3.js Initialization**: We initialize Web3 using Web3.givenProvider to connect to MetaMask. This allows the DApp to interact with the Ethereum network.
- **Load Account and Contract**: The app fetches the user's Ethereum account and the deployed smart contract using Web3.js, and loads the stored value from the blockchain.

- **User Interaction**: The user can input a number and update the stored value on the blockchain by sending a transaction to the smart contract.

Step 4: Running the DApp

1. **Start the React Development Server**:

bash
  Copy code
  npm start

1. **Connect MetaMask to the Correct Network**: Ensure MetaMask is connected to the same network (e.g., local Ganache or Ropsten test network) where the smart contract is deployed.
2. **Interact with the DApp**: Once the app is running, users can input a number and store it on the Ethereum blockchain, view the stored value, and interact with the decentralized storage.

Advanced DApp Features

To further enhance the DApp, additional features can be implemented, such as:

- **Real-Time Blockchain Events**: Use Web3.js to listen for events emitted by the smart contract, allowing the frontend to update in real time when a transaction is confirmed.
- **MetaMask Authentication**: Implement MetaMask as the login mechanism, so users can seamlessly authenticate and manage their blockchain accounts through the DApp.
- **Gas Fee Estimation**: Use Web3.js to estimate gas fees for transactions, providing users with more information about transaction costs.

Summary

In this section, we explored how to build a decentralized web application using React.js and Web3.js. By integrating Web3.js into a React frontend, developers can create fully functional DApps that interact with the Ethereum blockchain and smart contracts. This combination provides a powerful stack for building scalable and efficient decentralized applications, with React offering a flexible and dynamic user interface, and Web3.js enabling secure and transparent blockchain interactions.

As we move forward, we will delve deeper into integrating DApps with other popular web frameworks, managing user authentication, and handling complex smart contract interactions.

10.3 Handling Authentication and Transactions in DApps

In decentralized applications (DApps), handling authentication and trans-actions securely and efficiently is crucial. Given the nature of blockchain technology, traditional authentication methods (like username and password) are replaced by blockchain wallet solutions. This section will cover how to manage user authentication using wallets like MetaMask and how to facilitate transactions within your DApp.

User Authentication in DApps

Unlike traditional applications that rely on centralized servers for user authentication, DApps use blockchain wallets for authentication. Wallets like **MetaMask** allow users to manage their Ethereum accounts securely, providing a more decentralized approach.

Integrating MetaMask for Authentication

1. **Detecting MetaMask**: Check if MetaMask is installed in the user's browser.

javascript
Copy code

```
if (typeof window.ethereum !== 'undefined') {
console.log('MetaMask is installed!');
}
```

1. **Requesting Account Access**: Use eth_requestAccounts to prompt the

341

user to connect their MetaMask wallet.

javascript
```
Copy code
async function connectWallet() {
if (typeof window.ethereum !== 'undefined') {
try {
const accounts = await window.ethereum.request({ method: 'eth_requestA
ccounts' });
setAccount(accounts[0]); // Set the connected account
} catch (error) {
console.error('User denied account access:', error);
}
} else {
alert('Please install MetaMask!');
}
}
```

1. **Handling Account Changes**: Listen for account changes using the accountsChanged event. This ensures the UI updates if the user switches accounts.

javascript
```
Copy code
useEffect(() => {
if (window.ethereum) {
window.ethereum.on('accountsChanged', (accounts) => {
setAccount(accounts[0]);
});
}
}, []);
```
Advantages of Wallet Authentication

- **Decentralization**: Users retain control of their keys and accounts.
- **Security**: Private keys are stored securely in the wallet, reducing the risk of server-side attacks.
- **Ease of Use**: Users can interact with multiple DApps using a single wallet.

Handling Transactions in DApps

Transactions in DApps involve sending data to the blockchain, typically through smart contracts. Understanding how to manage these transactions, including sending, signing, and estimating gas costs, is vital for a seamless user experience.

Sending Transactions

To send a transaction to a smart contract, you need to:

1. **Prepare the Transaction**: Define the parameters and method to call on the smart contract.

javascript

```
Copy code
const handleSetValue = async () => {
const valueToSet = inputValue; // Assume inputValue is retrieved from user input
try {
await contract.methods.set(valueToSet).send({ from: account });
// Update stored value after transaction confirmation
const newValue = await contract.methods.get().call();
setStoredValue(newValue);
} catch (error) {
console.error('Transaction failed:', error);
}
};
```

1. **Estimating Gas**: Use Web3.js to estimate gas costs before sending a transaction. This helps users understand the potential cost.

javascript

Copy code

```
const estimateGas = async () => {
const gasEstimate = await contract.methods.set(inputValue).estimateGas({
from: account });
console.log('Estimated Gas:', gasEstimate);
};
```

1. **Handling Transaction Events**: Listen for transaction confirmations and handle success/failure notifications.

javascript

Copy code

```
const handleSetValue = async () => {
const valueToSet = inputValue;
try {
const tx = await contract.methods.set(valueToSet).send({ from: account });
console.log('Transaction successful with hash:', tx.transactionHash);
const newValue = await contract.methods.get().call();
setStoredValue(newValue);
} catch (error) {
console.error('Transaction failed:', error);
}
};
```

User Feedback on Transactions

Provide feedback to the user during and after the transaction process. This includes loading indicators, success messages, and error handling.

- **Loading Indicator**: Display a loading spinner when the transaction is being processed.
- **Success/Error Notifications**: Use alerts or UI components to notify users of the transaction status.

Best Practices for Handling Authentication and Transactions

1. **User Experience**: Ensure that the authentication process is intuitive and provides clear instructions for users who may not be familiar with wallets.
2. **Error Handling**: Implement comprehensive error handling for failed transactions and authentication issues to improve user confidence.
3. **Gas Fees Awareness**: Inform users about gas fees and provide gas estimates to prevent surprises during transaction execution.
4. **Security Best Practices**: Encourage users to secure their wallets and educate them about the importance of private key management.

Summary

In this section, we explored how to handle user authentication and transactions in decentralized applications (DApps) using MetaMask and Web3.js. By leveraging wallet authentication, DApps can provide a secure and user-friendly experience. Understanding how to manage transactions effectively is crucial for ensuring seamless interactions with the blockchain, enhancing the overall user experience.

10.4 Integrating Blockchain with REST APIs

Integrating blockchain technology with REST APIs allows developers to create flexible and scalable applications that can interact with blockchain networks while also leveraging traditional web services. This section will explore how to connect blockchain functionality with REST APIs to facilitate data exchange and streamline interactions between clients and the blockchain.

Understanding REST APIs

REST (Representational State Transfer) APIs are a standard way of providing interoperability between web services. They allow developers to communicate with a server over HTTP, using standard methods such as GET, POST, PUT, and DELETE. REST APIs can be used to access blockchain data, invoke smart contract functions, and manage transactions without requiring users to directly interact with the blockchain.

Key Characteristics of REST APIs

- **Stateless**: Each API request from the client to the server must contain all the information needed to understand and process the request.
- **Resource-Based**: APIs interact with resources (such as accounts, transactions, and smart contracts) using URIs (Uniform Resource Identifiers).
- **Flexible Formats**: Responses can be returned in various formats, commonly JSON, which is easy to work with in JavaScript.

Setting Up a REST API for Blockchain Interaction

To set up a REST API that interacts with a blockchain, you can use frameworks like **Express.js** to create the server and **Web3.js** or other blockchain SDKs for interacting with the blockchain.

1. Creating a Basic Express Server

First, set up a new Express server:

bash

Copy code

```
npm init -y
npm install express body-parser web3
```

Then, create a simple server in server.js:

javascript

Copy code

```
const express = require('express');
const bodyParser = require('body-parser');
const Web3 = require('web3');

const app = express();
const web3 = new Web3('https://mainnet.infura.io/v3/YOUR_INFURA_
PROJECT_ID');

app.use(bodyParser.json());

// Start the server
const PORT = process.env.PORT || 3000;
app.listen(PORT, () => {
```

```
console.log('Server is running on port ${PORT}');
});
```

2. Creating API Endpoints

Next, create endpoints to interact with the blockchain. For example, to retrieve the balance of an Ethereum address:

```javascript
Copy code
app.get('/api/balance/:address', async (req, res) => {
const address = req.params.address;
try {
const balance = await web3.eth.getBalance(address);
res.json({ address, balance: web3.utils.fromWei(balance, 'ether') });
} catch (error) {
res.status(500).json({ error: 'Failed to retrieve balance' });
}
});
```

3. Interacting with Smart Contracts via API

You can also create endpoints to interact with smart contracts. For instance, if you want to call a function from a smart contract:

```javascript
Copy code
const contractABI = [...]; // Your contract ABI
const contractAddress = '0xYourContractAddress';
const contract = new web3.eth.Contract(contractABI, contractAddress);

app.post('/api/setValue', async (req, res) => {
const { value, account } = req.body; // value to set and the account making the transaction
try {
const tx = await contract.methods.set(value).send({ from: account });
res.json({ success: true, transactionHash: tx.transactionHash });
} catch (error) {
res.status(500).json({ error: 'Transaction failed' });
```

```
}
});
```

Using REST APIs in Your DApp

After setting up the REST API, you can make HTTP requests from your DApp's frontend using **fetch** or **axios**. This allows users to interact with the blockchain seamlessly without needing direct blockchain knowledge.

Example: Fetching Balance from the Frontend

javascript

Copy code

```
async function getBalance() {
const response = await fetch('/api/balance/${account}');
const data = await response.json();
console.log('Balance:', data.balance);
}
```

Example: Sending Data to the Smart Contract

javascript

Copy code

```
async function setValue() {
const valueToSet = inputValue; // Assume inputValue is retrieved from user input
const response = await fetch('/api/setValue', {
method: 'POST',
headers: {
'Content-Type': 'application/json',
},
body: JSON.stringify({ value: valueToSet, account }),
});

const data = await response.json();
  if (data.success) {
  console.log('Transaction successful:', data.transactionHash);
  } else {
  console.error('Transaction failed:', data.error);
```

}
}
Best Practices for REST API Integration with Blockchain

1. **Rate Limiting**: Implement rate limiting to prevent abuse of the API and ensure fair usage.
2. **Error Handling**: Use consistent error handling mechanisms to provide meaningful feedback to users.
3. **Security**: Secure API endpoints to prevent unauthorized access, possibly using API keys or JWT (JSON Web Tokens) for authentication.
4. **Documentation**: Clearly document the API endpoints, request formats, and response structures to aid other developers using the API.

Summary

In this section, we explored how to integrate blockchain functionality with REST APIs, enabling a seamless interaction between traditional web services and blockchain networks. By using frameworks like Express.js, developers can create robust APIs that allow users to access blockchain data and interact with smart contracts efficiently.

10.5 Best Practices for UI/UX in Blockchain Applications

Creating a user-friendly interface and a positive user experience (UI/UX) is crucial for the success of blockchain applications (DApps). Since blockchain technology can be complex and intimidating for many users, prioritizing usability and accessibility is essential. This section will explore best practices for designing UI/UX in blockchain applications.

1. Simplify User Onboarding

- **Clear Instructions**: Provide clear and concise instructions for new users, guiding them through the process of creating accounts, connecting wallets, and understanding the application's features.
- **Minimal Setup**: Reduce the barriers to entry by minimizing the number of steps required for onboarding. Consider using tools like **MetaMask** to simplify wallet integration.

2. Intuitive Navigation

- **Logical Structure**: Organize the application's layout in a logical manner, ensuring that users can easily find important features and information.
- **Consistent Design**: Use consistent design elements throughout the application, such as buttons, colors, and fonts, to enhance familiarity and ease of use.

3. Clear Feedback and Notifications

- **Real-Time Updates**: Provide real-time feedback for user actions, such as transactions and interactions with smart contracts. Use visual cues (e.g., loaders or success messages) to inform users about the status of their actions.
- **Error Handling**: Display clear and actionable error messages when something goes wrong. Avoid technical jargon and provide steps for users to resolve the issue.

4. Minimize Complexity

- **Hide Complexity**: Abstract away complex blockchain concepts, such as gas fees or transaction hashes, unless they are necessary for the user's understanding. Present information in a simplified manner.
- **Use Familiar Terminology**: Utilize language and terms that are familiar to users, avoiding overly technical jargon when possible.

5. Focus on Security and Trust

- **Security Indicators**: Implement visual indicators that reassure users about the security of their transactions and data. For example, show secure connection indicators (like HTTPS) and trusted partner logos.
- **Privacy Practices**: Clearly communicate how user data is handled and ensure that privacy practices are followed. Users should feel secure using

your application.

6. Responsive Design

- **Cross-Device Compatibility**: Ensure that the application is responsive and works seamlessly on various devices, including desktops, tablets, and smartphones.
- **Accessibility Features**: Incorporate accessibility features (like text resizing and color contrast adjustments) to cater to users with disabilities.

7. Educate Users

- **Tooltips and Pop-ups**: Use tooltips and pop-up explanations to provide context for complex features, helping users understand their options without overwhelming them.
- **Tutorials and Guides**: Consider including tutorials or walkthroughs that guide users through key functionalities of the application, particularly for those unfamiliar with blockchain technology.

8. Use Engaging Visuals

- **Visual Hierarchy**: Create a clear visual hierarchy using typography, spacing, and color contrasts to direct users' attention to essential elements.
- **Interactive Elements**: Incorporate engaging visuals and animations that enhance the user experience without being distracting. This can include transitions and hover effects.

9. Monitor User Feedback

- **User Testing**: Conduct regular user testing sessions to gather feedback on usability and areas for improvement. Involve real users to identify pain points in the user journey.

- **Iterative Design**: Use an iterative design process that allows for continuous improvement based on user feedback. Adapt the application based on the insights gained.

Summary

Designing a successful UI/UX for blockchain applications requires a focus on user needs, clear communication, and thoughtful design principles. By simplifying user onboarding, providing intuitive navigation, and minimizing complexity, developers can create applications that are accessible to both blockchain enthusiasts and newcomers alike. Implementing these best practices will not only enhance the user experience but also contribute to the overall adoption of blockchain technology.

10.6 Real-World DApp Example: Voting System

In this section, we will walk through the creation of a decentralized application (DApp) for a voting system, which exemplifies the use of blockchain technology in ensuring secure, transparent, and tamper-proof electoral processes. The DApp will enable users to participate in elections, ensuring that their votes are counted accurately and cannot be altered.

Overview of the Voting System DApp

The voting system DApp will allow registered users to cast their votes on various candidates or propositions. This system leverages blockchain's immutable nature to guarantee that once a vote is cast, it cannot be changed or removed, fostering trust in the electoral process.

Key Features

1. **User Registration**:

- Users can register through the DApp using their Ethereum wallet addresses. Each registered user is uniquely identified on the blockchain.

1. **Vote Casting**:

- Registered users can select their preferred candidate or option and cast their vote, which is then securely recorded on the blockchain.

1. **Real-Time Vote Tracking**:

- The DApp provides real-time updates on the vote count, giving users immediate insight into the electoral process.

1. **Transparency and Security**:

- All votes are encrypted and stored on the blockchain, ensuring their integrity and preventing tampering. Each vote is publicly verifiable without revealing the voter's identity.

Architecture

- **Frontend**: Built using React.js, the frontend provides an intuitive user interface that interacts with the Ethereum blockchain via Web3.js.
- **Smart Contracts**: Written in Solidity, these contracts handle user registrations, vote casting, and result calculations.
- **Blockchain**: The Ethereum network serves as the underlying technology, providing a decentralized ledger to store all voting data.

Steps to Build the Voting System DApp

1. **Set Up the Development Environment**:

- Install Node.js, Truffle, and Ganache.
- Initialize a new Truffle project and configure it to connect to Ganache for local testing.

1. **Develop Smart Contracts**:

- Create a Solidity smart contract to manage the voting logic, including functions for user registration, vote casting, and tallying votes.

1. **Implement the Frontend**:

- Use React.js to build the user interface. Integrate Web3.js to connect the frontend to the Ethereum blockchain, allowing users to interact with the smart contract.

1. **Testing and Deployment**:

- Thoroughly test the DApp locally using Ganache. After confirming that everything works correctly, deploy the smart contracts to the Ethereum test network (Rinkeby or Ropsten).
- Ensure that users can connect their MetaMask wallets to the DApp and cast their votes securely.

1. **Launch and Monitor**:

- Once deployed, monitor the DApp for any issues and gather user feedback to improve functionality and user experience.

Conclusion

In this chapter, we explored the integration of blockchain technology with web development, focusing on creating decentralized applications (DApps). We covered key concepts such as using React.js for frontend development, handling authentication and transactions, and best practices for UI/UX in blockchain applications. The practical example of building a voting system DApp illustrated how these concepts come together to create a real-world application that leverages the benefits of blockchain technology.

By understanding how to effectively combine blockchain and web technologies, developers can create innovative solutions that enhance transparency, security, and user engagement in various domains. As blockchain technology continues to evolve, the demand for skilled developers who can navigate this intersection will only increase, opening new avenues for building impactful applications.

CHAPTER 11: SECURITY AND AUDITING IN BLOCKCHAIN APPLICATIONS

11.1 Common Blockchain Security Issues: Smart Contract Vulnerabilities

As the adoption of blockchain technology and decentralized applications (DApps) grows, so does the importance of security in this evolving landscape. Smart contracts, which are self-executing contracts with the terms of the agreement directly written into code, are particularly susceptible to vulnerabilities. Understanding these vulnerabilities is critical for developers to ensure the integrity and security of their blockchain applications.

Key Smart Contract Vulnerabilities

1. **Reentrancy Attacks**:

- This occurs when a malicious contract calls back into the original contract before the first invocation has completed, potentially draining funds. The infamous DAO hack in 2016 is a notable example of a reentrancy attack.

Mitigation: Use the Checks-Effects-Interactions pattern to update the contract state before calling external contracts, thereby minimizing reentrancy risks.

1. **Integer Overflow and Underflow**:

- In programming languages like Solidity, arithmetic operations can exceed the maximum size of an integer or drop below zero, leading to unintended behaviors.

Mitigation: Use safe math libraries (like OpenZeppelin's SafeMath) to handle arithmetic operations safely, preventing overflow and underflow conditions.

1. **Gas Limit and Loops**:

- Smart contracts have a gas limit, and if a function runs out of gas (due to excessive iterations in a loop), it can cause the transaction to fail, leading to potential denial of service.

Mitigation: Avoid using unbounded loops and keep function complexity in check. Consider using alternative data structures to minimize gas consumption.

1. **Access Control Issues**:

- Improperly configured access controls can lead to unauthorized access or manipulation of contract functions, enabling attackers to exploit the contract.

Mitigation: Implement strict access controls using modifiers, and regularly review permission settings to ensure only authorized users can execute sensitive functions.

1. **Timestamp Dependence**:

- If a smart contract relies on block timestamps for critical operations, it can be vulnerable to miners manipulating timestamps to their advantage.

Mitigation: Avoid using block timestamps for critical logic and instead use other methods to ensure fairness and randomness.

1. **Front-Running**:

- This vulnerability occurs when an attacker sees a pending transaction and places their own transaction with higher fees to be processed first, potentially manipulating outcomes.

Mitigation: Use commit-reveal schemes or time-locks to obscure sensitive information until after the transaction is confirmed.

1. **Phishing Attacks**:

- Users can be tricked into revealing their private keys or sensitive information, leading to the loss of funds.

Mitigation: Educate users on phishing risks, and encourage the use of hardware wallets and other secure methods for key management.

Best Practices for Smart Contract Security

- **Code Reviews**: Regularly review code for vulnerabilities, ideally involving multiple developers to catch overlooked issues.
- **Audits**: Engage third-party security firms to audit the smart contracts for potential vulnerabilities before deployment.
- **Testing**: Implement thorough testing, including unit tests and integration tests, to ensure the smart contract functions as intended under various scenarios.
- **Bug Bounties**: Consider setting up bug bounty programs to incentivize white-hat hackers to identify and report vulnerabilities in exchange for rewards.
- **Upgradable Contracts**: Design contracts to be upgradable, allowing for fixes and improvements to be implemented post-deployment if vulnerabilities are discovered.

By prioritizing security in the development lifecycle of smart contracts, developers can significantly reduce the risk of vulnerabilities and enhance the reliability and trustworthiness of blockchain applications.

Summary

Smart contracts play a pivotal role in the functionality of blockchain applications, but they also introduce unique security challenges that developers must navigate. Understanding the common vulnerabilities associated with smart contracts is essential for building secure applications. By implementing best practices, conducting rigorous testing, and fostering a security-first mindset, developers can mitigate risks and create robust, secure blockchain solutions that inspire user confidence. As the blockchain ecosystem continues to mature, a proactive approach to security will be critical in ensuring the long-term success and adoption of decentralized technologies.

11.2 Secure Coding Practices for JavaScript in Blockchain Development

As blockchain technology gains traction, the security of decentralized applications (DApps) has become paramount. JavaScript is often used to develop the frontend and backend of these applications, making it essential for developers to adopt secure coding practices. This section outlines key secure coding practices specifically tailored for JavaScript in the context of blockchain development.

1. Input Validation and Sanitization

One of the fundamental principles of secure coding is validating and sanitizing all user inputs. This helps prevent various attacks, including Cross-Site Scripting (XSS) and SQL injection.

- **Use Strong Validation Libraries**: Implement libraries like Joi or express-validator to enforce rules on input data, ensuring that only valid data is processed.
- **Sanitize Input Data**: Use libraries such as DOMPurify to clean user inputs and eliminate any malicious scripts or HTML tags that could compromise application security.

2. Avoiding JavaScript Injection

JavaScript injection is a type of attack where an attacker injects malicious scripts into a web application. To mitigate this risk:

- **Use Content Security Policy (CSP)**: Implement CSP headers to restrict the sources of content that can be executed, minimizing the risk of malicious scripts.
- **Avoid Inline JavaScript**: Inline JavaScript can be easily manipulated. Instead, link to external script files and utilize strict CSP rules.

3. Secure API Communication

When interacting with blockchain networks or external APIs, secure communication is crucial to protect sensitive information.

- **Use HTTPS**: Always use HTTPS for API calls to encrypt data in transit and protect against man-in-the-middle (MITM) attacks.
- **Authentication**: Implement strong authentication mechanisms (e.g., OAuth 2.0) for API access, ensuring only authorized users can interact with sensitive endpoints.

4. Managing Private Keys Safely

In blockchain applications, the security of private keys is paramount. Poor management of private keys can lead to loss of funds and unauthorized access.

- **Use Hardware Wallets**: Encourage users to store their private keys in hardware wallets rather than in software or web applications, which are more vulnerable to attacks.
- **Environment Variables**: Store sensitive keys and configuration settings in environment variables instead of hardcoding them in source code, reducing exposure.

5. Error Handling and Logging

Proper error handling can prevent attackers from gaining insights into application internals, which could lead to exploitation.

- **Generic Error Messages**: Avoid displaying detailed error messages to users. Use generic messages that do not disclose sensitive information about the application's inner workings.
- **Secure Logging**: Ensure that logs do not contain sensitive information, such as user credentials or private keys. Implement log rotation and access control to protect log files.

6. Regular Security Updates and Dependency Management

Keeping libraries and dependencies up to date is crucial for maintaining security in JavaScript applications.

- **Use Dependabot**: Tools like Dependabot can automatically check for outdated dependencies and security vulnerabilities in your project.
- **Review Dependencies**: Regularly audit third-party libraries for known vulnerabilities using tools such as npm audit or Snyk.

7. Implementing Smart Contract Security Measures

When interacting with smart contracts from JavaScript, it's essential to ensure that the contracts themselves are secure.

- **Understand Smart Contract Vulnerabilities**: Be aware of common vulnerabilities in smart contracts (as discussed in the previous section) and test interactions thoroughly.
- **Use Well-Audited Libraries**: Utilize libraries like OpenZeppelin for smart contracts to leverage secure implementations that have undergone rigorous testing.

8. Conducting Code Reviews and Security Audits

Incorporating peer reviews and security audits into the development process can help identify vulnerabilities before deployment.

- **Conduct Code Reviews**: Regularly review code with team members to catch potential security issues and improve overall code quality.
- **Engage Security Experts**: Consider hiring external security professionals to conduct thorough audits of your codebase and architecture.

Summary

Secure coding practices are essential for protecting blockchain applications built with JavaScript. By implementing input validation, securing API communications, and managing private keys responsibly, developers can significantly reduce the risk of vulnerabilities. Additionally, regularly updating dependencies and conducting thorough code reviews and audits are vital components of a robust security strategy. As the blockchain landscape continues to evolve, maintaining a proactive approach to security will be critical in safeguarding applications and fostering user trust in decentralized technologies.

11.3 Tools for Auditing Smart Contracts (MythX, Remix IDE)

Smart contract audits are critical in ensuring the security and functionality of decentralized applications (DApps) on blockchain platforms. Given the irreversible nature of blockchain transactions, any vulnerabilities in smart contracts can lead to significant financial losses and reputational damage. To mitigate these risks, developers should utilize specialized tools designed for auditing smart contracts. This section focuses on two prominent tools: MythX and Remix IDE.

1. MythX: Comprehensive Smart Contract Security Analysis

MythX is a leading security analysis service specifically designed for Ethereum smart contracts. It integrates seamlessly into the development workflow, providing developers with automated security assessments to identify vulnerabilities before deployment.

Key Features:

- **Automated Analysis**: MythX employs a combination of static and dynamic analysis techniques to scan smart contracts for known vulnerabilities, including reentrancy, overflow/underflow, and improper access controls.

- **Comprehensive Reports**: After analysis, MythX generates detailed reports that highlight potential issues, providing insights on how to remediate vulnerabilities effectively.
- **Integration with Development Tools**: MythX can be integrated with popular development tools like Truffle and Hardhat, enabling developers to perform security audits as part of their continuous integration and deployment (CI/CD) pipelines.
- **User-Friendly Interface**: The MythX web interface allows developers to upload contracts and view the analysis results easily, making it accessible for both beginners and experienced developers.

Usage Example:

To use MythX, developers can either submit their smart contracts through the web interface or integrate it into their development environment. By incorporating MythX into the development process, developers can catch vulnerabilities early, ensuring that contracts are secure before going live.

2. Remix IDE: An Integrated Development Environment for Smart Contracts

Remix IDE is a popular web-based integrated development environment for Ethereum smart contracts. While its primary purpose is to facilitate the development and testing of smart contracts, it also includes essential auditing features that developers can leverage.

Key Features:

- **In-Browser Development**: Remix allows developers to write, compile, and deploy smart contracts directly in the browser, streamlining the development process without the need for local setup.
- **Static Analysis**: The built-in static analysis tool scans contracts for common security issues and provides suggestions for improvement. It helps developers identify potential vulnerabilities before testing or deploying their contracts.
- **Unit Testing**: Remix enables developers to write and execute unit tests

for their smart contracts, ensuring that contracts behave as expected and meet predefined specifications.

- **Debugging Tools**: Remix offers powerful debugging features, including transaction tracing and event logging, which help developers troubleshoot issues in their contracts effectively.

Usage Example:

To audit a smart contract using Remix, developers can open the Remix IDE, paste their Solidity code, and enable the static analysis tool. After running the analysis, developers receive feedback on potential issues, allowing them to make necessary corrections before deploying the contract.

3. Comparison of MythX and Remix IDE

While both MythX and Remix IDE provide valuable tools for auditing smart contracts, they serve different purposes and audiences:

Summary

Using tools like MythX and Remix IDE is essential for conducting thorough audits of smart contracts. MythX provides a comprehensive security analysis that can identify vulnerabilities early in the development process, while Remix IDE offers a user-friendly environment for developing, testing, and debugging smart contracts. By leveraging these tools, developers can enhance the security of their DApps, reduce the risk of vulnerabilities, and ultimately build more reliable and trustworthy blockchain solutions. Incorporating these auditing practices into the development workflow will lead to a more secure blockchain ecosystem.

11.4 Protecting Private Keys and Wallets in DApps

In the world of blockchain and decentralized applications (DApps), the security of private keys and wallets is paramount. Private keys are the cornerstone of blockchain security, as they grant access to users' funds and assets. If compromised, users can lose everything. This section discusses best practices for protecting private keys and wallets in DApps, ensuring that developers build secure applications and users safeguard their digital assets.

1. Understanding Private Keys and Wallets

- **Private Keys**: A private key is a secret number that allows a user to access their cryptocurrency or blockchain assets. It is crucial never to share this key with anyone, as it grants complete control over the associated wallet.
- **Wallets**: A wallet is a software program or hardware device that stores a user's private and public keys. Wallets can be categorized into two main types:
- **Hot Wallets**: Connected to the internet, making them convenient for frequent transactions but more vulnerable to hacks.
- **Cold Wallets**: Offline storage methods, such as hardware wallets, providing enhanced security but requiring more effort to access funds.

2. Best Practices for Protecting Private Keys

- **Use Hardware Wallets**: For significant amounts of cryptocurrency, consider using hardware wallets, which store private keys offline and are less susceptible to hacking attempts.
- **Implement Strong Passwords**: Ensure that any wallet application is secured with a strong password. Encourage users to create complex passwords that are hard to guess.
- **Enable Two-Factor Authentication (2FA)**: Use 2FA in wallet applications to add an additional layer of security. Even if someone gains access to a user's password, they will need the second factor (like a mobile authentication app) to access the wallet.
- **Educate Users**: Provide clear instructions to users on how to manage and protect their private keys. Stress the importance of not sharing private keys and recognizing phishing attempts.
- **Encrypt Private Keys**: If storing private keys within the DApp or server, ensure they are encrypted. Use strong encryption algorithms to make it difficult for unauthorized parties to access the keys.

3. Secure Wallet Implementation in DApps

- **Use Established Libraries**: When building wallet functionalities in a

DApp, utilize established libraries such as Web3.js or Ethers.js. These libraries have built-in security features and are widely used by the community.

- **Limit Key Exposure**: Minimize the exposure of private keys in your application. Never store private keys in plaintext, and avoid displaying them in logs or error messages.
- **Use Wallet Connect or Similar Protocols**: Instead of requiring users to enter private keys directly into your DApp, implement WalletConnect or similar protocols that allow users to connect their wallets securely. This way, users can interact with your DApp without revealing their private keys.
- **Regular Security Audits**: Conduct regular security audits of your DApp to identify vulnerabilities related to wallet management and private key handling. Use automated tools and manual reviews to ensure security measures are effective.

4. Handling Recovery and Backup

- **Seed Phrases**: Educate users about seed phrases, which are backup phrases used to restore wallets. Emphasize the importance of securely storing these phrases, as losing them can result in irreversible loss of access to funds.
- **Backup Procedures**: Encourage users to back up their wallets regularly, including both hot and cold wallets. Provide clear instructions on how to create backups and securely store them.

Summary
Protecting private keys and wallets is critical for the security of DApps and their users. By implementing best practices such as using hardware wallets, strong passwords, two-factor authentication, and secure coding techniques, developers can significantly reduce the risk of unauthorized access to users' funds. Educating users on managing their private keys and recovery options is equally important in fostering a secure environment. In

the rapidly evolving blockchain landscape, prioritizing the security of private keys and wallets will help build trust and ensure the long-term success of decentralized applications.

11.5 Implementing Multi-Signature Wallets

Multi-signature (multisig) wallets represent a significant advancement in blockchain security, enabling a collaborative approach to managing cryptocurrency funds. These wallets require multiple signatures to authorize a transaction, providing an additional layer of protection against unauthorized access and theft. This section discusses the principles behind multi-signature wallets, their benefits, implementation strategies, and best practices for developers.

1. Understanding Multi-Signature Wallets

- **Definition**: A multi-signature wallet is a type of cryptocurrency wallet that requires more than one private key to authorize a transaction. For example, a 2-of-3 multisig wallet requires two out of three designated keys to sign a transaction before it can be executed.
- **Use Cases**: Multisig wallets are particularly useful in scenarios such as:
- **Joint Accounts**: Businesses or organizations where multiple stakeholders must agree on transactions.
- **Escrow Services**: Holding funds securely until specific conditions are met, requiring multiple parties to authorize the release of funds.
- **Enhanced Security**: Users can split their keys across different devices or individuals, reducing the risk of loss or theft.

2. Benefits of Multi-Signature Wallets

- **Increased Security**: By requiring multiple signatures, multisig wallets make it more challenging for a single compromised key to lead to unauthorized access to funds.
- **Reduction of Fraud**: In organizational settings, multisig wallets ensure that no single individual can unilaterally make transactions, reducing the risk of internal fraud.

- **Control and Transparency**: Multisig wallets provide clear accountability, as all parties involved must agree on transactions, making the process transparent.

3. Implementing Multi-Signature Wallets

- **Choosing the Right Configuration**: Determine the appropriate multisig configuration based on the needs of the users. Common configurations include:
- **2-of-3**: Requires two signatures from three total keys.
- **3-of-5**: Requires three signatures from five total keys.
- **n-of-m**: A flexible configuration where "n" signatures are required from "m" total keys.
- **Using Libraries**: Leverage existing libraries and frameworks for implementing multisig functionality. Popular libraries include:
- **BitcoinJS**: For Bitcoin multisig wallets.
- **Web3.js**: For Ethereum multisig wallets, allowing you to create and interact with multisig contracts.
- **Creating the Multisig Wallet**:

1. **Generate Keys**: Create the necessary key pairs for each participant in the wallet.
2. **Deploy a Multisig Smart Contract**: For blockchain platforms like Ethereum, deploy a multisig contract that defines the rules for transaction approvals.
3. **Add Participants**: Ensure that all parties' public keys are added to the multisig contract.

- **Transaction Authorization Process**:

1. **Initiate Transaction**: One participant proposes a transaction within the multisig wallet.
2. **Sign the Transaction**: Required participants sign the transaction using

their private keys.

3. **Broadcast Transaction**: Once the required number of signatures is reached, the transaction is broadcast to the blockchain for execution.

4. Best Practices for Multi-Signature Wallets

- **Secure Key Storage**: Ensure that private keys are stored securely using hardware wallets or secure environments to prevent unauthorized access.
- **Regular Security Audits**: Conduct periodic audits of multisig wallet implementations to identify vulnerabilities and ensure that best practices are followed.
- **User Education**: Provide thorough documentation and resources for users on how to manage their multisig wallets, including recovery processes and best security practices.
- **Backup Plans**: Implement backup strategies for the keys involved in the multisig wallet to prevent loss due to device failure or key compromise.

Summary

Implementing multi-signature wallets significantly enhances the security of cryptocurrency transactions, particularly for businesses and collaborative environments. By requiring multiple signatures for transaction authorization, these wallets reduce the risk of unauthorized access and promote accountability among participants. Developers must carefully consider the configuration, utilize reliable libraries, and follow best practices to ensure the secure implementation of multisig wallets. As the blockchain ecosystem evolves, the adoption of multi-signature technology will play a crucial role in fostering trust and enhancing the security of decentralized applications.

11.6 Disaster Recovery and Handling Failed Transactions

In the world of blockchain applications, ensuring robust disaster recovery mechanisms and effective handling of failed transactions is crucial for maintaining user trust and operational integrity. This section will discuss strategies for disaster recovery, methods for handling failed transactions, and best practices for blockchain developers.

1. Understanding Disaster Recovery in Blockchain

- **Definition**: Disaster recovery in the context of blockchain involves planning and implementing processes to recover data, application functionality, and service availability after catastrophic events, such as network failures, smart contract bugs, or cyberattacks.
- **Importance**: Given the immutable nature of blockchain transactions, once a transaction is recorded, it cannot be altered or deleted. This permanence means that developers must have strategies in place to deal with errors and recover from failures to minimize the impact on users and business operations.

2. Disaster Recovery Strategies

- **Data Backups**: Regularly back up critical data, including smart contract states, user data, and transaction logs. Utilize decentralized storage solutions like IPFS or traditional cloud backups to ensure data redundancy.
- **Multi-Node Architecture**: Deploy applications across multiple nodes to ensure redundancy. This way, if one node fails, the application can continue to operate through other nodes.
- **Failover Mechanisms**: Implement automated failover mechanisms to switch to backup systems or nodes in the event of a failure, ensuring minimal downtime.
- **Smart Contract Upgradeability**: Consider using proxy patterns or upgradeable contracts, allowing you to deploy new versions of contracts to fix bugs or vulnerabilities without losing the existing state.

3. Handling Failed Transactions

- **Identifying Failed Transactions**: Develop monitoring tools to detect failed transactions in real time. Use events emitted by smart contracts to trigger alerts when a transaction fails to execute.
- **User Notifications**: Inform users promptly about transaction failures,

providing clear explanations and potential next steps. Transparency helps maintain user trust.

- **Automatic Rollbacks**: For certain types of transactions, consider implementing rollback mechanisms where applicable. This could involve reverting to a previous state if a transaction fails, although it can be complex in the blockchain context due to immutability.
- **Retry Logic**: Implement retry logic for failed transactions, allowing users or systems to attempt the transaction again automatically after a specified interval. Ensure this is done cautiously to avoid double-spending.

4. Best Practices for Disaster Recovery and Transaction Handling

- **Document Recovery Processes**: Create comprehensive documentation outlining the steps for disaster recovery and handling transaction failures, ensuring that all team members are aware of protocols.
- **Test Recovery Plans**: Regularly conduct drills and tests of disaster recovery plans to ensure their effectiveness. Simulate various failure scenarios to identify potential weaknesses and improve response strategies.
- **User Education**: Provide users with information on what to do in case of transaction failures or service interruptions, including how to contact support and what information to provide.
- **Continuous Improvement**: Continuously evaluate and refine disaster recovery and transaction handling processes based on user feedback, incident reports, and emerging best practices in the blockchain space.

Conclusion

In the rapidly evolving blockchain landscape, security and auditing are paramount. This chapter has explored common security issues, secure coding practices, tools for auditing smart contracts, and strategies for protecting private keys and wallets. Implementing multi-signature wallets enhances transaction security, while robust disaster recovery mechanisms and effective handling of failed transactions are crucial for maintaining user trust and operational continuity. By following best practices and remaining vigilant against potential threats, developers can create resilient blockchain applications that stand the test of time, ensuring user confidence in decentralized solutions.

CHAPTER 12: TESTING AND DEPLOYMENT IN BLOCKCHAIN DEVELOPMENT

12.1 Unit Testing Smart Contracts with Truffle

Unit testing is an essential aspect of blockchain development, particularly for smart contracts. Given the immutable nature of blockchain, any errors in smart contract code can have significant repercussions. In this section, we will explore how to effectively use the Truffle framework to perform unit testing on smart contracts.

1. Introduction to Truffle

Truffle is a powerful development framework for Ethereum that simplifies the process of developing, testing, and deploying smart contracts. It provides a suite of tools that streamline the development workflow, making it easier to manage contracts, run tests, and interact with the Ethereum blockchain.

2. Setting Up Truffle

- **Installation**: To get started with Truffle, first ensure that you have Node.js installed. Then, install Truffle globally via npm:

bash
    Copy code
    npm install -g truffle

- **Create a New Project**: Initialize a new Truffle project in your desired directory:

bash

Copy code

mkdir MyBlockchainProject

cd MyBlockchainProject

truffle init

This command sets up the basic directory structure, including folders for contracts, migrations, and tests.

3. Writing Smart Contracts

Before diving into testing, you need to have a smart contract to work with. Create a simple smart contract in the contracts directory, for example, SimpleStorage.sol:

solidity

Copy code

```
// SPDX-License-Identifier: MIT
pragma solidity ^0.8.0;

contract SimpleStorage {
    uint256 private storedData;

function set(uint256 x) public {
    storedData = x;
    }

function get() public view returns (uint256) {
    return storedData;
    }
}
```

4. Writing Unit Tests

Truffle allows you to write tests in JavaScript or Solidity. For this example, we will use JavaScript.

- Create a new test file in the test directory, such as SimpleStorage.test.js, and write the following test cases:

javascript
  Copy code
  const SimpleStorage = artifacts.require("SimpleStorage");

```javascript
contract("SimpleStorage", (accounts) => {
  let simpleStorage;

beforeEach(async () => {
  simpleStorage = await SimpleStorage.new();
  });

it("should store the value correctly", async () => {
  await simpleStorage.set(42);
  const storedData = await simpleStorage.get();
  assert.equal(storedData.toString(), "42", "The stored value is incorrect.");
  });

it("should return 0 for an uninitialized storage", async () => {
  const storedData = await simpleStorage.get();
  assert.equal(storedData.toString(), "0", "The initial stored value should be
zero.");
  });
  });
```

5. Running Tests

To execute your tests, use the following command in your terminal:
bash
Copy code
truffle test

This command runs all the tests in the test directory and reports the results, helping you ensure that your smart contract behaves as expected.

6. Best Practices for Unit Testing

- **Test Coverage**: Aim for high test coverage by testing all functions and edge cases. Tools like solidity-coverage can help you measure coverage.
- **Isolate Tests**: Each test should be independent. Use the beforeEach hook to reset the state before each test runs.
- **Readable Tests**: Write tests that are easy to read and understand. Use descriptive names for your test cases to clarify their purpose.
- **Automated Testing**: Integrate testing into your continuous integration (CI) pipeline to ensure tests are run automatically whenever changes are made.

Summary

In this chapter, we have explored the crucial aspects of testing and deployment in blockchain development. We started with unit testing smart contracts using Truffle, emphasizing the importance of rigorous testing to ensure code correctness and security. By following best practices, developers can mitigate risks associated with deploying immutable smart contracts on the blockchain. As we move forward, understanding the deployment processes and tools will be essential for successfully launching blockchain applications in real-world scenarios.

12.2 Continuous Integration and Deployment (CI/CD) for Blockchain Applications

Continuous Integration (CI) and Continuous Deployment (CD) are essential practices in modern software development, enabling teams to deliver high-quality applications rapidly and efficiently. In the context of blockchain development, implementing CI/CD can significantly enhance the development workflow, ensuring that smart contracts and decentralized applications (DApps) are rigorously tested and deployed consistently.

1. Understanding CI/CD in Blockchain Development

- **Continuous Integration (CI)**: This involves automatically testing and integrating code changes into a shared repository multiple times a day.

For blockchain projects, CI ensures that any new changes to smart contracts or DApp code are immediately validated through automated tests, reducing the likelihood of introducing bugs or vulnerabilities.

- **Continuous Deployment (CD)**: This practice automatically deploys code changes to production once they pass all tests. In blockchain development, CD means that once smart contracts are tested and verified, they can be deployed to the blockchain without manual intervention, streamlining the release process.

2. Setting Up a CI/CD Pipeline

Creating an effective CI/CD pipeline for blockchain applications involves several key steps:

- **Source Code Management**: Use version control systems like Git to manage your smart contract and DApp code. Platforms like GitHub, GitLab, or Bitbucket can host your repository.
- **Automated Testing**: Integrate automated testing tools into your pipeline. For Ethereum smart contracts, you can use frameworks like Truffle or Hardhat. Ensure that your tests cover various scenarios, including unit tests, integration tests, and security tests.
- **Continuous Integration Service**: Use CI services like GitHub Actions, Travis CI, or CircleCI to automate the testing process. Configure your CI service to trigger tests every time code is pushed to the repository.

Example configuration for GitHub Actions (.github/workflows/ci.yml):

```yaml
Copy code
name: CI Pipeline

on:
  push:
    branches:
      - main
```

```
pull_request:
branches:
- main

jobs:
  test:
  runs-on: ubuntu-latest
  steps:
  - name: Checkout code
  uses: actions/checkout@v2

- name: Set up Node.js
  uses: actions/setup-node@v2
  with:
  node-version: '14'

- name: Install dependencies
  run: npm install

- name: Run tests
  run: npm test
```

3. Deployment Automation

Once your code passes all tests, the next step is to automate the deployment process.

- **Deployment Scripts**: Use deployment scripts to automate the deployment of smart contracts to the blockchain. For Ethereum, you can leverage Truffle migrations or Hardhat scripts.
- **Environment Configuration**: Maintain separate environments for development, testing, and production. Use environment variables to manage sensitive information, such as private keys and API endpoints.
- **Triggering Deployment**: Configure your CI/CD pipeline to trigger deployment automatically after passing tests. This can be done through

GitHub Actions or similar tools, ensuring that the latest code is always deployed.

Example deployment step in GitHub Actions:

```yaml
Copy code
deploy:
runs-on: ubuntu-latest
needs: test
steps:
- name: Checkout code
uses: actions/checkout@v2

- name: Set up Node.js
  uses: actions/setup-node@v2
  with:
  node-version: '14'

- name: Install dependencies
  run: npm install

- name: Deploy to Ethereum
  env:
  INFURA_API_KEY: ${{ secrets.INFURA_API_KEY }}
  DEPLOYER_PRIVATE_KEY: ${{ secrets.DEPLOYER_PRIVATE_KEY }}
  run: npx truffle migrate —network mainnet
```

4. Monitoring and Alerts

Once your CI/CD pipeline is in place, it's crucial to monitor the deployed applications actively. Consider implementing monitoring tools to track performance, identify errors, and receive alerts for critical issues. Services like Sentry or LogRocket can help you monitor DApp usage and detect anomalies.

5. Security Considerations

- **Secure Secrets Management**: Ensure that sensitive information, such as private keys and API tokens, are stored securely using the secrets management features provided by your CI/CD service.
- **Audit and Review**: Regularly audit your CI/CD pipeline and deployment processes. Implement code reviews and ensure that all changes are reviewed by multiple team members to maintain code quality.

Summary

In this chapter, we explored the critical role of Continuous Integration and Continuous Deployment (CI/CD) in blockchain development. By automating testing and deployment processes, developers can ensure that smart contracts and decentralized applications are released with higher quality and reliability. Implementing a robust CI/CD pipeline not only accelerates the development cycle but also enhances collaboration among team members. As we continue to advance in blockchain technology, embracing CI/CD practices will be vital for delivering secure and efficient solutions in the rapidly evolving landscape of decentralized applications.

12.3 Testing on Testnets (Ropsten, Kovan, and Rinkeby)

Testing smart contracts and decentralized applications (DApps) on testnets is a crucial step in the blockchain development process. Testnets are alternative Ethereum blockchains that allow developers to deploy and test their applications in a simulated environment without using real Ether (ETH). This chapter explores the three most popular Ethereum testnets—Ropsten, Kovan, and Rinkeby—discussing their features, use cases, and how to set up and test your applications on these networks.

1. Overview of Ethereum Testnets

Testnets provide a safe and cost-effective way to experiment with blockchain applications. Each testnet has unique characteristics that cater to different testing needs:

- **Ropsten**: A proof-of-work testnet that closely mimics the Ethereum mainnet. It uses the same consensus mechanism and allows for more realistic testing of applications that require gas fees and complex transactions.

However, due to its public nature, Ropsten can experience congestion and occasional instability.

- **Kovan**: A proof-of-authority testnet known for its fast block times and stability. It is maintained by the Parity team, which provides a reliable environment for testing DApps. Kovan is particularly useful for testing applications that require consistent performance and lower latency.
- **Rinkeby**: A proof-of-authority testnet that emphasizes security and reliability. Rinkeby uses a consensus mechanism that requires validators to perform additional steps to prevent spam attacks, making it a more secure environment for testing. It is ideal for developers who need a stable testing platform.

2. Setting Up Testnets for Development

To test your smart contracts on Ethereum testnets, follow these steps:

2.1. Install Dependencies

Ensure you have the necessary tools installed, such as Truffle, Hardhat, or any other Ethereum development framework.

bash

Copy code

npm install -g truffle

2.2. Create a Wallet and Obtain Test Ether

1. **Create a Wallet**: Use a wallet like MetaMask to create an Ethereum account. This wallet will hold your test Ether for transaction fees.
2. **Obtain Test Ether**: Use a faucet to get free test Ether. Each testnet has its own faucet:

- **Ropsten Faucet**: Ropsten Faucet
- **Kovan Faucet**: Kovan Faucet
- **Rinkeby Faucet**: Rinkeby Faucet

Simply enter your wallet address, and the faucet will send test Ether to your account.

2.3. Configure Your Development Environment

In your project directory, configure the Truffle or Hardhat settings to include the testnet. For Truffle, you can modify the truffle-config.js file:

javascript

Copy code

```
const HDWalletProvider = require('@truffle/hdwallet-provider');
const infuraKey = "YOUR_INFURA_KEY"; // Replace with your Infura key
const mnemonic = "YOUR_MNEMONIC"; // Replace with your wallet mnemonic

module.exports = {
  networks: {
    ropsten: {
      provider: () => new HDWalletProvider(mnemonic, 'https://ropsten.infura.io/v3/${infuraKey}'),
      network_id: 3,
      gas: 5500000,
      confirmations: 2,
      timeoutBlocks: 200,
      skipDryRun: true,
    },
    kovan: {
      provider: () => new HDWalletProvider(mnemonic, 'https://kovan.infura.io/v3/${infuraKey}'),
      network_id: 42,
      gas: 5500000,
      confirmations: 2,
      timeoutBlocks: 200,
      skipDryRun: true,
    },
    rinkeby: {
      provider: () => new HDWalletProvider(mnemonic, 'https://rinkeby.infura.
```

```
io/v3/${infuraKey}'),
   network_id: 4,
   gas: 5500000,
   confirmations: 2,
   timeoutBlocks: 200,
   skipDryRun: true,
   },
   },
 };
```

3. Deploying and Testing Smart Contracts on Testnets

Once your testnet is configured, you can deploy and test your smart contracts.

3.1. Deploying Smart Contracts

Use the following Truffle command to deploy your smart contracts to the selected testnet:

bash

Copy code

truffle migrate —network ropsten

Replace ropsten with kovan or rinkeby as needed.

3.2. Testing Smart Contracts

Use Truffle's built-in testing framework to run tests:

bash

Copy code

truffle test —network ropsten

This command executes your test suite against the smart contracts deployed on the testnet.

4. Benefits of Testing on Testnets

- **Cost-Efficiency**: Testing on testnets is free, allowing developers to experiment without the financial risk associated with deploying to the mainnet.
- **Realistic Environment**: Testnets like Ropsten provide a more accurate simulation of how smart contracts will perform on the main Ethereum

network.

- **Debugging Opportunities**: Developers can identify and fix issues in their smart contracts before deploying to the mainnet, minimizing the risk of costly errors.
- **User Feedback**: Developers can share their DApps on testnets to gather feedback from users, allowing for iterative improvements before the final release.

Summary

Testing on Ethereum testnets is a fundamental practice for blockchain developers, enabling them to validate their smart contracts and DApps in a risk-free environment. By understanding the characteristics of Ropsten, Kovan, and Rinkeby, developers can choose the most suitable testnet for their applications and ensure a smooth transition to the mainnet. With proper setup and deployment processes, testing on these networks helps to build more reliable, secure, and efficient blockchain solutions.

12.4 Deploying Smart Contracts to Mainnet

Deploying smart contracts to the Ethereum mainnet is a critical step in the blockchain development process. This chapter outlines the considerations, steps, and best practices for successfully launching smart contracts on the main Ethereum network.

1. Preparing for Mainnet Deployment

Before deploying your smart contracts to the mainnet, ensure that you have adequately tested your contracts on testnets and addressed any issues. Here are some key preparations:

1.1. Review Smart Contract Code

Conduct a thorough review of your smart contract code to ensure that it meets the following criteria:

- **Security**: Check for vulnerabilities, such as reentrancy attacks, integer overflow/underflow, and gas limit issues. Use established security practices and tools to analyze your code.
- **Gas Efficiency**: Optimize your code to minimize gas costs during

deployment and execution. Avoid unnecessary computations and data storage.

- **Logic Accuracy**: Confirm that the logic within your contracts behaves as intended. Ensure that all functions perform as expected and that edge cases are handled.

1.2. Choose the Right Time for Deployment

Consider deploying during times of lower network congestion to reduce transaction fees and improve the likelihood of timely confirmations. Tools like EthGasStation can help you monitor gas prices and choose the best time to deploy.

1.3. Create a Wallet and Fund It with ETH

Ensure you have a wallet capable of interacting with the Ethereum mainnet, such as MetaMask or a hardware wallet. Fund your wallet with enough ETH to cover gas fees for deployment. It's essential to account for the cost of deploying your contracts and executing any initial transactions.

2. Deploying Smart Contracts

Once you are prepared, follow these steps to deploy your smart contracts to the mainnet:

2.1. Configure Your Deployment Settings

Ensure that your Truffle or Hardhat configuration file is set to deploy to the mainnet. Here is an example configuration for Truffle:

```javascript
Copy code
const HDWalletProvider = require('@truffle/hdwallet-provider');
const infuraKey = "YOUR_INFURA_KEY"; // Replace with your Infura key
const mnemonic = "YOUR_MNEMONIC"; // Replace with your wallet mnemonic

module.exports = {
  networks: {
    mainnet: {
```

```
provider: () => new HDWalletProvider(mnemonic, 'https://mainnet.infura
.io/v3/${infuraKey}'),
network_id: 1, // Mainnet ID
gas: 5500000, // Gas limit
gasPrice: 20000000000, // Set a gas price (20 gwei)
confirmations: 2,
timeoutBlocks: 200,
skipDryRun: true,
},
},
};
```

2.2. Deploy Your Smart Contracts

With your configuration set up, you can deploy your contracts to the Ethereum mainnet. Use the following command:

bash

Copy code

```
truffle migrate —network mainnet
```

This command will execute your migration scripts, deploying your contracts and saving their addresses on the blockchain.

2.3. Verify Your Smart Contracts

After deployment, it's essential to verify your smart contracts on Etherscan or similar block explorers. This allows users to read the contract code and interact with it directly. Use the following Truffle command for verification:

bash

Copy code

```
truffle run verify YourContractName —network mainnet
```

3. Interacting with Deployed Contracts

Once your contracts are deployed, you can interact with them using libraries like Web3.js or Ethers.js. This interaction typically involves sending transactions, calling contract functions, and monitoring events. Here's a brief example using Web3.js:

javascript

Copy code

```
const Web3 = require('web3');
const web3 = new Web3('https://mainnet.infura.io/v3/YOUR_INFURA_
KEY');
const contractAddress = 'YOUR_CONTRACT_ADDRESS';
const abi = [ /* ABI array here */ ];

const contract = new web3.eth.Contract(abi, contractAddress);

// Example of calling a function
contract.methods.yourFunction().call()
.then(result => {
console.log(result);
})
.catch(error => {
console.error(error);
});
```

4. Post-Deployment Considerations

After deploying your smart contracts, consider the following:

4.1. Monitor Contract Activity

Use blockchain explorers like Etherscan to monitor contract activity, including transactions and event emissions. You can also set up alerts for specific events or actions to stay updated on the contract's usage.

4.2. Addressing Issues

Be prepared to handle any issues that may arise post-deployment. This could involve interacting with users who encounter problems or managing unexpected contract behaviors.

4.3. Plan for Upgrades

Consider how you will manage contract upgrades in the future. Ethereum smart contracts are immutable once deployed, so you may need to implement a proxy pattern or use upgradable contract patterns to facilitate changes without losing state.

Summary

Deploying smart contracts to the Ethereum mainnet is a significant milestone in the blockchain development journey. By thoroughly preparing, following best practices, and maintaining post-deployment vigilance, developers can ensure a successful launch. Proper deployment not only enhances the security and functionality of the smart contracts but also builds trust and reliability within the Ethereum ecosystem, paving the way for robust decentralized applications.

12.5 Monitoring and Managing Smart Contracts Post-Deployment

Once your smart contracts are successfully deployed on the Ethereum mainnet, ongoing monitoring and management are essential for ensuring their security, performance, and functionality. This section covers key practices and tools to effectively manage your smart contracts post-deployment.

1. Continuous Monitoring of Smart Contracts

Monitoring your smart contracts allows you to track their activity, performance, and any potential issues that may arise. Here are some strategies for effective monitoring:

1.1. Use Blockchain Explorers

Blockchain explorers such as Etherscan provide detailed information about your smart contracts, including:

- **Transaction History**: Track all transactions related to your smart contract, including function calls and value transfers.
- **Event Emissions**: Monitor events emitted by your smart contracts, which can indicate significant state changes or actions taken by users.
- **Gas Usage**: Analyze gas consumption for transactions involving your contracts, helping you understand the cost of interactions.

1.2. Implement Logging and Analytics Tools

Using logging and analytics tools can help you gather insights about user interactions and contract performance. Tools like Tenderly and Fortmatic provide features such as:

- **Transaction Monitoring**: Track all transactions and visualize their execution status, gas consumption, and execution paths.

- **Alerts**: Set up alerts for specific events or transaction types, allowing you to respond quickly to issues or significant activity.

1.3. Use On-Chain Monitoring Services

On-chain monitoring services offer tools and dashboards specifically designed for smart contract monitoring. These services can alert you to issues like high gas costs, pending transactions, and unexpected contract states. Popular options include:

- **Dune Analytics**: Create custom dashboards to visualize data from your smart contracts and track specific metrics over time.
- **Nansen**: Offers insights into wallet activities and on-chain behaviors, providing context around your smart contracts' usage.

2. Managing Smart Contracts Post-Deployment

Post-deployment management involves addressing issues, implementing updates, and ensuring user satisfaction. Here are some key management practices:

2.1. Handling Issues and Feedback

Stay responsive to user feedback and issues that may arise. Encourage users to report bugs, unexpected behaviors, or security concerns. Establishing communication channels, such as Discord or GitHub, allows you to engage with your community effectively.

2.2. Upgrade Strategies

Since deployed smart contracts are immutable, you may need to consider upgrade strategies to introduce new features or fix bugs. Some common upgrade patterns include:

- **Proxy Contracts**: Use a proxy contract to delegate calls to an implementation contract. This allows you to change the implementation while keeping the same address.
- **Admin Controls**: Implement administrative functions that allow designated accounts to upgrade the contract or migrate to a new contract.

2.3. Governance Mechanisms

If applicable, establish governance mechanisms to allow stakeholders to participate in decision-making regarding contract upgrades or changes. Decentralized governance can be facilitated through voting mechanisms or token-based governance models.

2.4. Security Audits and Reviews

Regularly conduct security audits and code reviews to identify vulnerabilities or areas for improvement. Engaging third-party auditors can provide an additional layer of scrutiny and confidence in your smart contracts' security.

3. Performance Optimization

Monitor your smart contracts' performance to identify areas for optimization. This can include:

- **Gas Efficiency**: Analyze transactions to identify functions that consume excessive gas and refactor code to improve efficiency.
- **State Management**: Optimize how data is stored and managed within your contracts to reduce gas costs and improve responsiveness.

Summary

Monitoring and managing smart contracts post-deployment is a crucial aspect of blockchain development. By implementing robust monitoring strategies, engaging with users, and adopting upgrade strategies, developers can ensure their contracts remain secure, efficient, and relevant in a rapidly evolving landscape. Continuous improvement and responsiveness to user needs will ultimately enhance the trust and reliability of the decentralized applications built on Ethereum and other blockchain platforms.

12.6 Case Study: Launching a Token on Ethereum

In this section, we will walk through a case study of launching a token on the Ethereum blockchain. This practical example will highlight key considerations, best practices, and steps involved in deploying a token, illustrating the process from development to post-deployment monitoring.

1. Defining the Token

Before writing any code, it's essential to define the purpose and features of the token. This involves:

- **Token Name and Symbol**: Choose a name and symbol that represent your token. For example, "MyToken" (MTK).
- **Total Supply**: Decide the total number of tokens that will ever be created. This can be fixed or adjustable based on your token's design.
- **Token Standards**: Determine whether your token will adhere to ERC-20 (fungible tokens) or ERC-721 (non-fungible tokens) standards, depending on its intended use.

2. Writing the Smart Contract

Using Solidity, you can write a smart contract for the token. Here's a simplified example of an ERC-20 token contract:

solidity
Copy code
pragma solidity ^0.8.0;

```
import "@openzeppelin/contracts/token/ERC20/ERC20.sol";

contract MyToken is ERC20 {
    constructor(uint256 initialSupply) ERC20("MyToken", "MTK") {
    _mint(msg.sender, initialSupply);
    }
}
```

This contract initializes the token with a specified supply and mints the tokens to the contract creator's address.

3. Testing the Smart Contract

Before deployment, thoroughly test the smart contract using frameworks like Truffle or Hardhat:

- **Unit Tests**: Write tests to cover all functions, including transfers, allowances, and minting.
- **Simulate Transactions**: Use local test networks to simulate token

transactions and validate the contract's behavior.

4. Deploying the Token

Once testing is complete, deploy the token contract to the Ethereum mainnet:

- **Deploy Script**: Use a migration script in Truffle or Hardhat to deploy the contract. Example using Truffle:

javascript
Copy code
```
const MyToken = artifacts.require("MyToken");

module.exports = function (deployer) {
deployer.deploy(MyToken, 1000000); // Mint 1,000,000 tokens
};
```

- **Transaction Fees**: Be prepared to pay gas fees for the deployment. Monitor the network conditions to choose an optimal time for deployment.

5. Post-Deployment Monitoring and Management

After deployment, monitor the token's performance and user interactions:

- **Blockchain Explorers**: Use Etherscan to track transactions, holders, and token transfers.
- **Community Engagement**: Establish communication channels (e.g., Discord, Telegram) for user support and feedback.

6. Marketing and Adoption

To ensure your token gains traction:

- **Marketing Strategy**: Create a marketing plan to promote the token, explaining its benefits and use cases.

- **Community Building**: Engage with the community through social media, forums, and events to drive awareness and adoption.

Conclusion

In this chapter, we explored the vital aspects of testing and deploying blockchain applications, emphasizing the significance of robust testing practices and continuous integration. Through the case study of launching a token on Ethereum, we demonstrated the end-to-end process from defining a token's purpose to its deployment and post-deployment monitoring.

Effective testing, proper deployment strategies, and ongoing management practices are essential for the success of blockchain applications. By implementing these practices, developers can enhance the security, reliability, and performance of their decentralized applications, ensuring they meet the needs of users and the demands of the evolving blockchain landscape. The knowledge gained in this chapter serves as a foundation for building and deploying successful blockchain solutions.

CHAPTER 13: BLOCKCHAIN INTEROPERABILITY AND ORACLES

13.1 What is Blockchain Interoperability?

Blockchain interoperability refers to the ability of different blockchain networks to communicate, share data, and interact with one another seamlessly. As the blockchain ecosystem grows, it becomes increasingly important for these diverse networks to interoperate, allowing for greater flexibility, functionality, and user experience.

1. The Need for Interoperability

Blockchain networks operate independently, each with its own protocols, consensus mechanisms, and governance structures. This siloed nature limits the potential for cross-chain transactions and data sharing. Interoperability addresses these challenges by enabling:

- **Cross-Chain Transactions**: Facilitating transactions and asset transfers across different blockchain platforms.
- **Data Sharing**: Allowing applications on one blockchain to access and utilize data from another, enhancing functionality.
- **Decentralized Applications (DApps)**: Building DApps that can leverage multiple blockchains, creating richer user experiences and more robust functionalities.

2. Benefits of Interoperability

- **Increased Flexibility**: Users can select the best blockchain for their specific needs without being limited to a single network.
- **Enhanced Security**: By spreading data and transactions across multiple blockchains, the risk of attacks on a single network can be mitigated.
- **Broader Adoption**: Interoperable solutions can appeal to a wider audience, promoting greater adoption of blockchain technology.

3. Challenges to Interoperability

While interoperability offers numerous benefits, it also presents significant challenges:

- **Technical Complexity**: Different blockchain protocols may use distinct data formats, consensus algorithms, and security models, complicating integration.
- **Scalability**: Ensuring that interoperability solutions can scale efficiently as networks grow is crucial for widespread adoption.
- **Governance Issues**: Aligning governance structures and decision-making processes across multiple blockchains can be challenging.

4. Approaches to Achieving Interoperability

Various approaches are being explored to facilitate blockchain interoperability:

- **Atomic Swaps**: Allowing users to exchange cryptocurrencies from different blockchains directly, without the need for intermediaries.
- **Cross-Chain Bridges**: Creating bridges that connect two or more blockchain networks, enabling seamless communication and asset transfer.
- **Interoperability Protocols**: Developing standards and protocols, such as Polkadot and Cosmos, designed specifically to enable communication between different blockchains.

This overview of blockchain interoperability highlights its importance and the various methods being developed to facilitate seamless interactions between blockchain networks. In the following sections, we will explore oracles and their role in enhancing interoperability, providing real-world data to smart contracts and applications.

13.2 Cross-Chain Communication between Ethereum, Hyperledger, and Corda

Cross-chain communication is a crucial component in achieving blockchain interoperability, especially between major blockchain platforms like Ethereum, Hyperledger, and Corda. These platforms serve distinct use cases, but enabling communication between them opens up new possibilities for collaboration, innovation, and more efficient workflows.

1. Why Cross-Chain Communication is Important

Each blockchain platform has its own strengths:

- **Ethereum**: Known for its public, decentralized nature and the ability to deploy smart contracts.
- **Hyperledger Fabric**: A permissioned blockchain used for enterprise applications, offering privacy, scalability, and permissioned access control.
- **Corda**: Aimed at the financial sector, offering a permissioned environment optimized for secure and transparent business transactions.

Enabling these platforms to communicate ensures that enterprises and developers can utilize the most appropriate platform for each specific task while still leveraging the strengths of others. This enhances overall flexibility and functionality in the blockchain ecosystem.

2. Challenges in Cross-Chain Communication

There are several key challenges in enabling communication between these platforms:

- **Different Consensus Mechanisms**: Ethereum uses Proof of Stake (previously Proof of Work), Hyperledger Fabric uses Byzantine Fault Tolerance, and Corda uses a unique consensus model focused on legal finality. These varying consensus mechanisms make direct interaction between the platforms difficult.

- **Data Structures**: Ethereum, Hyperledger, and Corda utilize different formats for transactions, contracts, and states, making it necessary to translate or bridge these differences for effective communication.
- **Privacy Requirements**: While Ethereum is a public blockchain, both Hyperledger Fabric and Corda are permissioned networks designed to handle private transactions. Facilitating communication between these environments while maintaining privacy is a complex challenge.
- **Governance**: Cross-chain governance is another challenge, as each platform follows its own governance model and rules for consensus, upgrades, and decisions.

3. Methods and Solutions for Cross-Chain Communication

Various solutions are emerging to tackle the challenge of cross-chain communication between Ethereum, Hyperledger, and Corda:

a. Blockchain Bridges

Blockchain bridges are one of the most promising approaches to enable cross-chain communication. They act as intermediaries between two or more blockchain platforms, translating and transferring data, assets, or contracts. These bridges can allow:

- Asset transfers (e.g., moving tokens between Ethereum and Corda)
- Data sharing (e.g., supply chain data between Hyperledger and Ethereum-based applications)
- Cross-chain smart contract execution

Examples include Cosmos and Polkadot, which are designed to enable communication across different blockchain networks.

b. Atomic Swaps

Atomic swaps allow direct, peer-to-peer exchanges of assets across different blockchains without intermediaries. This method ensures that a transaction either happens fully on both chains or not at all, thereby providing security and trust for cross-chain exchanges.

c. Oracle Solutions

Oracles can serve as intermediaries for cross-chain communication. By acting as trusted third parties, oracles can facilitate the movement of data or assets between platforms, ensuring consistency and trustworthiness.

d. API Gateways

APIs can be used to facilitate communication between blockchains by translating data formats and functions into compatible outputs for other platforms. While this may not offer real-time, decentralized communication like atomic swaps or bridges, it can be highly effective for specific use cases, such as connecting enterprise applications running on Hyperledger with public smart contracts on Ethereum.

4. Current Initiatives and Projects

Several projects are working on enabling cross-chain communication between major platforms:

- **Polkadot**: A platform built to enable seamless cross-chain communication, allowing different blockchains to exchange data and assets.
- **Cosmos**: Focuses on creating an "Internet of Blockchains" by allowing independent blockchains to communicate with each other.
- **Hyperledger Cactus**: A framework under the Hyperledger umbrella specifically designed to enable interoperability between various blockchains, including Ethereum, Hyperledger, and Corda.

5. Use Cases for Cross-Chain Communication

- **Supply Chain Management**: A Hyperledger-based supply chain management system could interact with Ethereum smart contracts to enable public transparency on certain transactions while keeping other data private.
- **Financial Services**: Corda could be used for private financial transactions, while Ethereum could handle decentralized finance (DeFi) components of the same ecosystem.
- **Enterprise Solutions**: Corporations may use Hyperledger for internal,

permissioned applications while interacting with Ethereum for broader, public use cases like token issuance or decentralized applications.

Cross-chain communication between Ethereum, Hyperledger, and Corda is a key step toward fully realizing the potential of blockchain technology across industries. While challenges remain, solutions like blockchain bridges, oracles, and atomic swaps are paving the way for seamless interactions between these diverse platforms.

13.3 Using Oracles in Smart Contracts

Smart contracts, by design, are self-executing agreements with the terms directly written into code. They function autonomously on blockchain platforms like Ethereum, Hyperledger, and Corda. However, smart contracts are inherently limited to interacting with data that exists on the blockchain. This presents a challenge when external data, such as weather reports, stock prices, or event outcomes, is needed for contract execution. Oracles provide a solution to this problem.

1. What are Oracles?

Oracles are trusted third-party services or decentralized networks that act as a bridge between the blockchain and the outside world. They provide smart contracts with the ability to access off-chain data or communicate with external systems. Essentially, oracles fetch real-world information and feed it into the blockchain environment so that smart contracts can interact with external events and data.

There are different types of oracles, including:

- **Data Oracles**: These provide real-time information such as price feeds, weather data, or sports results.
- **Payment Oracles**: These handle payments to external systems or bank accounts.
- **Event Oracles**: These trigger contract execution based on real-world events, such as stock price changes or election outcomes.
- **Cross-Chain Oracles**: These enable data sharing between different blockchain platforms, which is particularly useful for interoperability.

2. How Oracles Work with Smart Contracts

When a smart contract requires external data, an oracle fetches the required information from a reliable source and delivers it to the contract on the blockchain. Here's a step-by-step breakdown of how oracles interact with smart contracts:

1. **Smart Contract Requests Data**: The smart contract sends a request to an oracle when it requires off-chain information. This request is typically encoded into the blockchain.
2. **Oracle Fetches Data**: The oracle service retrieves the requested data from the external source or system. This could be a web API, a data feed, or any other source of real-world information.
3. **Oracle Submits Data to the Blockchain**: The oracle sends the fetched data back to the blockchain, which then gets incorporated into the smart contract.
4. **Smart Contract Execution**: Based on the received data, the smart contract performs its logic and either completes a transaction, triggers an action, or enforces the contract terms.

For example, in a weather-based insurance contract, an oracle could provide weather data to the smart contract. If the oracle reports rainfall exceeding a certain threshold, the smart contract could trigger an insurance payout to the affected party.

3. Types of Oracles

a. Centralized Oracles

Centralized oracles are single entities that provide data to a smart contract. While they offer simplicity and speed, centralized oracles pose a risk of being a single point of failure. If the centralized oracle becomes compromised or provides incorrect data, the smart contract could malfunction or execute inaccurately.

b. Decentralized Oracles

Decentralized oracles involve multiple independent nodes or sources providing data to the smart contract. They aim to reduce reliance on a single entity and increase trust in the data provided. Decentralized oracles aggregate data from several sources and use consensus mechanisms to ensure the integrity of the information.

A popular example of decentralized oracles is **Chainlink**, which uses multiple oracles to fetch and verify data before providing it to smart contracts.

c. Hardware Oracles

Hardware oracles interact with physical sensors and devices in the real world. For instance, a hardware oracle could be connected to a sensor that monitors the temperature in a storage facility. When the temperature exceeds a certain threshold, the oracle could send this data to a smart contract, triggering an alert or action.

d. Inbound and Outbound Oracles

- **Inbound Oracles**: These retrieve off-chain data and send it into the blockchain. For example, retrieving current exchange rates for a financial smart contract.
- **Outbound Oracles**: These send data from the blockchain to an external system. For example, a smart contract might use an outbound oracle to trigger a payment in a traditional banking system.

4. Use Cases for Oracles in Smart Contracts

Oracles open up a wide range of use cases for smart contracts, making them more versatile and applicable to real-world scenarios:

- **Decentralized Finance (DeFi)**: DeFi protocols rely heavily on oracles for obtaining accurate price feeds for assets like cryptocurrencies, stocks, and commodities. Oracles are essential for enabling features like lending, borrowing, and yield farming.
- **Insurance Contracts**: Smart contracts can automatically trigger payouts based on real-world events such as flight delays or natural disasters. Oracles provide the necessary data for verifying these events.
- **Prediction Markets**: Platforms like Augur and Gnosis use oracles to settle bets or predictions based on real-world outcomes, such as election

results or sports scores.

- **Supply Chain Management**: Oracles can be used to track the movement of goods in a supply chain, ensuring that smart contracts execute when certain conditions are met, such as delivery confirmation.

5. Challenges with Oracles

While oracles extend the functionality of smart contracts, they also introduce some challenges:

a. Trust and Security

The biggest challenge with oracles is trust. Smart contracts are designed to be trustless, but if an oracle provides inaccurate or manipulated data, it can compromise the entire system. Decentralized oracles help mitigate this risk, but they still rely on the quality of external data sources.

b. Oracle Manipulation

Oracle manipulation occurs when malicious actors attempt to alter the data being provided by an oracle. This is a significant risk in financial applications, where price manipulation could lead to large-scale financial loss. Some decentralized oracle networks have developed incentive models to ensure honest data reporting.

c. Latency and Speed

Oracles can introduce latency into smart contracts. Fetching and validating external data, especially from decentralized sources, can take time, which may slow down the execution of smart contracts.

Oracles are a vital tool for extending the functionality of smart contracts, allowing them to interact with real-world data and events. They serve as bridges between the blockchain and the outside world, enabling smart contracts to be more dynamic and applicable across industries. However, ensuring the reliability and security of oracles is key to maintaining trust in blockchain systems.

13.4 Integrating External Data into Smart Contracts with Chainlink

Chainlink is a decentralized oracle network that enables smart contracts to securely interact with external data sources, APIs, and off-chain systems. As blockchain-based applications evolve, many of them require real-world data to function effectively. Chainlink acts as a bridge between blockchain platforms and external data providers, ensuring that data fed into smart contracts is trustworthy and tamper-proof.

In this section, we will explore how to integrate external data into smart contracts using Chainlink.

1. What is Chainlink?

Chainlink is a decentralized network of oracles designed to securely connect smart contracts with off-chain data sources. By using multiple independent oracles to retrieve data, Chainlink ensures that the information provided to smart contracts is accurate and trustworthy, preventing manipulation and single points of failure. This makes it one of the most widely used oracle services in the decentralized finance (DeFi) ecosystem.

Some key features of Chainlink include:

- **Decentralization**: Unlike centralized oracles that rely on a single data provider, Chainlink uses a decentralized network of nodes to gather and verify external data.
- **Data Aggregation**: Chainlink aggregates data from multiple sources to ensure accuracy and protect against outliers or faulty data.
- **Tamper-Resistant**: Chainlink's decentralized architecture ensures that the data provided is resistant to tampering and manipulation.

2. Why Use Chainlink for Smart Contracts?

Many blockchain applications, such as DeFi protocols, insurance contracts, and supply chain solutions, require reliable real-world data to operate. For example, a DeFi application might need accurate price data to determine the collateralization ratio of a loan. Smart contracts can't access this data natively because they are isolated from the outside world.

Chainlink solves this problem by providing a secure way for smart contracts to fetch external data, such as:

- **Cryptocurrency prices**: To support DeFi applications like lending, borrowing, and derivatives.

- **Weather data**: For use in parametric insurance contracts.
- **Event outcomes**: To trigger conditional actions in prediction markets.
- **APIs**: Allowing smart contracts to communicate with external services like payment systems or data providers.

3. How Chainlink Works

When a smart contract requires off-chain data, the Chainlink oracle network follows a series of steps to fetch and deliver the required information:

1. **Smart Contract Request**: A smart contract issues a request for external data via a Chainlink Requesting Contract.
2. **Oracle Selection**: Chainlink selects a set of independent oracles that are trusted to fetch the required data. These oracles are chosen based on criteria like reputation and historical performance.
3. **Data Fetching**: Each oracle fetches the requested data from one or more external sources, such as APIs or web services.
4. **Data Aggregation**: Chainlink aggregates the data provided by multiple oracles and calculates a consensus result. This aggregation ensures that the final data is accurate and reduces the risk of manipulation by any single oracle.
5. **Data Delivery**: The aggregated data is then sent back to the smart contract, which can use it to execute its logic and perform actions based on the received data.

4. Integrating Chainlink with Ethereum Smart Contracts

To integrate external data using Chainlink, developers can use Chainlink's smart contract libraries to interact with the Chainlink network. Here's an example of how to use Chainlink to get data from an off-chain API.

Step 1: Install Chainlink Libraries

Before you can use Chainlink in your Ethereum smart contract, you need to install the Chainlink client libraries. In a typical project using the Truffle framework, you would add Chainlink to your project dependencies:
bash

Copy code

npm install @chainlink/contracts

Step 2: Create a Chainlink Smart Contract

Here's an example of a simple smart contract that uses Chainlink to fetch the latest price of Ether (ETH) in USD from an external price feed.

solidity

Copy code

```
// SPDX-License-Identifier: MIT
pragma solidity ^0.8.0;

import "@chainlink/contracts/src/v0.8/interfaces/AggregatorV3Interface.sol";

contract PriceConsumerV3 {

AggregatorV3Interface internal priceFeed;

constructor() {
    // Chainlink Price Feed address for ETH/USD on Ethereum Mainnet
    priceFeed = AggregatorV3Interface(0x5f4eC3Df9cbd43714FE2740f5E3616155c5b8419);
}

/**
 * Returns the latest price of ETH in USD
 */
function getLatestPrice() public view returns (int) {
    (
        ,
        int price,
        ,
        ,
```

```
) = priceFeed.latestRoundData();
  return price;
  }
  }
```

In this example:

- The contract imports the AggregatorV3Interface from Chainlink's contract library.
- The contract interacts with Chainlink's ETH/USD price feed aggregator to get the latest price of Ether in USD.
- The getLatestPrice() function returns the latest ETH/USD price.

Step 3: Deploy and Use the Smart Contract

Once the contract is written, it can be deployed to the Ethereum network using standard tools like Remix, Truffle, or Hardhat. After deployment, you can call the getLatestPrice() function to fetch the current ETH price in USD, as provided by the Chainlink oracles.

5. Chainlink Data Feeds

Chainlink provides pre-built, decentralized data feeds for various types of data, such as cryptocurrency prices, commodities, and market indices. These data feeds are available on multiple blockchain networks, including Ethereum, Binance Smart Chain, and Polygon. Developers can integrate these feeds directly into their smart contracts to get real-time, tamper-resistant data.

Example: Using Chainlink's ETH/USD Price Feed

Here's how you can use Chainlink's ETH/USD price feed in a smart contract to retrieve the price of Ether.

```
solidity
Copy code
// SPDX-License-Identifier: MIT
pragma solidity ^0.8.0;

import "@chainlink/contracts/src/v0.8/interfaces/AggregatorV3Interface.sol";
```

```
contract GetETHPrice {

AggregatorV3Interface internal ethUsdPriceFeed;

constructor() {
  ethUsdPriceFeed = AggregatorV3Interface(0x5f4eC3Df9cbd43714FE2740
f5E3616155c5b8419); // ETH/USD price feed on mainnet
  }

function getETHUSDPrice() public view returns (int) {
  (, int price,,,) = ethUsdPriceFeed.latestRoundData();
  return price / 10 ** 8; // Adjust for 8 decimals in Chainlink price feed
  }
  }
```

6. Decentralized Oracle Networks

Chainlink operates a decentralized oracle network (DON) where data is
fetched and verified by multiple independent oracle nodes. This decentralized
approach ensures high data integrity and trust, which is critical for applications in sectors like decentralized finance (DeFi), insurance, and gaming.

- **Price Feeds**: Chainlink offers ready-to-use price feeds for assets like
  cryptocurrencies, foreign exchange rates, and commodities.
- **Verifiable Randomness**: Chainlink's Verifiable Random Function (VRF)
  provides on-chain random number generation, which is particularly
  useful for gaming applications.
- **External API Access**: Developers can build custom oracles that fetch
  data from any public API, making Chainlink highly versatile.

7. Advantages of Chainlink Integration

- **Security**: Chainlink's decentralized oracle network ensures that data is
  tamper-proof and resistant to manipulation.
- **Trust**: By using multiple data sources, Chainlink ensures that smart

407

contracts get reliable and accurate data.

- **Interoperability**: Chainlink works across various blockchain platforms, making it suitable for a wide range of decentralized applications.

Integrating external data into smart contracts using Chainlink opens up a world of possibilities for decentralized applications. By bridging the gap between blockchains and real-world data, Chainlink enables smart contracts to become more dynamic and applicable across various industries.

13.5 Building an Oracle-Powered DApp

Building a decentralized application (DApp) powered by oracles allows developers to incorporate real-world data into their blockchain-based applications. Oracles, such as Chainlink, serve as intermediaries between smart contracts and off-chain data, making DApps more versatile and capable of handling use cases beyond the on-chain ecosystem. In this section, we'll walk through the process of building an oracle-powered DApp, including setting up oracles, integrating them into smart contracts, and deploying the DApp.

1. Overview of the Oracle-Powered DApp

Oracle-powered DApps are decentralized applications that utilize external data feeds provided by oracles to execute certain functions within a smart contract. A common example of such a DApp could be:

- **Prediction Markets**: Where external data like sports results, election outcomes, or financial markets influence payouts.
- **DeFi Platforms**: That rely on external price feeds for loan collateralization, asset swapping, or liquidation triggers.
- **Insurance Contracts**: Where real-world events like weather conditions determine the payout.

For this example, we'll focus on building a **decentralized lottery DApp** that uses Chainlink's **Verifiable Random Function (VRF)** to randomly select a winner. This ensures that the winner selection process is secure, fair, and completely random.

2. Components of an Oracle-Powered DApp

An oracle-powered DApp consists of several components:

- **Smart Contract**: A Solidity contract deployed on a blockchain network (e.g., Ethereum) that uses oracles to access external data.
- **Oracle Service**: Such as Chainlink, which provides a secure, decentralized feed of data.
- **Frontend**: A user interface built with web technologies (e.g., React.js) that interacts with the smart contract.
- **Backend (optional)**: An off-chain service that processes additional logic or interacts with the DApp, but for decentralized apps, most logic is handled on-chain.

3. Chainlink VRF: Ensuring Randomness

Chainlink's VRF is a service that provides on-chain verifiable randomness, which is useful for applications that require fair randomness, such as lotteries, games, or giveaways. Chainlink VRF ensures that randomness is not tampered with, as the result is provable on-chain, guaranteeing fairness.

4. Building the Smart Contract

Let's write a simple lottery contract that uses Chainlink VRF to randomly select a winner.

Step 1: Install Chainlink Contracts

Add the Chainlink contract libraries to your project:

bash

Copy code

npm install @chainlink/contracts

Step 2: Write the Lottery Contract

Here's a Solidity smart contract for a lottery system using Chainlink VRF:

solidity

Copy code

// SPDX-License-Identifier: MIT

pragma solidity ^0.8.0;

```solidity
import "@chainlink/contracts/src/v0.8/interfaces/VRFCoordinatorV2Interface.sol";
    import "@chainlink/contracts/src/v0.8/VRFConsumerBaseV2.sol";


contract Lottery is VRFConsumerBaseV2 {
    address public owner;
    address payable[] public players;
    address public recentWinner;


uint256 public lotteryId;
    uint256 public randomness;


VRFCoordinatorV2Interface COORDINATOR;
    uint64 s_subscriptionId;
    bytes32 keyHash;
    uint32 callbackGasLimit = 100000;
    uint16 requestConfirmations = 3;
    uint32 numWords = 1;


constructor(
    address vrfCoordinator,
    uint64 subscriptionId,
    bytes32 _keyHash
    ) VRFConsumerBaseV2(vrfCoordinator) {
    owner = msg.sender;
    COORDINATOR = VRFCoordinatorV2Interface(vrfCoordinator);
    s_subscriptionId = subscriptionId;
    keyHash = _keyHash;
    }


function enterLottery() public payable {
    require(msg.value == 0.01 ether, "Must send exactly 0.01 ETH");
    players.push(payable(msg.sender));
```

```
}

function startLottery() public onlyOwner {
  require(players.length > 0, "No players entered");
  requestRandomWinner();
  }

function requestRandomWinner() internal {
  COORDINATOR.requestRandomWords(
  keyHash,
  s_subscriptionId,
  requestConfirmations,
  callbackGasLimit,
  numWords
  );
  }

function fulfillRandomWords(uint256, uint256[] memory randomWords)
internal override {
  uint256 indexOfWinner = randomWords[0] % players.length;
  recentWinner = players[indexOfWinner];
  players[indexOfWinner].transfer(address(this).balance);
  // Reset players array
  players = new address payable randomness = randomWords[0];
  lotteryId++;
  }

modifier onlyOwner() {
  require(msg.sender == owner, "Only the owner can call this function");
  _;
  }
  }
  In this contract:
```

- Players can enter the lottery by sending 0.01 ETH.
- The lottery owner can start the lottery and request a random winner using Chainlink's VRF.
- The fulfillRandomWords() function is called once Chainlink VRF provides a random number, and this number is used to select a winner.
- The winner receives the entire balance of the contract.

Step 3: Deploy the Contract

The contract can be deployed to an Ethereum testnet (e.g., Rinkeby) or mainnet using development tools like Truffle or Hardhat.

Step 4: Request and Use Randomness

To use Chainlink VRF, you need to subscribe to Chainlink's services and get a **Subscription ID** from their platform. You will also need to fund your contract with LINK tokens, which are used to pay for oracle services.

5. Building the Frontend with React.js

We can create a simple frontend for the lottery DApp using React.js to interact with the Ethereum smart contract. The frontend will allow users to:

- Enter the lottery.
- View the current players.
- Start the lottery (if you are the owner).

Here's how you can set up the frontend:

1. **Install Dependencies**: Install the required packages for web3 integration:

bash
Copy code
npm install web3 @metamask/detect-provider

1. **Create the Frontend Logic**: Use Web3.js to interact with the lottery smart contract:

```javascript
Copy code
import React, { useState, useEffect } from 'react';
import Web3 from 'web3';
import detectEthereumProvider from '@metamask/detect-provider';
import Lottery from './Lottery.json'; // ABI of Lottery contract

const web3 = new Web3(window.ethereum);

function App() {
  const [account, setAccount] = useState('');
  const [lotteryContract, setLotteryContract] = useState(null);
  const [players, setPlayers] = useState([]);
  const [winner, setWinner] = useState('');

useEffect(() => {
  async function loadBlockchainData() {
  const provider = await detectEthereumProvider();
  if (provider) {
  const accounts = await web3.eth.requestAccounts();
  setAccount(accounts[0]);
  const networkId = await web3.eth.net.getId();
  const deployedNetwork = Lottery.networks[networkId];
  const contract = new web3.eth.Contract(Lottery.abi, deployedNetwork
&& deployedNetwork.address);
  setLotteryContract(contract);
  }
  }
  loadBlockchainData();
  }, []);

const enterLottery = async () => {
  await lotteryContract.methods.enterLottery().send({
```

```javascript
      from: account,
      value: web3.utils.toWei('0.01', 'ether')
    });
  };

  const startLottery = async () => {
    await lotteryContract.methods.startLottery().send({ from: account });
  };

  const fetchPlayers = async () => {
    const playerList = await lotteryContract.methods.getPlayers().call();
    setPlayers(playerList);
  };

  const fetchWinner = async () => {
    const recentWinner = await lotteryContract.methods.recentWinner().call();
    setWinner(recentWinner);
  };

  return (
    <div>
      <h1>Lottery DApp</h1>
      <p>Account: {account}</p>
      <button onClick={enterLottery}>Enter Lottery</button>
      <button onClick={startLottery}>Start Lottery</button>
      <button onClick={fetchPlayers}>Get Players</button>
      <button onClick={fetchWinner}>Get Winner</button>
      <div>
      <h2>Players:</h2>
      {players.map((player, index) => (
      <p key={index}>{player}</p>
      ))}
      </div>
```

```
<div>
<h2>Recent Winner: {winner}</h2>
</div>
</div>
);
}
```

export default App;

In this React component:

- Users can interact with the contract via MetaMask (or any other Ethereum provider).
- Users can enter the lottery, and the owner can start the lottery to select a random winner.

6. Conclusion

By using Chainlink as an oracle provider, developers can create decentralized applications that integrate real-world data, ensuring trust and security. In this example, we built a lottery DApp that used Chainlink VRF to provide provable randomness. This architecture can be extended to various other applications that require external data, such as DeFi, insurance, and prediction markets. The combination of oracles and smart contracts opens up vast possibilities for decentralized, data-driven applications.

13.6 Challenges in Blockchain Interoperability and Solutions

As blockchain technology continues to evolve, the need for interoperability between different blockchains has become increasingly critical. However, achieving seamless interaction between distinct blockchain networks presents significant challenges, primarily due to the differences in their underlying technologies, consensus mechanisms, and governance models. In this section, we will explore some of the key challenges in blockchain interoperability and the potential solutions that are being developed to overcome them.

1. Challenges in Blockchain Interoperability

a. Lack of Standardization

Different blockchain platforms, such as Ethereum, Hyperledger, and Corda, have been developed with varying protocols, consensus mechanisms, and data structures. This diversity creates difficulties in creating standardized ways to communicate between these platforms. The lack of universal standards for how blockchains should operate and interact with each other limits interoperability.

b. Security Risks

Interoperability mechanisms, such as cross-chain bridges and oracles, introduce new security risks. These mechanisms are often targets for attacks, as they are responsible for transferring assets or data between blockchains. If an attacker compromises an interoperability protocol, they can manipulate data, causing inconsistencies between chains or leading to loss of funds.

c. Scalability Concerns

Interoperability solutions must handle a large volume of transactions and data exchanges between chains. As the number of chains and the volume of transactions increase, scalability becomes a major concern. Ensuring that cross-chain communication is efficient, fast, and capable of handling high throughput is a significant challenge.

d. Consensus Compatibility

Different blockchains often use different consensus mechanisms (e.g., Proof of Work, Proof of Stake, Practical Byzantine Fault Tolerance), which makes it challenging to achieve consensus when communicating between chains. Ensuring compatibility between these consensus mechanisms is essential for ensuring the integrity of cross-chain transactions.

e. Data Privacy and Confidentiality

Certain blockchains, like Hyperledger, are designed for private, permissioned environments, where data privacy and confidentiality are paramount. However, public blockchains like Ethereum operate transparently, meaning data is visible to all participants. Balancing the privacy requirements of private blockchains with the transparency of public ones is a critical challenge for interoperability.

2. Solutions to Blockchain Interoperability Challenges

a. Cross-Chain Bridges

Cross-chain bridges are one of the most common solutions for enabling interoperability. These bridges act as connectors between two different blockchain networks, allowing the transfer of assets and information. For example, a bridge between Ethereum and Binance Smart Chain enables users to transfer tokens between these two networks. However, ensuring the security and reliability of these bridges remains a major concern.

b. Blockchain Protocols and Standards

Various organizations and developers are working towards creating interoperability protocols and standards that different blockchains can adopt. **Polkadot** and **Cosmos** are two prominent projects working on interoperability. Polkadot enables the creation of parachains that are interoperable with the Polkadot relay chain, while Cosmos uses the Inter-Blockchain Communication (IBC) protocol to connect independent blockchains.

c. Atomic Swaps

Atomic swaps enable the direct exchange of cryptocurrencies between two different blockchains without the need for an intermediary or third-party service. Atomic swaps use smart contracts to ensure that the exchange happens in a trustless manner. If either party does not fulfill their part of the agreement, the transaction is canceled, ensuring no loss of funds.

d. Oracles for Cross-Chain Data Transfer

Oracles, such as Chainlink, are also key to interoperability, allowing blockchains to interact with external data and other chains. Oracles can help facilitate the exchange of data and assets across multiple blockchains, improving the functionality and reliability of cross-chain interactions.

e. Layer 2 Solutions

Layer 2 solutions, such as **rollups** and **state channels**, offer scalability improvements by processing transactions off the main chain, reducing the load on blockchain networks. When combined with interoperability solutions, Layer 2 technologies can help scale cross-chain transactions more efficiently and at lower costs.

f. Interoperability-Focused Projects

Several projects are building blockchain networks from the ground up with interoperability in mind. Projects like **Cosmos** and **Polkadot** offer frameworks that allow various blockchains to interact and share information seamlessly. These platforms serve as hubs for different blockchains, providing tools and protocols to enhance cross-chain communication.

3. The Future of Blockchain Interoperability

The need for seamless interoperability between blockchains will only grow as the number of decentralized applications (DApps) and blockchain platforms increases. In the future, we can expect further advancements in cross-chain protocols, enhanced security for bridges and oracles, and improved consensus compatibility across different blockchain systems. Achieving secure, scalable, and efficient interoperability will unlock new possibilities for decentralized finance (DeFi), supply chain management, enterprise applications, and beyond.

Conclusion

Blockchain interoperability is essential for the growth and evolution of the decentralized ecosystem. As blockchain networks become more fragmented and specialized, the need for cross-chain communication and data exchange has intensified. This chapter explored the fundamentals of blockchain interoperability, the role of oracles in enhancing smart contracts with external data, and real-world use cases where these technologies come together to power decentralized applications (DApps).

We began by discussing the definition and importance of blockchain interoperability, highlighting key challenges such as standardization, security, scalability, and privacy. We then delved into potential solutions, including cross-chain bridges, atomic swaps, interoperability-focused projects like Polkadot and Cosmos, and the role of oracles such as Chainlink in facilitating external data integration into smart contracts.

Furthermore, we explored the practicalities of building an oracle-powered DApp and the mechanisms that drive the secure interaction between blockchains. By examining a real-world decentralized application, such as an oracle-powered lottery DApp, we illustrated how blockchain interoperability and oracle services can be leveraged to create powerful, decentralized, and fair applications.

The future of blockchain interoperability is promising, with ongoing innovations aimed at overcoming the challenges that still exist. As interoperability improves, it will pave the way for more complex, interconnected DApps that span multiple blockchain networks, opening up new opportunities in decentralized finance, governance, supply chains, and beyond.

This chapter emphasized that seamless cross-chain communication and the integration of real-world data are crucial for blockchain's continued growth, setting the stage for a truly decentralized and interoperable future.

CHAPTER 14: ADVANCED TOPICS IN BLOCKCHAIN DEVELOPMENT

14.1 Layer 2 Solutions: Off-Chain Scaling with Sidechains and Rollups

As blockchain adoption grows, the limitations of on-chain scaling become more apparent, particularly on public blockchains like Ethereum and Bitcoin. High transaction fees, long confirmation times, and scalability bottlenecks can hinder the usability of decentralized applications (DApps) and the overall efficiency of blockchain networks. To address these challenges, **Layer 2 solutions** have emerged as an essential component of blockchain scalability, providing off-chain scaling techniques that alleviate the strain on the main blockchain (Layer 1) while maintaining its security and decentralization.

Layer 2 solutions operate as protocols built on top of the base Layer 1 blockchain. These solutions handle a portion of the blockchain's transactions or computation off-chain, reducing congestion and improving performance. Two major Layer 2 scaling solutions are **sidechains** and **rollups**, both of which play critical roles in optimizing blockchain scalability.

Sidechains

A **sidechain** is an independent blockchain that is interoperable with a main blockchain (Layer 1) through a two-way peg or bridge. This allows assets and data to be transferred between the two chains. Sidechains can have their own consensus mechanisms, which are often optimized for speed and scalability. The main blockchain ensures security and decentralization, while the sidechain handles more transactions or complex computations.

Advantages of Sidechains:

- **Scalability**: Sidechains can process a high volume of transactions without congesting the main chain.
- **Customizability**: Developers can design sidechains with different consensus mechanisms and features suited to specific use cases (e.g., faster finality, lower fees).
- **Interoperability**: Assets and data can be transferred between sidechains and the main chain, enhancing functionality.

Challenges of Sidechains:

- **Security**: The security of sidechains relies on their consensus mechanisms, which may not be as robust as the main blockchain.
- **Complexity**: Implementing cross-chain communication can be complex, and ensuring seamless interaction between the sidechain and main chain is a technical challenge.

Rollups

Rollups are another type of Layer 2 solution that bundles or "rolls up" multiple off-chain transactions into a single batch, which is then submitted to the main chain for verification. The idea behind rollups is to offload the majority of the computational work off-chain, while still using the Layer 1 blockchain to ensure security and finality. Rollups can be categorized into two types: **Optimistic Rollups** and **ZK-Rollups** (Zero-Knowledge Rollups).

Optimistic Rollups:

Optimistic rollups assume that off-chain transactions are valid by default and only submit the final state to the main chain. Validators can challenge any fraudulent transactions through a fraud-proof mechanism, where they present proof of an invalid transaction.

ZK-Rollups:

ZK-Rollups use zero-knowledge proofs to verify the validity of off-chain transactions. Instead of submitting all transactions to the main chain, ZK-Rollups generate cryptographic proof (a succinct proof) that verifies the batch of transactions as correct. This proof is then submitted to the main chain, which verifies it without needing to process every individual transaction.

Advantages of Rollups:

- **Security**: Rollups inherit the security of the main chain (e.g., Ethereum) since all transactions are ultimately settled on the Layer 1 blockchain.
- **Scalability**: Rollups can significantly reduce the computational load on the main chain by processing multiple transactions off-chain and submitting only compressed data or proofs.
- **Lower Fees**: Since fewer transactions are directly processed on Layer 1, transaction fees can be reduced.

Challenges of Rollups:

- **Latency**: With Optimistic Rollups, there can be a delay in finalizing transactions due to the time required for fraud proofs.
- **Complexity**: Rollup solutions require sophisticated cryptographic mechanisms, particularly ZK-Rollups, which can be challenging to implement and verify.

Layer 2 solutions are critical to the future of blockchain scalability. By offloading transactions and computations from the main chain, sidechains and rollups can increase throughput, reduce fees, and improve user experience. Both sidechains and rollups have distinct strengths and trade-offs, and they offer scalable solutions for different types of decentralized applications. As adoption grows, these Layer 2 solutions will continue to evolve and address the needs of developers, users, and enterprises seeking efficient blockchain solutions.

14.2 Sharding and its Impact on Blockchain Scaling

Sharding is a prominent scaling solution aimed at improving the capacity and throughput of blockchain networks by dividing the blockchain into smaller, more manageable parts, called **shards**. Each shard operates as a separate chain within the network and processes its own subset of transactions and smart contracts, allowing for parallel transaction processing across multiple shards. This method enhances the blockchain's overall performance by reducing congestion and increasing scalability.

Sharding is particularly important for blockchains like Ethereum, which have faced significant scaling issues as the number of users and decentralized applications (DApps) has increased. Ethereum 2.0 (now referred to as Ethereum's consensus layer) is one of the major networks planning to implement sharding as part of its long-term scaling roadmap.

How Sharding Works

In a sharded blockchain, the network is split into distinct shards, each responsible for processing a specific set of transactions. Each shard has its own ledger, smart contracts, and validators. However, the entire network maintains an overarching consensus protocol, which ensures that all shards remain synchronized and secure.

Instead of every node processing every transaction (as is the case with most Layer 1 blockchains), sharding allows nodes to only process transactions on a single shard, reducing the computational burden on each node. As a result, the blockchain can handle many more transactions per second (TPS) without compromising decentralization or security.

Cross-Shard Communication

Sharding introduces the challenge of **cross-shard communication**. Since each shard processes its own transactions independently, there must be mechanisms for data and value to be transferred between shards. This requires a protocol that facilitates communication between different shards to maintain consistency and avoid double-spending or conflicting transactions.

There are several approaches to achieving cross-shard communication, including:

- **Atomic cross-shard transactions**: Ensures that transactions affecting multiple shards are executed atomically (all-or-nothing), meaning the transaction either succeeds on all involved shards or fails completely.
- **Shard collators**: Specialized nodes that help validate and synchronize transactions across different shards.

Impact of Sharding on Blockchain Scaling

Sharding has the potential to dramatically increase the scalability of blockchains by allowing the network to process transactions in parallel across multiple shards. The main benefits include:

- **Higher Throughput**: Sharding enables a blockchain to process transactions across many shards simultaneously, significantly increasing the number of transactions the network can handle. Instead of being limited by the processing power of a single chain, the network's total transaction capacity grows with the number of shards.
- **Reduced Congestion**: By distributing transactions across shards, sharding reduces the likelihood of network congestion. This leads to faster confirmation times and lower transaction fees, making the network more efficient for users and DApps.
- **Decentralization**: Sharding maintains decentralization by allowing nodes to validate transactions on a single shard rather than the entire blockchain. This reduces the computational and storage requirements for participating in the network, potentially increasing the number of validators and contributing to greater decentralization.
- **Improved Scalability without Sacrificing Security**: Sharding scales the blockchain without compromising security because each shard remains connected to the overarching consensus layer. This ensures that the network remains secure even as it scales.

Challenges and Risks of Sharding

While sharding presents a promising solution for blockchain scalability, it also introduces challenges and risks, including:

- **Cross-Shard Communication Complexity**: Ensuring seamless communication and synchronization between shards is technically challenging. Developing protocols that securely transfer data and assets across shards without introducing vulnerabilities requires careful design.
- **Security of Individual Shards**: Each shard operates independently,

which may create opportunities for attackers to target less-secure shards. For example, a shard with fewer validators could be more susceptible to a 51% attack. To mitigate this risk, sharded networks often use random validator assignment to ensure that no shard can be easily compromised.

- **Validator Coordination**: Validators need to be dynamically assigned to different shards over time to prevent collusion or attacks on specific shards. This requires coordination and mechanisms to randomly assign validators to shards while ensuring network security.

Sharding in Ethereum 2.0

Ethereum's implementation of sharding is one of the most anticipated upgrades in the blockchain space. In Ethereum 2.0, the network is expected to be divided into multiple shards, each of which can process its own transactions. The Ethereum mainnet will act as a beacon chain, coordinating the shards and managing the network's overall consensus.

Ethereum 2.0's sharding will involve a multi-phase rollout:

- **Phase 1**: Introduction of the beacon chain and sharding infrastructure.
- **Phase 2**: Full implementation of shard chains, allowing for parallel transaction processing across shards.
- **Phase 3**: Cross-shard communication protocols, enabling smooth interaction between different shards.

Summary

Sharding is a transformative scaling solution that can significantly improve the performance and capacity of blockchain networks by distributing the transaction load across multiple parallel shards. While it introduces technical complexities, particularly in terms of cross-shard communication and security, the potential benefits are immense. Sharding can increase transaction throughput, reduce network congestion, and improve the user experience, making blockchains more suitable for large-scale applications.

As blockchain networks like Ethereum and others continue to evolve, sharding will likely play a key role in addressing the scaling challenges that have hindered widespread adoption. By enabling parallel processing while maintaining the security and decentralization of the underlying network, sharding holds the potential to unlock the next generation of decentralized applications and blockchain-based solutions.

14.3 Zero-Knowledge Proofs (zk-SNARKs) in Blockchain

Zero-Knowledge Proofs (ZKPs) are cryptographic protocols that enable one party (the prover) to prove to another party (the verifier) that a statement is true without revealing any information about the statement itself. This concept has profound implications for privacy and security in blockchain technology, where transparency and immutability are fundamental but can pose challenges when sensitive information needs to remain confidential.

One of the most popular types of ZKPs used in blockchain is **zk-SNARKs**, which stands for **Zero-Knowledge Succinct Non-Interactive Arguments of Knowledge**. zk-SNARKs are an advanced form of zero-knowledge proofs that enable efficient, non-interactive verification of computations while preserving privacy.

Key Features of zk-SNARKs

1. **Zero-Knowledge**: The verifier learns nothing beyond the validity of the statement being proven. For example, in the context of a blockchain transaction, the verifier can confirm that a transaction is valid without learning the sender, receiver, or the amount being transferred.
2. **Succinct**: zk-SNARKs generate short proofs that can be verified quickly, making them efficient in terms of computational overhead. This is crucial for blockchain applications where scalability and performance are important considerations.
3. **Non-Interactive**: Traditional zero-knowledge proofs often require multiple rounds of communication between the prover and verifier. In contrast, zk-SNARKs are non-interactive, meaning the proof can be generated and verified in a single communication step, which is more practical for distributed networks like blockchains.
4. **Arguments of Knowledge**: zk-SNARKs prove that the prover actually possesses the knowledge of the statement they are proving, rather than

simply asserting its validity. This ensures the integrity of the proof.

How zk-SNARKs Work

In zk-SNARKs, a **trusted setup** is required to initialize the cryptographic system. This involves generating a set of cryptographic parameters (often referred to as the "public parameters") that are used to create and verify the zero-knowledge proofs. The trusted setup must be performed securely because any compromise could undermine the security of the system.

Once the system is initialized, zk-SNARKs allow the following:

- The **prover** generates a proof that demonstrates they have computed a certain function or statement correctly.
- The **verifier** can check the proof's validity without needing to know the inputs or details of the computation itself.

zk-SNARKs are particularly useful in situations where sensitive data needs to be processed or verified on a public blockchain without exposing the underlying information.

Applications of zk-SNARKs in Blockchain

1. **Privacy-Preserving Transactions**

- One of the earliest and most well-known applications of zk-SNARKs is in the cryptocurrency **Zcash**, which uses zk-SNARKs to allow private transactions on a public blockchain. With zk-SNARKs, Zcash can validate transactions without revealing any details about the sender, receiver, or transaction amount, enabling true financial privacy while maintaining the integrity of the network.

1. **Scalability Solutions**

- zk-SNARKs can also be used to improve blockchain scalability by enabling succinct proofs of complex computations. For example, zk-

Rollups (an Ethereum Layer 2 scaling solution) use zk-SNARKs to bundle many transactions into a single proof that can be verified quickly on the main chain. This reduces the computational load on the blockchain and increases transaction throughput.

1. Decentralized Identity

- zk-SNARKs are useful in decentralized identity systems, where they can prove certain attributes about a user (e.g., age or residency) without revealing their full identity. This can be particularly beneficial in decentralized finance (DeFi) applications or KYC (Know Your Customer) compliance systems that require verification of user information while maintaining privacy.

1. Auditable Elections

- zk-SNARKs can be applied to create transparent and verifiable voting systems where individual votes can be validated without revealing the identity of the voter or their choice. This ensures that elections remain secure, private, and auditable.

Advantages of zk-SNARKs in Blockchain

- **Enhanced Privacy**: zk-SNARKs allow for private transactions and computations on a public blockchain, preserving user privacy without sacrificing security or transparency.
- **Efficiency**: The succinct nature of zk-SNARKs enables fast and efficient verification of proofs, making them practical for real-time applications on blockchain networks.
- **Scalability**: zk-SNARKs reduce the amount of data that needs to be processed and stored on the blockchain, improving network performance and scalability.
- **Trustless Verification**: zk-SNARKs allow verifiers to confirm the

correctness of computations or transactions without trusting the prover or knowing the underlying data.

Challenges of zk-SNARKs

- **Trusted Setup**: One of the main criticisms of zk-SNARKs is the need for a trusted setup. If the initial setup is compromised or not performed securely, the entire system's security could be jeopardized. This has led to research into alternative zero-knowledge proof systems, such as zk-STARKs, which do not require a trusted setup.
- **Complexity**: zk-SNARKs are mathematically and computationally complex, which can make implementation and optimization challenging for developers.
- **Overhead**: While zk-SNARKs are more efficient than traditional zero-knowledge proofs, they still introduce some computational and bandwidth overhead, particularly in the case of generating proofs.

Future of zk-SNARKs in Blockchain

The adoption of zk-SNARKs is growing rapidly, especially in privacy-focused cryptocurrencies and Layer 2 scaling solutions. As the technology matures and becomes more accessible to developers, zk-SNARKs will likely play an increasingly important role in enabling privacy, scalability, and security in blockchain applications. Additionally, research into new types of zero-knowledge proofs, such as zk-STARKs (Scalable Transparent Arguments of Knowledge), aims to address some of the limitations of zk-SNARKs, particularly the need for a trusted setup.

Summary

Zero-knowledge proofs, particularly zk-SNARKs, represent a powerful tool for enhancing privacy and scalability in blockchain networks. By allowing proofs of computation to be verified without revealing underlying data, zk-SNARKs offer a way to build privacy-preserving, efficient, and scalable blockchain applications. While there are challenges, including the need for a trusted setup and the complexity of implementation, zk-SNARKs have proven their utility in real-world applications like Zcash and zk-Rollups. As blockchain technology evolves, zk-SNARKs are expected to become a cornerstone of secure and private decentralized systems, paving the way for more sophisticated applications in finance, identity, and beyond.

14.4 Implementing Decentralized Identity (DID) with Blockchain

Decentralized Identity (DID) is a new model for identity management that enables individuals, organizations, and devices to have secure and verifiable digital identities without relying on centralized authorities, such as governments or corporations. Instead, identities are managed by users themselves through cryptographic keys and blockchain technology, giving them full control over their personal data and how it's shared.

Blockchain plays a crucial role in **DID systems** by providing a trustless, immutable, and distributed ledger for managing identity credentials. With blockchain, DIDs can be securely registered, verified, and used across different applications and platforms without the need for intermediaries.

Key Concepts in Decentralized Identity

1. **Self-Sovereign Identity (SSI):**

- SSI allows individuals to own and control their identity data. Instead of relying on centralized databases or identity providers, users can create and manage their digital identities on decentralized networks, using cryptographic keys for authentication and verification.

1. **Decentralized Identifiers (DIDs):**

- DIDs are unique, self-owned, and globally resolvable identifiers that users can generate and control. A DID typically consists of a string of characters (e.g., "did:example:123456789") and points to a document that contains cryptographic material, such as public keys or proofs, for authentication.

1. **Verifiable Credentials:**

- Verifiable credentials are tamper-proof digital credentials that are cryptographically signed by trusted entities (issuers) and presented by users (holders) to third parties (verifiers). Examples include digital passports, driver's licenses, or educational certificates. These credentials are issued and verified in a decentralized manner using blockchain.

1. **DID Documents**:

- A DID document is a JSON-LD (JavaScript Object Notation for Linked Data) file that contains essential information about the DID, including cryptographic keys, endpoints for interaction, and other metadata. It serves as a public record for verifying the identity associated with a DID.

1. **Decentralized Identity Networks**:

- These are blockchain-based networks where DIDs are registered, managed, and verified. Common examples include **Sovrin, uPort**, and **Microsoft's ION**, all of which use public or permissioned blockchains to provide a decentralized infrastructure for identity management.

How Decentralized Identity Works with Blockchain

1. **Generating a DID**:

- The process starts with an individual or entity generating a DID using a decentralized identity platform. The DID is created along with a pair of cryptographic keys (private and public), with the private key securely stored by the user and the public key being made available for verification.

1. **Registering the DID on the Blockchain**:

- The DID is registered on a blockchain to create a tamper-proof, immutable record. This registration process does not store personal information on the blockchain, but it associates the DID with a public key, ensuring that anyone can verify the owner's identity.

1. **Issuing Verifiable Credentials**:

- Once the DID is created, trusted issuers (such as governments, banks, or educational institutions) can issue verifiable credentials to the user. These credentials are digitally signed by the issuer and can be stored in a secure digital wallet by the user.

1. **Presenting and Verifying Credentials**:

- When a user needs to prove their identity or qualifications (for example, to a job interviewer), they can present their verifiable credentials. The verifier can use the DID and public key to cryptographically verify the credential without needing to rely on the issuing entity directly.

1. **Ensuring Privacy**:

- A key advantage of DID systems is that they enable users to control who gets access to their data. Using techniques like **zero-knowledge proofs**, users can prove certain facts (e.g., they are over 18) without revealing their full identity or any other personal information. This allows for privacy-preserving authentication and verification.

Advantages of Decentralized Identity (DID)

- **User Control**:
- With DID, individuals have full control over their identity and data, removing the need to rely on centralized entities like governments or corporations. Users decide what information they want to share and with whom.
- **Security**:

- DIDs and verifiable credentials are secured using cryptography, reducing the risk of identity theft, data breaches, or tampering. The blockchain provides an immutable ledger to prevent unauthorized changes to identity records.
- **Interoperability**:
- DIDs are designed to be platform-agnostic, meaning they can work across different blockchains, networks, and applications. This ensures that identities can be easily used in a wide range of scenarios, from logging into websites to accessing government services.
- **Privacy-Preserving**:
- Unlike traditional identity systems, DID ensures that personal data is not stored on centralized servers or distributed publicly. Instead, only the necessary credentials are shared, and privacy-preserving techniques like zero-knowledge proofs can further protect sensitive information.
- **Resilience**:
- Since DID systems rely on decentralized networks, they are more resilient to failures, hacks, or censorship compared to centralized systems that depend on a single point of control.

Challenges of Decentralized Identity

- **Adoption**:
- The decentralized identity model is still in its early stages, and widespread adoption requires cooperation between governments, institutions, and enterprises. Many organizations are hesitant to adopt new identity paradigms that require a shift in how identity management is traditionally done.
- **Trust Frameworks**:
- To ensure that verifiable credentials are trusted across different networks and countries, common trust frameworks and standards need to be established. These frameworks define who can issue credentials, how they are verified, and what legal protections are in place.
- **Key Management**:

- In a decentralized identity system, users are responsible for managing their private keys. If a user loses access to their private key, they could lose control over their identity, which is a significant risk in self-sovereign identity systems.
- **Scalability**:
- Depending on the underlying blockchain used for DID, there can be concerns about scalability and transaction costs. For example, using a public blockchain like Ethereum for identity management could become expensive if gas fees are high.

Implementing Decentralized Identity with Blockchain

Several projects and standards are pushing forward the implementation of DID systems:

1. **Sovrin**:

- Sovrin is a permissioned blockchain specifically designed for decentralized identity management. It allows users to create DIDs, issue verifiable credentials, and present them for verification.

1. **uPort**:

- Built on the Ethereum blockchain, uPort allows users to create and manage their own digital identity, store verifiable credentials, and interact with decentralized applications (DApps) that support DID.

1. **Microsoft ION**:

- ION is a decentralized identity system built on top of Bitcoin that allows for the creation of DIDs without relying on a centralized authority. Microsoft has integrated ION with its Azure Active Directory to provide decentralized identity services.

1. **W3C Decentralized Identifier (DID) Standard**:

- The W3C (World Wide Web Consortium) has developed a standard for decentralized identifiers (DIDs) to ensure that they are interoperable and can be used across different platforms. This standard is crucial for making DID systems compatible with global applications.

Future of Decentralized Identity (DID)

The future of DID lies in its ability to revolutionize how individuals interact with the digital world. As blockchain technology matures and DID systems become more user-friendly, they could replace traditional identity management systems in finance, healthcare, education, and government services. Self-sovereign identity, powered by blockchain, has the potential to democratize identity, giving individuals greater control over their personal information while ensuring security and privacy.

Summary

Decentralized identity (DID) offers a transformative approach to managing digital identities, placing control in the hands of individuals and reducing reliance on centralized entities. By leveraging blockchain technology, DIDs provide a secure, private, and tamper-proof way of verifying identity and credentials. While there are challenges to adoption, such as key management and interoperability, the benefits of user control, privacy, and security make DID a promising solution for the future of digital identity. As the technology continues to evolve, it has the potential to reshape industries and empower individuals to take control of their personal data.

14.5 Governance Models in Decentralized Systems

Governance models in decentralized systems are frameworks that define how decisions are made within a blockchain network or decentralized application (DApp). In traditional systems, governance is typically centralized, with decisions being made by a small group of people or institutions. However, in decentralized systems, governance needs to be distributed among the participants to maintain the decentralized nature of the network.

Effective governance in decentralized systems is critical for maintaining trust, ensuring security, and promoting the continuous evolution of the network. As these systems evolve, governance plays a key role in managing conflicts, adapting to new challenges, and upgrading protocols.

Types of Governance Models in Decentralized Systems

1. **On-Chain Governance**

- On-chain governance refers to the process where all decisions and changes to the blockchain protocol are voted on by stakeholders directly on the blockchain. This model is transparent, and the decision-making process is enforced by smart contracts.
- **Example**: Tezos and Polkadot use on-chain governance where token holders vote on protocol upgrades, and decisions are automatically implemented based on the outcome of the votes.

1. **Off-Chain Governance**

- Off-chain governance occurs outside the blockchain and relies on informal mechanisms like community discussions, forums, and developer meetings to make decisions. The process is more flexible, but it often lacks the transparency and automated enforcement found in on-chain governance.
- **Example**: Bitcoin and Ethereum primarily use off-chain governance, where decisions about protocol upgrades are made through community consensus and developer proposals, such as Bitcoin Improvement Proposals (BIPs) or Ethereum Improvement Proposals (EIPs).

1. **Hybrid Governance**

- Hybrid governance models combine elements of both on-chain and off-chain governance to leverage the benefits of each approach. In these models, some decisions may be made on-chain, while others are discussed off-chain before being formalized in the system.

- **Example**: MakerDAO uses a hybrid governance model where token holders vote on-chain for changes in the system, but the community first discusses the proposals off-chain in forums.

Key Components of Governance Models

1. **Voting Mechanisms**

- Decentralized systems use various voting mechanisms to ensure that decisions are made democratically. Some common voting models include:
- **Token-weighted voting**: Voting power is proportional to the number of tokens held by participants.
- **Quadratic voting**: Voters can allocate multiple votes to issues they care most about, with the cost of each additional vote increasing quadratically.
- **Delegated voting**: Token holders can delegate their voting power to trusted individuals or groups who vote on their behalf.

1. **Consensus Mechanisms**

- Consensus mechanisms are crucial in decentralized governance, as they determine how agreement is reached on decisions. Common mechanisms include:
- **Proof of Stake (PoS)**: Validators stake tokens as collateral to participate in governance decisions. Their voting power is often proportional to the amount staked.
- **Proof of Work (PoW)**: Miners who validate transactions in PoW blockchains typically don't participate in governance directly, but they influence the system by choosing which version of the protocol to mine.
- **Delegated Proof of Stake (DPoS)**: Token holders elect a small group of representatives who make decisions on behalf of the entire network.

1. **Proposals and Improvements**

- In decentralized systems, any participant can propose changes to the protocol or application through a formal proposal process. These proposals are then voted on by the community. For example, Ethereum uses **Ethereum Improvement Proposals (EIPs)**, while Tezos uses **Tezos Amendment Proposals**.

1. **Incentive Structures**

- For decentralized governance to function efficiently, incentive structures need to be carefully designed. Participants need to be incentivized to act in the best interest of the network. This often involves rewarding voters or penalizing bad actors through staking mechanisms.

1. **Checks and Balances**

- Decentralized systems need mechanisms to prevent governance from being captured by a small group of participants (e.g., token whales). These checks and balances might include quorum requirements (a minimum number of votes needed for a decision), time delays before decisions are enacted, or limits on voting power.

Challenges of Decentralized Governance

1. **Voter Apathy**

- A common problem in decentralized governance is **voter apathy**, where only a small percentage of participants actively engage in voting or decision-making. This can lead to governance being dominated by a few large stakeholders or delegates.

1. **Centralization Risks**

- Although decentralized governance aims to distribute decision-making, it can sometimes lead to centralization if a small group of wealthy participants controls the majority of voting power. This can undermine the decentralized nature of the system.

1. **Complexity**

- Governance in decentralized systems can be complex, especially in systems that use sophisticated mechanisms like quadratic voting or multi-layered governance structures. This complexity can make it difficult for average participants to engage meaningfully in governance.

1. **Hard Forks and Conflicts**

- Governance decisions can sometimes lead to hard forks, where the network splits into two separate blockchains due to irreconcilable differences. For example, Bitcoin's fork into Bitcoin and Bitcoin Cash resulted from disagreements over scaling solutions.

1. **Incentive Misalignment**

- If governance incentives are not aligned with the long-term interests of the network, participants may act in self-interest, leading to poor decision-making and potential harm to the system's sustainability.

Best Practices for Governance in Decentralized Systems

1. **Transparency**

- Governance processes should be transparent and open to the community. All proposals, voting results, and decision-making steps should be publicly accessible and verifiable.

1. **Inclusivity**

- Effective governance should be inclusive, encouraging participation from all stakeholders, regardless of their technical expertise or token holdings. This can be achieved by simplifying voting processes and ensuring diverse representation.

1. **Incentivization**

- Proper incentives should be in place to encourage active participation in governance. This may involve rewarding voters or providing incentives for well-informed decision-making.

1. **Governance Education**

- Providing participants with the tools and knowledge to understand the governance process is essential. This includes educating users about how proposals work, how to vote, and the impact of their decisions on the network.

1. **Flexibility**

- Decentralized governance should be adaptable, allowing the system to evolve over time. Governance models should be open to changes and upgrades, as the needs of the network and its participants evolve.

Examples of Governance Models in Decentralized Systems

1. **Tezos**

- Tezos has one of the most robust on-chain governance models, allowing token holders to vote on protocol upgrades and changes. Tezos uses a **liquid proof-of-stake** mechanism where participants can delegate their voting power to others if they don't wish to vote directly.

1. MakerDAO

- MakerDAO, the protocol behind the DAI stablecoin, uses a hybrid governance model where token holders vote on key decisions related to the protocol, such as interest rates and collateral types. Governance decisions are proposed and discussed off-chain before being implemented on-chain.

1. Polkadot

- Polkadot uses a sophisticated governance model that combines **referenda**, **council voting**, and **technical committees**. Token holders can vote directly on referenda, while the elected council helps manage the protocol.

Summary

Governance models in decentralized systems are a critical aspect of ensuring the long-term sustainability, security, and adaptability of blockchain networks and applications. Whether on-chain, off-chain, or hybrid, these models determine how decisions are made, how conflicts are resolved, and how networks evolve. As decentralized systems continue to grow, governance will remain a focal point for ensuring that these networks remain truly decentralized, secure, and fair to all participants. However, challenges such as voter apathy, centralization risks, and the complexity of governance mechanisms must be addressed to create robust and inclusive governance systems for the future.

14.6 Real-World Case Study: Decentralized Finance (DeFi) Applications

Decentralized Finance (DeFi) has emerged as one of the most transformative applications of blockchain technology, reshaping traditional financial services by providing open, permissionless, and transparent alternatives. This case study explores how various DeFi applications exemplify the principles of decentralization, governance, and the use of advanced blockchain technologies.

Key DeFi Applications

1. Uniswap

- **Overview**: Uniswap is a decentralized exchange (DEX) that allows users to trade cryptocurrencies directly from their wallets without relying on a centralized authority. It utilizes an automated market-making (AMM) model, where users can provide liquidity in exchange for fees.
- **Governance**: Uniswap's governance is driven by the UNI token, allowing holders to propose and vote on changes to the protocol. This model empowers the community to shape the future of the platform, demonstrating on-chain governance in action.

1. Aave

- **Overview**: Aave is a decentralized lending and borrowing platform that enables users to lend their crypto assets to others and earn interest or borrow against their collateral. It operates through smart contracts that automatically manage loans and interest rates.
- **Governance**: Aave employs a governance model where AAVE token holders can vote on protocol upgrades, risk parameters, and new asset listings. This decentralized approach ensures that the platform evolves according to the needs of its users.

1. Compound

- **Overview**: Compound is another prominent DeFi lending platform that allows users to earn interest on their cryptocurrency holdings or borrow assets. It utilizes a system of collateralized loans and algorithmically determined interest rates.
- **Governance**: Compound has adopted a governance model where COMP token holders can vote on protocol changes, making it a community-

driven platform. This model fosters engagement and encourages users to participate actively in decision-making processes.

1. **MakerDAO**

- **Overview**: MakerDAO is a decentralized stablecoin platform that issues DAI, a stablecoin pegged to the US dollar, through a system of collateralized debt positions (CDPs). Users lock up collateral in smart contracts to generate DAI, enabling them to access stable funds without selling their assets.
- **Governance**: The Maker governance system allows MKR token holders to vote on critical parameters, such as collateral types and stability fees. This governance structure empowers the community to manage the stability and risk of the DAI ecosystem.

1. **Yearn.Finance**

- **Overview**: Yearn.Finance is a DeFi yield aggregator that optimizes yield farming strategies for users. By automatically shifting users' assets between different lending platforms, it maximizes returns.
- **Governance**: The YFI token grants holders governance rights, enabling them to propose and vote on changes to the protocol, including the addition of new strategies and integrations with other DeFi platforms.

Impact of DeFi on Traditional Finance

DeFi applications are challenging the status quo of traditional finance by providing several key benefits:

- **Accessibility**: DeFi platforms are open to anyone with an internet connection, removing barriers to entry for financial services that are often restricted by geography, credit scores, or regulatory requirements.
- **Transparency**: All transactions and governance processes in DeFi applications are recorded on the blockchain, providing an unprecedented

level of transparency and auditability.

- **Interoperability**: Many DeFi projects are built on Ethereum and leverage composability, allowing them to interact seamlessly with one another. This creates a vibrant ecosystem where users can move assets and services across platforms without friction.
- **Innovation**: DeFi fosters a culture of innovation, with new financial products and services emerging rapidly. This dynamism encourages experimentation and allows users to benefit from cutting-edge financial technologies.

Challenges Facing DeFi

Despite its potential, the DeFi space is not without challenges:

- **Smart Contract Risks**: DeFi applications rely heavily on smart contracts, which are prone to vulnerabilities and bugs. Hacks and exploits can lead to significant financial losses.
- **Regulatory Uncertainty**: As DeFi grows, regulators are beginning to take notice. The future of DeFi may be impacted by forthcoming regulations that could affect the legality and operation of these platforms.
- **Market Volatility**: The cryptocurrency market is known for its volatility, which can impact the value of collateral in lending platforms and the stability of stablecoins like DAI.

Conclusion

The rise of Decentralized Finance (DeFi) applications showcases the transformative power of blockchain technology in reshaping financial systems. By leveraging decentralized governance, transparency, and innovative solutions, DeFi has opened up new opportunities for individuals worldwide. As these applications continue to evolve, they present both tremendous potential and significant challenges. The ongoing development and adoption of DeFi will require careful consideration of security, regulatory, and operational challenges to ensure a sustainable and equitable financial future for all participants.

Chapter 14 explored advanced topics in blockchain development, including Layer 2 solutions, sharding, zero-knowledge proofs, decentralized identity, and governance models in decentralized systems. Through real-world case studies, particularly in the realm of Decentralized Finance (DeFi), we highlighted the practical applications and implications of these advanced concepts.

As blockchain technology continues to mature, understanding these advanced topics is crucial for developers, businesses, and policymakers aiming to harness the full potential of decentralized systems. By embracing innovative governance structures, enhancing scalability through Layer 2 solutions, and implementing privacy-preserving technologies like zero-knowledge proofs, the blockchain ecosystem can evolve to meet the demands of a diverse range of applications.

In the coming years, the lessons learned from these advanced topics and real-world applications will guide the future development of blockchain technologies, ensuring they remain secure, efficient, and beneficial for all stakeholders involved.

CHAPTER 15: FUTURE OF BLOCKCHAIN AND JAVASCRIPT

15.1 Emerging Trends in Blockchain Development

As blockchain technology continues to evolve, several emerging trends are shaping the future of its development, particularly in the context of JavaScript and web technologies. This section highlights key trends that developers and businesses should watch for in the coming years.

1. **Increased Adoption of Layer 2 Solutions**

- **Overview**: Layer 2 solutions, such as rollups and state channels, are gaining traction as they help address the scalability challenges faced by major blockchains like Ethereum. By processing transactions off-chain and then settling them on the main chain, these solutions can significantly reduce congestion and lower transaction fees.
- **Implications for JavaScript**: Developers will increasingly use JavaScript frameworks and libraries to integrate Layer 2 solutions into decentralized applications (DApps), enabling seamless interactions and improved user experiences.

1. **Rise of Decentralized Finance (DeFi) and Decentralized Autonomous Organizations (DAOs)**

- **Overview**: DeFi has already disrupted traditional financial systems, and its growth shows no signs of slowing down. Similarly, DAOs are transforming governance structures, allowing communities to manage resources and decision-making through decentralized models.

- **Implications for JavaScript**: As DeFi and DAOs continue to proliferate, JavaScript developers will need to create sophisticated interfaces and integration points with various DeFi protocols and DAO governance tools, enhancing user engagement and accessibility.

1. **Interoperability Between Blockchains**

- **Overview**: As the number of blockchain networks grows, interoperability has become crucial for allowing seamless communication between different chains. Projects focused on cross-chain solutions are gaining momentum, enabling assets and data to move freely between various platforms.
- **Implications for JavaScript**: Developers will leverage JavaScript to build tools and libraries that facilitate cross-chain transactions, enhancing user experience and expanding the utility of blockchain applications.

1. **Integration of Artificial Intelligence (AI) and Machine Learning (ML)**

- **Overview**: The integration of AI and ML with blockchain technology is becoming a significant trend, enabling smarter contracts and automated decision-making processes. These technologies can enhance data analysis and improve the overall efficiency of blockchain applications.
- **Implications for JavaScript**: JavaScript developers will increasingly work with AI/ML libraries alongside blockchain frameworks, creating applications that can autonomously execute tasks based on data-driven insights.

1. **Focus on Privacy and Security Solutions**

- **Overview**: As blockchain technology matures, there is a growing emphasis on privacy and security, particularly concerning user data and transactions. Solutions such as zero-knowledge proofs and privacy-focused blockchains are gaining popularity.
- **Implications for JavaScript**: Developers will need to incorporate privacy-enhancing features into their DApps, utilizing JavaScript libraries that support advanced cryptographic techniques to protect user data and ensure secure transactions.

1. **Regulatory Developments and Compliance**

- **Overview**: As governments and regulatory bodies pay closer attention to blockchain technology, compliance will become a key concern for developers and businesses. Navigating the regulatory landscape will be essential for ensuring the longevity and legitimacy of blockchain projects.
- **Implications for JavaScript**: Developers will need to implement features that facilitate compliance with regulations, such as KYC/AML checks, within their JavaScript-based applications, ensuring that they adhere to legal requirements while maintaining user experience.

1. **Growth of Non-Fungible Tokens (NFTs)**

- **Overview**: NFTs have emerged as a powerful application of blockchain technology, allowing for the tokenization of unique assets. From digital art to virtual real estate, NFTs are transforming ownership and value representation in the digital realm.
- **Implications for JavaScript**: JavaScript developers will play a pivotal role in creating user-friendly interfaces for NFT marketplaces and platforms, as well as tools for minting, trading, and managing NFTs, making these assets more accessible to a broader audience.

1. **Enhanced User Experiences with Web3 Technologies**

- **Overview**: The transition to Web3, characterized by decentralized applications and user-controlled data, is revolutionizing how users interact with the internet. Enhanced user experiences through intuitive interfaces and seamless interactions are critical for driving adoption.
- **Implications for JavaScript**: JavaScript developers will need to focus on building responsive, engaging interfaces that leverage Web3 technologies, ensuring that users can easily navigate and interact with blockchain applications.

Summary

Chapter 15 explored the emerging trends in blockchain development that are shaping the future of the technology, particularly in relation to JavaScript. The evolution of Layer 2 solutions, the rise of DeFi and DAOs, the push for interoperability, and the integration of AI and ML highlight the dynamic nature of the blockchain ecosystem.

As the demand for decentralized applications grows, JavaScript developers must adapt to these trends by embracing new tools and frameworks, implementing privacy and security measures, and ensuring compliance with evolving regulations. The future of blockchain development presents exciting opportunities and challenges, and those who stay ahead of the curve will play a crucial role in shaping the next generation of decentralized technologies.

With a strong foundation in JavaScript and a keen understanding of these trends, developers will be well-positioned to innovate and contribute to the transformative potential of blockchain technology in various sectors.

15.2 The Role of JavaScript in Future Blockchain Architectures

As blockchain technology matures and new architectures emerge, JavaScript is poised to play a vital role in shaping the future landscape of blockchain development. This section explores how JavaScript can influence and integrate with future blockchain architectures, highlighting its versatility, community support, and alignment with modern web technologies.

1. Universal Language for Frontend Development

- **Overview**: JavaScript has long been the dominant language for frontend web development, powering interactive and dynamic user interfaces. As DApps become more prevalent, the demand for seamless user experiences will grow. JavaScript will remain a primary choice for developers building intuitive interfaces that interact with blockchain backends.

- **Implication**: Developers can leverage popular JavaScript frameworks like React, Vue, and Angular to create rich user interfaces that facilitate user interactions with blockchain applications. The extensive libraries and tools available in the JavaScript ecosystem will support faster and more efficient development cycles.

2. Integration with Web3 Technologies

- **Overview**: With the emergence of Web3, which emphasizes decentralization, privacy, and user ownership of data, JavaScript is well-positioned to lead the way. JavaScript libraries such as Web3.js and Ethers.js enable developers to connect their applications to various blockchain networks, simplifying the process of interacting with smart contracts and decentralized storage solutions.

- **Implication**: The continued evolution of Web3 technologies will encourage JavaScript developers to adopt and implement best practices for building decentralized applications, fostering a community that prioritizes user control and data privacy.

3. Server-Side Development with Node.js

- **Overview**: Node.js allows JavaScript to be used for server-side development, providing an environment for building scalable applications. As blockchain applications increasingly require backend support, Node.js can serve as a bridge between blockchain networks and user-facing applications.

- **Implication**: By leveraging Node.js, developers can create APIs that interact with smart contracts, manage user sessions, and handle data processing for DApps. This versatility enables a full-stack JavaScript development approach, reducing the need for multiple programming languages.

4. Real-Time Data Processing and Events

- **Overview**: JavaScript excels in handling real-time data processing, making it an ideal choice for applications that require immediate feedback and updates. In blockchain applications, this can be crucial for tracking transactions, smart contract events, and other on-chain activities.
- **Implication**: Using libraries like Socket.io, developers can implement real-time communication in DApps, enhancing user engagement and providing instant updates on blockchain events, such as transaction confirmations and changes in state.

5. Interoperability with Other Technologies

- **Overview**: As blockchain systems evolve, the need for interoperability between various protocols and platforms will become increasingly important. JavaScript's flexibility allows it to interact with other languages and frameworks, facilitating cross-chain solutions and multi-platform applications.
- **Implication**: Developers can create JavaScript-based middleware solutions that communicate between different blockchain networks, enabling seamless asset transfers and data sharing. This can help bridge the gap between public and private blockchains, fostering collaboration among diverse ecosystems.

6. Emergence of Smart Contract Development Frameworks

- **Overview**: The growth of blockchain development has led to the creation of various frameworks for building and deploying smart contracts. JavaScript-based frameworks like Truffle and Hardhat provide developers with robust tools for managing the entire development lifecycle.

451

- **Implication**: These frameworks simplify the process of writing, testing, and deploying smart contracts, allowing developers to focus on building innovative applications rather than wrestling with underlying infrastructure. The continued evolution of these tools will streamline the development process and empower more developers to enter the blockchain space.

7. Focus on User Experience and Accessibility

- **Overview**: The future of blockchain technology will hinge on user adoption, which requires a strong emphasis on user experience and accessibility. JavaScript's extensive libraries and frameworks allow developers to create applications that are not only functional but also user-friendly and accessible to a broader audience.
- **Implication**: By prioritizing UX/UI design in DApps and utilizing JavaScript to implement responsive interfaces, developers can attract non-technical users, ultimately driving greater adoption of blockchain technologies.

Summary

JavaScript's role in the future of blockchain architectures is poised to be significant. As the technology evolves, its adaptability, extensive ecosystem, and strong community support will enable developers to create innovative solutions that enhance user experiences and drive the adoption of decentralized applications.

From frontend development to server-side integration and real-time data processing, JavaScript will remain a cornerstone of blockchain development, empowering developers to build versatile, user-friendly, and efficient applications. As the demand for blockchain solutions grows, JavaScript will continue to adapt, helping to shape the next generation of decentralized technologies.

15.3 Quantum-Resistant Cryptography and Blockchain

As quantum computing continues to advance, the potential implications for cryptography and blockchain technology are significant. Quantum computers possess the capability to perform complex calculations at speeds far exceeding those of classical computers, which raises concerns about the security of current cryptographic algorithms that underpin blockchain systems. This section explores the intersection of quantum computing and blockchain technology, focusing on the need for quantum-resistant cryptography and its potential implementations.

1. Understanding Quantum Computing

- **Overview**: Quantum computers leverage the principles of quantum mechanics, utilizing qubits instead of traditional bits to perform calculations. This allows them to process vast amounts of data simultaneously, making them particularly powerful for specific tasks, such as factoring large numbers and solving complex mathematical problems.
- **Implication**: The advent of practical quantum computers poses a threat to widely-used cryptographic algorithms, particularly those based on asymmetric cryptography, such as RSA and ECC (Elliptic Curve Cryptography). These algorithms are essential for securing transactions and identities in blockchain networks.

2. The Threat to Current Cryptographic Algorithms

- **Overview**: Many existing blockchain systems rely on public-key cryptography to secure transactions and protect user identities. Quantum computers could potentially break these cryptographic systems using algorithms like Shor's algorithm, which can factor large integers exponentially faster than classical algorithms.
- **Implication**: If quantum computers become capable of executing Shor's algorithm effectively, they could compromise the integrity of blockchain networks, allowing malicious actors to forge signatures, steal funds, and disrupt the entire ecosystem.

3. The Need for Quantum-Resistant Cryptography

- **Overview**: To safeguard blockchain technology against quantum threats, the development and implementation of quantum-resistant cryptographic algorithms are essential. These algorithms must be secure against both classical and quantum attacks, ensuring the long-term integrity of blockchain systems.
- **Implication**: The adoption of quantum-resistant cryptography can provide a robust defense against potential vulnerabilities, allowing blockchain networks to maintain their trustless and decentralized nature even in a post-quantum world.

4. Types of Quantum-Resistant Cryptographic Approaches

- **Post-Quantum Cryptography (PQC)**:
- Researchers are exploring new cryptographic algorithms that can withstand quantum attacks. This includes lattice-based cryptography, hash-based signatures, code-based cryptography, and multivariate-quadratic-equations (MQ) cryptography. These methods do not rely on integer factorization or discrete logarithms, making them more resilient to quantum threats.
- **Hybrid Approaches**:
- Some proposed solutions involve using a combination of classical and quantum-resistant algorithms to provide an additional layer of security. By implementing both types of algorithms in tandem, blockchain networks can enhance their defenses against potential quantum attacks while maintaining compatibility with existing systems.

5. Integrating Quantum-Resistant Algorithms into Blockchain

- **Overview**: Transitioning existing blockchain networks to quantum-resistant cryptographic algorithms will require careful planning and execution. This includes updating consensus mechanisms, modifying smart contracts, and ensuring compatibility with current infrastructure.
- **Implication**: Blockchain projects must adopt a proactive approach by

exploring and integrating quantum-resistant algorithms before quantum computers become practical. This involves collaboration between researchers, developers, and blockchain communities to establish standards and best practices.

6. Case Studies and Current Developments

- **Overview**: Several blockchain projects are actively researching and implementing quantum-resistant cryptographic solutions. For example, initiatives like Quantum Resistant Ledger (QRL) and other protocols are specifically designed to be secure against quantum attacks.
- **Implication**: These projects can serve as models for future blockchain developments, providing insights into effective strategies for integrating quantum-resistant technologies. As awareness of quantum threats grows, more blockchain projects will likely follow suit, prioritizing the security of their systems.

Summary

Quantum-resistant cryptography represents a crucial area of focus for the future of blockchain technology. As quantum computing continues to evolve, the need for robust cryptographic solutions that can withstand potential quantum threats becomes increasingly urgent.

By developing and implementing quantum-resistant algorithms, blockchain networks can enhance their security posture, ensuring the integrity of transactions and user identities in an uncertain future. The proactive approach of integrating these solutions will not only safeguard existing blockchain systems but also pave the way for the next generation of decentralized applications that can thrive in a post-quantum world.

As the landscape of cryptography shifts with the advent of quantum computing, collaboration and innovation will be key to maintaining the trust and security that underpin blockchain technology.

15.4 Impact of AI and IoT on Blockchain

The convergence of Artificial Intelligence (AI), the Internet of Things (IoT), and blockchain technology is reshaping various industries by enhancing efficiency, security, and transparency. This section explores how AI and IoT integrate with blockchain, their potential benefits, and the challenges that arise from this convergence.

1. Understanding AI and IoT

- **Overview of AI**: AI refers to the simulation of human intelligence in machines, enabling them to learn, reason, and make decisions. It encompasses various technologies, including machine learning, natural language processing, and computer vision.
- **Overview of IoT**: IoT refers to the network of interconnected devices that communicate and exchange data over the internet. These devices, ranging from sensors to smart appliances, collect and share real-time data, facilitating automation and improved decision-making.

2. The Role of Blockchain in AI and IoT

- **Data Integrity and Security**: Blockchain provides a decentralized and immutable ledger that ensures data integrity and security. In IoT, devices can securely share data on a blockchain, reducing the risk of tampering and enhancing trust in the information exchanged.
- **Enhanced Transparency**: By recording all transactions on a transparent ledger, blockchain can enhance accountability in both AI and IoT systems. This is particularly beneficial in supply chain management, where tracking the provenance of goods is essential for ensuring authenticity and compliance.
- **Decentralization**: Blockchain's decentralized nature allows for peer-to-peer interactions among IoT devices without the need for a central authority. This can streamline processes, reduce costs, and enhance operational efficiency.

3. AI-Powered Blockchain Applications

- **Improved Decision-Making**: AI can analyze vast amounts of data stored on a blockchain to derive insights and make predictions. This capability enhances decision-making in various sectors, such as finance, healthcare, and logistics, where data-driven insights are crucial.
- **Smart Contracts**: AI can optimize smart contracts by enabling them to adapt based on real-time data. For example, a smart contract could automatically adjust terms based on market conditions or user behavior, enhancing flexibility and efficiency.

4. IoT-Enabled Blockchain Solutions

- **Data Collection and Sharing**: IoT devices generate massive amounts of data. By integrating blockchain, organizations can securely collect and share this data, ensuring its authenticity and reliability for analytics and decision-making.
- **Automated Transactions**: IoT devices can trigger transactions on a blockchain based on predefined conditions. For instance, a smart meter could automatically execute a payment transaction when energy consumption reaches a certain threshold, streamlining billing processes.

5. Real-World Use Cases

- **Supply Chain Management**: Combining blockchain, AI, and IoT can create end-to-end visibility in supply chains. IoT sensors can track products in real-time, while AI analyzes this data to optimize logistics and inventory management. Blockchain ensures that all data is secure and verifiable, enhancing trust among stakeholders.
- **Healthcare**: In healthcare, IoT devices can monitor patient vitals and record data on a blockchain for secure sharing among medical professionals. AI can analyze this data to identify trends, predict health outcomes, and recommend personalized treatment plans.

6. Challenges and Considerations

- **Scalability**: The integration of AI, IoT, and blockchain poses scalability challenges, particularly in handling large volumes of data generated by IoT devices. Solutions such as Layer 2 scaling and off-chain processing may be necessary to address these issues.
- **Interoperability**: Ensuring interoperability among various blockchain platforms, IoT devices, and AI systems is critical for seamless integration. Standardization efforts are needed to establish common protocols and frameworks.
- **Data Privacy and Security**: While blockchain enhances data security, the combination of AI and IoT raises concerns about data privacy. Organizations must implement robust security measures to protect sensitive information while leveraging these technologies.

Summary

The intersection of AI, IoT, and blockchain technology presents immense opportunities for innovation and efficiency across various industries. By harnessing the strengths of each technology, organizations can enhance data integrity, security, and transparency, leading to improved decision-making and streamlined processes.

However, the convergence of these technologies also introduces challenges that must be addressed to ensure successful implementation. As the landscape evolves, collaboration among stakeholders, continuous research, and the development of standards will be essential for unlocking the full potential of AI and IoT in the blockchain ecosystem. Embracing these advancements can lead to transformative solutions that redefine traditional business models and create new value propositions in the digital age.

15.5 How Blockchain Will Evolve in the Next Decade

As we look towards the future, blockchain technology is set to undergo significant transformations that will reshape its applications, scalability, governance, and integration with other emerging technologies. This section explores the anticipated evolution of blockchain over the next decade, highlighting key trends and potential breakthroughs.

1. Increased Scalability Solutions

- **Layer 2 Technologies**: Solutions like Rollups and state channels will continue to gain traction, allowing blockchains to process more transactions off-chain while maintaining security and decentralization. This will significantly enhance throughput, making blockchain more viable for high-demand applications.
- **Sharding**: This technique, which involves splitting a blockchain into smaller, manageable pieces (shards), will likely be implemented more widely. By distributing the network load, sharding can greatly increase transaction speeds and reduce congestion on the main chain.

2. Greater Interoperability

- **Cross-Chain Solutions**: The development of protocols that facilitate seamless communication between different blockchain networks will enable more integrated and versatile applications. This interoperability will allow assets and data to flow freely across platforms, fostering collaboration and innovation.
- **Standardization Efforts**: As the blockchain ecosystem matures, standardization will become essential for interoperability. Initiatives aimed at creating common protocols and frameworks will promote compatibility and ease of integration among various blockchain systems.

3. Integration with Emerging Technologies

- **Artificial Intelligence**: The synergy between AI and blockchain will deepen, enabling smarter contracts that can adapt based on real-time data analysis. This integration will enhance decision-making, automation, and predictive capabilities in various sectors.
- **Internet of Things (IoT)**: As IoT devices proliferate, blockchain will play a critical role in ensuring secure data sharing and transaction execution. The combination of blockchain and IoT will lead to smarter, more efficient systems across industries, from supply chain management to smart cities.

4. Regulatory Evolution

- **Adaptation to Legal Frameworks**: As blockchain technology matures, regulatory frameworks will evolve to address emerging challenges and opportunities. Governments and regulatory bodies will likely develop clearer guidelines for the use of blockchain, particularly in areas like digital currencies, data privacy, and smart contracts.
- **Increased Collaboration**: The blockchain community will increasingly engage with regulators to establish cooperative frameworks that balance innovation with compliance. This collaboration will foster a more supportive environment for blockchain adoption.

5. Mainstream Adoption

- **Enterprise Solutions**: More businesses will recognize the value of blockchain for enhancing transparency, security, and efficiency in operations. Sectors such as finance, healthcare, and supply chain will adopt blockchain solutions to streamline processes, reduce costs, and improve trust among stakeholders.
- **Consumer Applications**: As user-friendly blockchain applications emerge, everyday consumers will become more engaged with the technology. Decentralized finance (DeFi), non-fungible tokens (NFTs), and digital identities will become more accessible, leading to broader adoption among the general public.

6. Sustainability Initiatives

- **Energy Efficiency**: The blockchain industry will increasingly prioritize sustainability by adopting energy-efficient consensus mechanisms, such as Proof of Stake (PoS) and exploring new technologies that reduce the carbon footprint of blockchain operations.
- **Environmental Impact**: As awareness of environmental issues grows, blockchain applications focused on sustainability will gain popularity.

Projects aimed at tracking carbon credits, sustainable supply chains, and renewable energy sources will leverage blockchain to enhance transparency and accountability.

7. Enhanced Privacy Features

- **Privacy-Enhancing Technologies**: The need for privacy in blockchain transactions will drive the development of advanced cryptographic techniques, such as zero-knowledge proofs, to ensure data confidentiality while maintaining transparency.
- **User-Controlled Data**: Individuals will increasingly demand control over their personal data. Blockchain can empower users to manage their identities and data sharing, enhancing privacy while enabling trusted interactions with organizations.

Summary

The next decade promises significant advancements in blockchain technology, driven by the need for scalability, interoperability, and integration with emerging technologies like AI and IoT. As the industry evolves, businesses, developers, and regulators will collaborate to create a more robust and adaptable ecosystem.

Embracing these changes will enable blockchain to fulfill its potential as a transformative force across industries, reshaping how we transact, interact, and manage information. The evolution of blockchain will pave the way for innovative solutions that address real-world challenges, fostering a more connected, secure, and efficient future.

15.6 Preparing for the Future as a Blockchain Developer

As blockchain technology continues to evolve, aspiring developers must equip themselves with the knowledge, skills, and adaptability to thrive in this dynamic landscape. Here are key steps to prepare for a successful future in blockchain development:

1. Stay Informed on Trends and Innovations

- Regularly follow industry news, attend webinars, and participate in blockchain conferences to stay updated on emerging trends, tools, and best practices. Engaging with the community through forums, social media, and meetups can also provide valuable insights.

2. Deepen Your Technical Skills

- Continuously improve your programming skills in languages relevant to blockchain development, such as Solidity for Ethereum, Go for Hyperledger Fabric, or Java for Corda. Familiarize yourself with popular frameworks and libraries, including Web3.js, Truffle, and Chaincode.
- Embrace learning about complementary technologies, such as decentralized storage solutions (e.g., IPFS), smart contract auditing tools, and security practices to enhance your expertise.

3. Engage in Hands-On Projects

- Practical experience is invaluable. Work on personal projects, contribute to open-source initiatives, or collaborate with others in the blockchain community. Building real-world applications will deepen your understanding of the technology and showcase your skills to potential employers.

4. Understand Regulatory and Ethical Considerations

- As blockchain matures, understanding the regulatory landscape and ethical implications of blockchain applications will be critical. Stay informed about legal developments and incorporate ethical considerations into your development process to foster trust and transparency.

5. Adaptability and Lifelong Learning

- The blockchain landscape is fast-paced and ever-changing. Cultivating a mindset of adaptability and a commitment to lifelong learning will enable you to pivot and embrace new technologies and methodologies as they emerge.

6. Network and Collaborate

- Building a professional network in the blockchain space can open doors to opportunities and collaborations. Engage with other developers, entrepreneurs, and industry leaders to share knowledge, seek mentorship, and explore partnerships.

Summary

In Chapter 15, we explored the future of blockchain technology and the essential role of JavaScript in shaping its evolution. Key trends include increased scalability through Layer 2 solutions, enhanced interoperability among blockchain networks, and the integration of emerging technologies like AI and IoT.

As blockchain continues to mature, developers will see a growing demand for innovative applications across various sectors, driven by a focus on sustainability, privacy, and user empowerment. Additionally, we highlighted the importance of preparing for the future as a blockchain developer by staying informed, deepening technical skills, engaging in hands-on projects, and understanding regulatory considerations.

By adopting a proactive approach and embracing the evolving landscape, developers can position themselves for success in a technology that is poised to transform industries and redefine how we interact with digital assets and data.

Conclusion

Summary of Key Learnings

In this book, we have explored the multifaceted world of blockchain technology and its integration with JavaScript for building decentralized applications. We delved into fundamental concepts such as blockchain architecture, smart contracts, and decentralized applications (DApps), along with specific platforms like Ethereum, Hyperledger, and Corda.

Throughout our journey, we covered essential tools and frameworks, including Web3.js, Truffle, and various SDKs, which are crucial for developing and deploying blockchain applications. We also examined the importance of security, testing, and best practices in blockchain development, as well as advanced topics such as interoperability and the future implications of blockchain technology.

Final Thoughts on Blockchain and JavaScript Development

The synergy between blockchain technology and JavaScript presents a unique opportunity for developers to create innovative solutions that challenge traditional paradigms. As blockchain continues to disrupt industries, JavaScript's versatility allows developers to build user-friendly interfaces and robust backend systems. Embracing this powerful combination will enable developers to contribute to a more decentralized and equitable digital future.

Next Steps for Blockchain Developers

For developers looking to further their blockchain journey, consider the following next steps:

- Engage in hands-on projects and contribute to open-source blockchain initiatives to apply your knowledge in real-world scenarios.
- Stay current with the latest trends and advancements in blockchain technology through webinars, online courses, and industry news.
- Collaborate with other developers and experts in the field to expand your network and share insights.
- Explore emerging technologies and methodologies that complement blockchain, such as decentralized finance (DeFi), non-fungible tokens (NFTs), and Layer 2 solutions.

Resources for Continued Learning

To support your ongoing learning in blockchain and JavaScript development, consider the following resources:

- **Online Learning Platforms:** Websites like Coursera, Udemy, and edX offer courses on blockchain development and JavaScript.

- **Documentation and Tutorials:** The official documentation for Ethereum, Hyperledger, Corda, and Web3.js provides comprehensive guides and examples.
- **Books:** Look for additional books focusing on specific areas of blockchain, smart contracts, and DApps.
- **Community and Forums:** Join forums such as Stack Overflow, Reddit, and Discord channels dedicated to blockchain development for peer support and knowledge sharing.
- **Conferences and Meetups:** Participate in blockchain conferences and local meetups to network with other professionals and learn about the latest developments.

By embracing these resources and actively engaging with the blockchain community, you will be well-equipped to navigate the evolving landscape of blockchain development and make meaningful contributions to this transformative technology.

APPENDIX A: GLOSSARY OF BLOCKCHAIN TERMS

This glossary provides definitions for key terms related to blockchain technology and development:

- **Blockchain:** A decentralized and distributed digital ledger that records transactions across many computers in such a way that the registered transactions cannot be altered retroactively.
  - **Smart Contract:** Self-executing contracts with the terms of the agreement directly written into code, which automatically execute when predetermined conditions are met.
  - **DApp (Decentralized Application):** Applications that run on a peer-to-peer network rather than being hosted on centralized servers.
  - **Token:** A digital asset created on a blockchain that can represent ownership or access rights to a specific resource or service.
  - **Consensus Mechanism:** A protocol used to achieve agreement on a single data value among distributed processes or systems, such as Proof of Work (PoW) or Proof of Stake (PoS).
  - **Ledger:** A record-keeping system that maintains the transaction history of an asset or account.
  - **Fork:** A change to the protocol of a blockchain that can lead to a split into two separate chains, often occurring due to differing opinions within the community.

APPENDIX B: JAVASCRIPT SYNTAX REFERENCE

T his reference includes essential JavaScript syntax and structures frequently used in blockchain development:

- **Variables:**
- Declaration: let, const, var
- Example: const transactionAmount = 100;
- **Functions:**
- Function Declaration:

javascript
Copy code
```
function add(a, b) {
return a + b;
}
```

- Arrow Function:

javascript
Copy code
```
const add = (a, b) => a + b;
```

- **Objects:**

- Object Literal:

javascript
```
Copy code
const user = {
name: 'Alice',
age: 25,
isActive: true
};
```

- **Promises:**
- Creating a Promise:

javascript
```
Copy code
const myPromise = new Promise((resolve, reject) => {
// asynchronous code
});
```

APPENDIX C: ETHEREUM GAS PRICING AND OPTIMIZATION TECHNIQUES

Understanding gas pricing and optimization is crucial for efficient Ethereum transactions:

- **Gas:** The unit of measure for computational work on the Ethereum network. Gas prices fluctuate based on network demand.
  - **Gas Limit:** The maximum amount of gas a user is willing to spend on a transaction.
  - **Optimization Techniques:**
  - **Minimize State Changes:** Fewer state changes reduce gas costs.
  - **Use Efficient Data Structures:** Choose data types that consume less gas, such as bytes instead of string.
  - **Batch Transactions:** Group multiple operations into a single transaction to save on gas fees.

APPENDIX D: HYPERLEDGER FABRIC CONFIGURATION GUIDE

quick reference guide to setting up and configuring Hyperledger Fabric:

1. **Install Prerequisites:**

- Docker
- Docker Compose
- Go Programming Language
- Node.js

1. **Download Hyperledger Fabric Samples:**

bash
Copy code
git clone https://github.com/hyperledger/fabric-samples.git
cd fabric-samples

1. **Set Up the Network:**

- Use the sample configurations provided in the fabric-samples repository to launch the network.
- Deploy the sample applications to test the configuration.

APPENDIX E: ADDITIONAL RESOURCES AND LEARNING MATERIALS

To enhance your knowledge and skills in blockchain development and JavaScript, consider exploring the following resources:

- **Books:**
- "Mastering Ethereum" by Andreas M. Antonopoulos
- "Blockchain Basics" by Daniel Drescher
- **Online Courses:**
- "Ethereum and Solidity: The Complete Developer's Guide" on Udemy
- "Blockchain Fundamentals" on Coursera
- **Documentation:**
- Ethereum: Ethereum.org
- Hyperledger: Hyperledger Fabric Documentation
- **Communities:**
- Join blockchain developer communities on platforms like Reddit, Discord, and Stack Overflow to connect with peers and experts.